Take the Next Step in Your IT Career

T0292977

Save 10%
on Exam Vouchers*

(up to a $35 value)

*Some restrictions apply. See web page for details.

CompTIA.

CompTIA® Tech+ CertMike

Prepare. Practice. Pass the Test! Get Certified!

Second Edition

CompTIA® Tech+ CertMike

Prepare. Practice. Pass the Test! Get Certified!

Exam FC0-U71

Second Edition

Mike Chapple

To all of my students at Notre Dame. The energy, enthusiasm, and experiences you bring to the classroom makes me a better teacher and writer.

—Mike

ACKNOWLEDGMENTS

I'd first like to thank the people who helped shape the vision for this series. The original idea was hatched over breakfast with two very supportive editors from the Wiley team: Ken Brown and Jim Minatel. I've worked with both Jim and Ken on many books over many years, and they're both insightful industry experts who know what it takes to produce a great book.

I'd also like to extend a special thank-you to my agent, Carole Jelen of Waterside Productions. Carole is also an experienced industry pro who can deftly navigate the murky waters of publishing. Carole is the one who pushed me to create my own series.

Of course, the creation of any book involves a tremendous amount of effort from many people other than the author. I truly appreciate the work of Adaobi Obi Tulton, the project editor. Adaobi and I have now worked together on many books, and she keeps the train on the tracks! I'd also like to thank Chris Crayton, the technical editor, who provided insightful advice and gave wonderful feedback throughout the book, and Magesh Elangovan, production editor, who guided me through layouts, formatting, and final cleanup to produce a great book. I would also like to thank the many behind-the-scenes contributors, including the graphics, production, and technical teams who make the book and companion materials into a finished product.

Finally, I would like to thank my family, who supported me through the late evenings, busy weekends, and long hours that a book like this requires to write, edit, and get to press.

ABOUT THE AUTHOR

Mike Chapple, Ph.D., CySA+, is author of the best-selling *CISSP (ISC2) Certified Information Systems Security Professional Official Study Guide* (Sybex, 2024) and the *CISSP (ISC2) Official Practice Tests* (Sybex, 2024). He is an information technology professional with over 25 years of experience in higher education, the private sector, and government.

Mike currently serves as Teaching Professor in the IT, Analytics, and Operations department at the University of Notre Dame's Mendoza College of Business, where he teaches undergraduate and graduate courses on cybersecurity, cloud computing, data management, and business analytics.

Before returning to Notre Dame, Mike served as executive vice president and chief information officer of the Brand Institute, a Miami-based marketing consultancy. Mike also spent four years in the information security research group at the National Security Agency and served as an active duty intelligence officer in the U.S. Air Force.

Mike has written more than 50 books. He earned both his B.S. and Ph.D. degrees from Notre Dame in computer science and engineering. Mike also holds an M.S. in computer science from the University of Idaho and an MBA from Auburn University. Mike holds the Tech+, Cybersecurity Analyst+ (CySA+), Data+, Security+, Certified Information Security Manager (CISM), Certified Cloud Security Professional (CCSP), and Certified Information Systems Security Professional (CISSP) certifications.

Learn more about Mike and his other security certification materials at his website, `https://www.certmike.com`.

About the Technical Editor

Chris Crayton, MCSE, CISSP, CASP+, PenTest+, CySA+, Cloud+, S+, N+, A+, ITF+ is a technical consultant, trainer, author, and industry-leading technical editor. He has worked as a computer technology and networking instructor, information security director, network administrator, network engineer, and PC specialist. Chris has served as technical editor and content contributor on numerous technical titles for several of the leading publishing companies. He has also been recognized with many professional and teaching awards.

CONTENTS

INTRODUCTION

If you're preparing to take the Tech+ exam, you might find yourself overwhelmed with information. This exam covers a very broad range of topics, and it's possible to spend weeks studying each one of them. Fortunately, that's not necessary!

As part of the CertMike Get Certified series, this book is designed to help you focus on the specific knowledge that you'll need to pass the Tech+ exam. CompTIA publishes a detailed list of exam objectives, and this book is organized around those objectives. Each chapter clearly states the single objective that it covers and then, in a few pages, covers the material you need to know about that objective.

You'll find two important things at the end of each chapter: CertMike Exam Essentials and Practice Questions. The CertMike Exam Essentials distill the major points from the chapter into just a few bullet points. Reviewing these CertMike Exam Essentials is a great way to prepare yourself right before taking the exam.

I've also recorded an audio version of the CertMike Exam Essentials that you can access online at www.wiley.com/go/sybextestprep after registering and logging on. You can listen to the audio review when you're in the car, at the gym, or mowing the lawn!

Each chapter concludes with two practice questions that are designed to give you a taste of what it's like to take the exam. You'll find that they're written in the same style as the Tech+ exam questions and have very detailed explanations to help you understand the correct answer. Be sure to take your time and thoroughly study these questions.

Finally, the book's online test bank (www.wiley.com/go/sybextestprep) includes a full-length practice exam that you can use to assess your knowledge when you're ready to take the test. Good luck on the Tech+ exam!

> **NOTE**
>
> Don't just study the questions and answers! The questions on the actual exam will be different from the practice questions included in this book. The exam is designed to test your knowledge of a concept or objective, so use this book to learn the objectives behind the questions.

THE TECH+ EXAM

The Tech+ exam is designed to be a vendor-neutral certification for those seeking to enter the information technology field. CompTIA recommends this certification for three types of people:

- ▶ Students considering starting a career in information technology
- ▶ Professionals working in fields that require an understanding of information technology
- ▶ Sales, marketing, and operations professionals in IT-focused companies

The exam covers six major domains of knowledge:

1. IT Concepts and Terminology
2. Infrastructure
3. Applications and Software
4. Software Development Concepts
5. Data and Database Fundamentals
6. Security

These six areas include a range of topics, from installing printers to securing networks, while focusing heavily on the basic knowledge expected of all IT professionals. That's why CompTIA recommends the Tech+ certification for those in any IT-related field.

The Tech+ exam uses only standard multiple-choice questions. Unlike other CompTIA exams, you won't find performance-based questions (PBQs) on the Tech+ exam. This exam is designed to be straightforward and not to trick you. If you know the material in this book, you will pass the exam.

The exam costs $138 in the United States, with roughly equivalent prices in other locations around the globe. More details about the Tech+ exam and how to take it can be found at www.comptia.org/certifications/tech.

You'll have 60 minutes to take the exam and will be asked to answer up to 75 questions during that time period. Your exam will be scored on a scale ranging from 100 to 900, with a passing score of 650.

> **NOTE**
>
> CompTIA frequently does what is called *item seeding*, which is the practice of including unscored questions on exams. It does so to gather psychometric data, which is then used when developing new versions of the exam. Before you take the exam, you will be told that your exam may include these unscored questions. So, if you come across a question that does not appear to map to any of the exam objectives—or for that matter, does not appear to belong in the exam—it is likely a seeded question. You never really know whether or not a question is seeded, however, so always make your best effort to answer every question.

Taking the Exam

Once you are fully prepared to take the exam, you can visit the CompTIA website to purchase your exam voucher:

https://store.comptia.org

Currently, CompTIA offers two options for taking the exam: an in-person exam at a testing center and an at-home exam that you take on your own computer.

> **TIP**
>
> This book includes a coupon that you may use to save 10 percent on your CompTIA exam registration.

In-Person Exams

CompTIA partners with Pearson VUE's testing centers, so your next step will be to locate a testing center near you. In the United States, you can do this based on your address or your ZIP code, while non-U.S. test takers may find it easier to enter their city and country. You can search for a test center near you at the Pearson Vue website, where you will need to navigate to "Find a test center":

`www.pearsonvue.com/comptia`

Now that you know where you'd like to take the exam, simply set up a Pearson VUE testing account and schedule an exam on their site.

On the day of the test, take two forms of identification, and make sure to show up with plenty of time before the exam starts. Remember that you will not be able to take your notes, electronic devices (including smartphones and watches), or other materials in with you.

At-Home Exams

CompTIA began offering online exam proctoring in 2020 in response to the coronavirus pandemic. Candidates using this approach will take the exam at their home or office and be proctored over a webcam by a remote proctor.

Due to the rapidly changing nature of the at-home testing experience, candidates wishing to pursue this option should check the CompTIA website for the latest details.

After the Tech+ Exam

Once you have taken the exam, you will be notified of your score immediately, so you'll know if you passed the test right away. You should keep track of your score report with your exam registration records and the email address you used to register for the exam.

After you earn the Tech+ certification, you're certified for life! Unlike many other CompTIA certifications that must be renewed on a periodic basis, the Tech+ certification is permanent and remains with you throughout your career.

Many people who earn the Tech+ credential use it as a steppingstone to earning other certifications in their areas of interest. Those interested in technical support roles pursue the A+ certification, those interested in networking work toward the Network+ credential, and the Security+ certification is a gateway to a career in cybersecurity.

WHAT DOES THIS BOOK COVER?

This book covers everything you need to know to pass the Tech+ exam. It is organized into six parts, each corresponding to one of the six Tech+ domains.

Part I: IT Concepts and Terminology

Chapter 1: Computing Basics

Chapter 2: Notational Systems

Chapter 3: Units of Measure

Chapter 4: Troubleshooting

CertMike Get Certified Series Elements

Each book in the CertMike Get Certified series uses a number of common elements to help you prepare. These include the following:

Exam Tips   Throughout each chapter, I've sprinkled practical exam tips that help focus your reading on topics that are particularly confusing or important to understand for the exam.

CertMike Exam Essentials   The exam essentials focus on major exam topics and critical knowledge that you should take into the test. The exam essentials focus on the exam objectives provided by CompTIA.

Practice Questions   Two questions at the end of each chapter help you assess your knowledge and if you are ready to take the exam based on your knowledge of that chapter's topics.

Practice Exam and Audio Review

This book comes with online study tools: a practice exam and audio review to help you prepare for the exam.

> **NOTE**
> Go to www.wiley.com/go/sybextestprep to register and gain access to
> the online study tools.

Practice Exam

The book includes a practice exam. You can test your knowledge of the Tech+ objectives that are covered in the chapters in their entirety or randomized. It's your choice!

Audio Review

I've recorded an audio review where I read each of the 40 sets of CertMike Exam Essentials. This review provides a helpful recap of the main topics covered on the exam, which you can listen to while you're commuting, working out, or relaxing.

> **NOTE**
>
> Like all exams, the Tech+ certification from CompTIA is updated periodically and may eventually be retired or replaced. At some point after CompTIA is no longer offering this exam, the old editions of our books and online tools will be retired. If you have purchased this book after the exam was retired, or are attempting to register in the Sybex online learning environment after the exam was retired, please know that we make no guarantees that this exam's online Sybex tools will be available once the exam is no longer available.

EXAM FC0-U71 EXAM OBJECTIVES

CompTIA goes to great lengths to ensure that its certification programs accurately reflect the IT industry's best practices. They do this by establishing committees for each of its exam programs. Each committee consists of a small group of IT professionals, training providers, and publishers who are responsible for establishing the exam's baseline competency level and who determine the appropriate target-audience level.

Once these factors are determined, CompTIA shares this information with a group of hand-selected subject matter experts (SMEs). These folks are the true brainpower behind the certification program. The SMEs review the committee's findings, refine them, and shape them into the objectives that follow this section. CompTIA calls this process a job-task analysis (JTA).

Finally, CompTIA conducts a survey to ensure that the objectives and weightings truly reflect job requirements. Only then can the SMEs go to work writing the hundreds of questions needed for the exam. Even so, they have to go back to the drawing board for further refinements in many cases before the exam is ready to go live in its final state. Rest assured that the content you're about to learn will serve you long after you take the exam.

CompTIA also publishes relative weightings for each of the exam's objectives. The following table lists the six Tech+ objective domains and the extent to which they are represented on the exam.

Domain	% of Exam
1.0 IT Concepts and Terminology	13%
2.0 Infrastructure	24%
3.0 Applications and Software	18%
4.0 Software Development Concepts	13%
5.0 Data and Database Fundamentals	13%
6.0 Security	19%

FC0-U71 CERTIFICATION EXAM OBJECTIVE MAP

Objective	Chapter(s)
1.0 IT Concepts and Terminology	
1.1 Explain the basics of computing	1
1.2 Identify notational systems	2
1.3 Compare and contrast common units of measure	3
1.4 Explain the troubleshooting methodology	4
2.0 Infrastructure	
2.1 Explain common computing devices and their purposes	5
2.2 Explain the purpose of common internal computing components	6
2.3 Compare and contrast storage types	7
2.4 Given a scenario, install and configure common peripheral devices	8
2.5 Compare and contrast common types of input/output device interfaces	9

Objective	Chapter(s)
6.0 Security	
6.1 Explain fundamental security concepts and frameworks	32, 33, 34
6.2 Explain methods to secure devices and security best practices	33, 35, 36, 37
6.3 Explain password best practices	38
6.4 Identify common use cases for encryption	39
6.5 Given a scenario, configure security settings for a small wireless network	40

> **NOTE**
> Exam objectives are subject to change at any time without prior notice and at CompTIA's discretion. Please visit CompTIA's website (www.comptia.org) for the most current listing of exam objectives.

HOW TO CONTACT THE PUBLISHER

If you believe you've found a mistake in this book, please bring it to our attention. At John Wiley & Sons, we understand how important it is to provide our customers with accurate content, but even with our best efforts an error may occur.

In order to submit your possible errata, please email it to our Customer Service Team at wileysupport@wiley.com with the subject line "Possible Book Errata Submission."

Domain 1.0: IT Concepts and Terminology

IT Concepts and Terminology is the first domain of CompTIA's Tech+ exam. It provides the foundational knowledge that anyone in information technology needs to understand as they begin their careers. This domain has four objectives:

1.1 Explain the basics of computing

1.2 Identify notational systems

1.3 Compare and contrast common units of measure

1.4 Explain the troubleshooting methodology

Questions from this domain make up 13% of the questions on the Tech+ exam, so you should expect to see approximately 10 questions on your test covering the material in this part.

Domain 1.0: IT Concepts and Terminology

## CHAPTER 1

Computing Basics

Objective 1.1: Explain the basics of computing

Computers perform four basic operations on data: They accept *input* from users and devices, *process* data by performing calculations and other operations, *store* data obtained from input and processing, and provide *output* of their results.

In this chapter, you'll learn everything you need to know about Tech+ objective 1.1, including the following topics:

▶ **Input**
▶ **Processing**
▶ **Output**
▶ **Storage**

COMPUTER ACTIONS

Any computing device performs four basic operations: obtaining input, storing data, processing data, and providing output. This is true whether you're dealing with a laptop or desktop computer, a server, a smartphone, a tablet, or another specialized computing device.

Input

Input is when we provide information to the device to help us do our work. Input often comes from users, and we provide that input in a variety of ways. If we're using a laptop or desktop computer, we might provide input by typing on the keyboard or moving and clicking the mouse. On a tablet or smartphone, we're used to interacting by tapping or swiping on the screen or by using our voices.

Input doesn't have to come directly from a person. Computers can also receive input from other computers, from stored data, or even from sensors. For example, the thermostat in your home is a computer. It receives input from a built-in thermometer that tells it the current temperature in your home. It also receives input from residents when they change the temperature setting on the thermostat screen.

Processing

Processing is when the computer analyzes data and performs operations on it. For example, if the computer calculates the total amount of a customer order by adding together the prices of individual products and computing taxes and discounts, that's an example of processing.

Computers can also process data in other ways. When a computer manipulates an image file, plays a video file stored on disk, or predicts the weather, all of those actions are examples of processing.

In most computer systems, processing is done by a special chip inside the computer called the *central processing unit (CPU)*. We'll cover CPUs and other ways of processing data in Chapter 6, "Internal Computing Components."

Output

For a computer to be useful to us, it needs some way to provide us with *output*. Output is simply the computer reporting back to us on the results of its processing.

Output can come in many forms. The simplest form of output is simply showing the results of processing data on the screen, where we can read it. We can also use a printer to create a paper record of output.

Output can also come in other forms. Instead of providing us with the output of its calculations for us to read, a computer might use output to provide instructions to another device on how it should perform.

Storage

When a computer receives input, it can do two different things with that input: It can store the data directly or it might perform some processing on that data (discussed in the next section) and then store it.

Storage mechanisms allow computers to maintain data that they will need later. Computers can store data in two different ways. They might keep some data stored in memory, where the computer can quickly access it on a temporary basis, or they might write the data to a hard drive, cloud storage service, or other storage location where it may be kept more permanently.

> **EXAM TIP**
> You should be prepared to answer exam questions asking you to read the description of an action and classify it as one of the four basic computing actions. Know the differences between input, storage, processing, and output.

Tying It All Together

Let's tie that all together by returning to the thermostat example from earlier.

Input

A thermostat is a computer that receives input from two different sources. You might provide input to the thermostat by telling it the temperature you'd like to have in your home. You might set your thermostat to 74 degrees Fahrenheit. The thermostat also receives input from its built-in thermometer, telling it the actual temperature in your home, which might be 77 degrees on a warm day.

Processing

The thermostat then performs some processing on that input. Basically, it asks the question, is the current temperature lower than the desired temperature, equal to the desired temperature, or above the desired temperature?

Output

The thermostat provides some output in the form of instructions to other devices. If the current temperature is lower than our desired temperature, that means that your house is too cool and the thermostat tells the furnace to turn on and generate heat. If it's too warm in the house, the thermostat turns on the air conditioning to cool down the temperature.

These four actions—input, processing, storage, and output—are the basic activities carried out by any computing system. For example, think about the computer that you use most often. It likely has the following:

- ▶ Input devices, including a keyboard, mouse/trackpad, microphone, and video camera/webcam
- ▶ Processing capability in its CPU
- ▶ Storage capacity in memory and a hard disk drive (HDD) or solid-state drive (SSD)
- ▶ An output device, such as a display or printer

Storage

The thermostat might store the current temperature in memory so that it can later show you data on the temperature in your house over time.

CERTMIKE EXAM ESSENTIALS

- ▶ Computers receive input from a variety of sources, including directly from users and from other devices.
- ▶ After receiving input, computers may perform processing on that input to perform computation or decision-making. They may then store the original data and/or processed data in memory or on disk.
- ▶ Computers provide output in the form of data displayed to end users on monitors or printers as well as in the form of commands sent to other devices.

Practice Question 1

You are assisting a manager who is trying to print a PDF report saved on their laptop for distribution to their employees at a staff meeting in a few hours. The manager is frustrated because the printer keeps jamming, preventing them from printing the report.

What basic computing action is causing this problem?

A. Input
B. Processing
C. Output
D. Storage

Practice Question 2

You are working with a front desk technician at a hotel and troubleshooting an issue that guests are having with the hotel's check-in kiosks. The kiosks use a touchscreen to interact with guests. The touchscreens are correctly displaying information, but when users tap buttons on the screen, the device does not respond.

What basic computing action is causing this problem?

A. Input
B. Processing
C. Output
D. Storage

Practice Question 1 Explanation

This question asks us to evaluate the situation and decide whether it involves input, processing, output, or storage. Let's walk through each of the possibilities.

Input is when a user or system provides data to a computer. In this case, we don't need to gather any new data. The information the manager wants is already present in a PDF report.

Processing is when the computer performs computation or analysis on data. Again, we already have a PDF report that would contain the results of that analysis, so processing seems to be working fine.

Storage is when the computer saves data for later use. Once again, the report is already generated and saved on the device, so there is no storage issue.

The core issue here is that the printer is not creating the report. That's an output issue because the printer is an output device. The manager can't generate the report to provide to their team.

Correct Answer: C. Output

Practice Question 2 Explanation

This question also calls for the classification of this activity into one of the categories of input, processing, output, and storage. Let's walk through each of the categories.

The use of a touchscreen makes this a very interesting question because touchscreens are both input *and* output devices. They accept input from users in the form of touches, and they provide output on the screen. With this knowledge that touchscreens perform input and output, we can quickly eliminate processing and storage as possible answers.

We don't seem to have an output problem here because the touchscreens are correctly displaying information. We do have an input problem because the devices are not responding when users attempt to input information by tapping buttons on the screen.

Correct Answer: A. Input

## CHAPTER 2

Notational Systems
Objective 1.2: Identify notational systems

Computers are designed to store and manipulate data in binary form, but that format isn't often convenient or appropriate for humans or software applications. *Notational systems* provide us with ways to use binary data storage technologies to represent numbers, text, and other data formats.

In this chapter, you'll learn everything you need to know about Tech+ objective 1.2, including the following topics:

▶ **Binary**
▶ **Hexadecimal**
▶ **Decimal**
▶ **Octal**

STORING DATA

As we dive into the world of information technology, it's important to understand how computers store and work with data. Let's begin that discussion by talking about the basic units of storage in a computer system.

Binary Data

You've probably heard that computers work with *binary* data, or data that is stored as simply 0s and 1s. Everything that happens inside a computer system uses combinations of 0s and 1s. From the operating system and software that we run to our Microsoft Word documents or even a video file, everything is encoded in binary format. The reason for this is that computers can easily use this binary format to store data on disk, keep it in memory, or send it over a network.

The basic unit of binary storage in any computer system is the *bit*. A bit is a single binary digit that can be either 1 or 0. Those are the only two possible values for a bit. You can't put the number 2 or the letter Z in a bit. It can only be a 1 or a 0, as shown in Figure 2.1

FIGURE 2.1   A single bit can hold only one of two possible values: 0 and 1.

When we store data on a magnetic hard drive, the computer divides the drive up into billions of tiny little spaces, each designed to store a single bit. If the value of the bit is 1, the computer places a magnetic charge in the location used by that bit. If the value of the bit is 0, the computer leaves no magnetic charge in that location.

When data is stored on a *solid-state drive (SSD)* or in memory, the process works the same way but uses electricity instead of magnetism. If the value of a bit in memory is 1, a small electrical charge changes the value in that memory location to the "on" position. If the value of the bit is 0, the value in that position is set to the "off" position.

Now, computers may think in 0s and 1s, but that's not the way that we human beings think. We'd much prefer to think of our data in terms of letters and numbers! Computers store the data that we're more familiar with by combining multiple bits together.

If we have 2 bits of data, we can use them together to represent four different values, as shown in Figure 2.2.

0	0
0	1
1	0
1	1

FIGURE 2.2   Two bits can hold four possible values.

We could use the 2-bit values in Figure 2.2 to store whole numbers between 0 and 3. We simply assign each of the 2-bit binary possibilities a whole-number equivalent. Table 2.1 shows the standard conversion for these 2-bit values.

If we have 3 bits of data, we can use them to store eight possible values: 000, 001, 010, 011, 100, 101, 110, and 111. These convert to decimal values ranging from 0 to 7, as shown in Table 2.2.

Similarly, if we have 4 bits of data, we can store 16 possible values, and as we increase the number of bits, we increase the number of values. Once we get up to 8 bits, we find ourselves able to store 256 possible values, ranging from 0 to 255. That's an important number because we can store all of the possible characters and digits used by a computer system in this range.

This combination of 8 bits is known as a *byte*, and the byte is the second important unit of binary data storage. When you're thinking about text data, you can think of each character as being a single byte, made up of 8 bits.

TABLE 2.1 Decimal conversion of 2-bit values

Binary value	Decimal value
00	0
01	1
10	2
11	3

TABLE 2.2 Decimal conversion of 3-bit values

Binary value	Decimal value
000	0
001	1
010	2
011	3
100	4
101	5
110	6
111	7

Decimal Data

Whether or not you know it, you're already familiar with *decimal notation*. This is the numbering system that we use in our everyday lives, and it's based off multiples of the number 10.

In a decimal number, each digit can take on 10 possible values, ranging from 0 to 9, as shown in Figure 2.3.

0	5
1	6
2	7
3	8
4	9

FIGURE 2.3 One decimal digit can hold 10 possible values.

When we grow to two decimal digits, we can represent one hundred values, ranging from 0 to 99. Adding a third digit allows us to store numbers between 0 and 999. Every time that we add another digit, we increase the number of values we can store by 10.

Hexadecimal Data

Unless you've worked with computer memory before, you're probably not familiar with *hexadecimal notation*. In this notation, each value can store 16 possible values, ranging from 0 to 15. Now you're probably wondering how we can put a two-digit number like 10 or 15 into a single location. That's a good question!

We do this by using the values 0 through 9 to represent the numbers 0 through 9 but then using the values A through F to represent 10 through 15. Figure 2.4 shows the 16 possible values that may be stored in a single hexadecimal digit.

0	4	8	C
1	5	9	D
2	6	A	E
3	7	B	F

FIGURE 2.4 A single hexadecimal digit can hold 16 possible values.

Octal Data

Octal notation is another method used by computers to represent data, sitting between the simplicity of binary and the more complex hexadecimal system. In octal notation, each position can hold eight possible values, ranging from 0 to 7, as shown in Figure 2.5. This system works well for computers because 8 is a power of 2, which aligns closely with how computers process data using bits.

FIGURE 2.5 A single octal digit can hold 8 possible values.

Table 2.3 provides some examples of the same numbers expressed in decimal, binary, hexadecimal, and octal forms.

TABLE 2.3 Decimal, binary, hexadecimal, and octal equivalent values

Decimal value	Binary value	Hexadecimal value	Octal value
0	0	0	0
5	101	5	5
10	1010	A	12
123	1111011	7B	173

The math here gets a little complicated, but the good thing is that you won't be asked to convert these values on the exam. What you want to understand is that if you see a value consisting of 0s and 1s, that's binary. If you see values made up of the digits 0 through 9, that's decimal. If the values contain only the digits 0 through 7, you may be looking at octal values. And if you see the letters A through F mixed in with those digits, that's hexadecimal.

EXAM TIP

Expect to see exam questions that ask you to identify the best notational system for a given situation. If the question asks about values that can be encoded as 0 or 1, true or false, off or on, yes or no, or similar two-value options, that's a key indicator that binary data storage is appropriate.

CHARACTER ENCODING

We've discussed four notation systems: binary, decimal, hexadecimal, and octal. Those are the different ways that we can represent numbers. But we often want to store and process text values instead of numbers when we're working with data. The way that we do this is to encode text characters as numbers.

You may remember when we first discussed binary data, I mentioned that computers typically work in units of bytes and that each byte consists of 8 bits. Bytes can store decimal numbers from 0 to 255, and we use 1 byte to store one character of text. We do this by using standard codes to describe how we encode each character as a number.

When we're using English or another language that uses our alphabet, we use a code called the American Standard Code for Information Interchange, or *ASCII*. This code describes what numeric value to use for each of the uppercase and lowercase letters, digits, punctuation, and other symbols commonly used in the English language. ASCII was originally designed as a 7-bit code, but modern computers use an extended version of ASCII that uses 8-bit bytes.

If you're working in languages other than English, you need to have more characters available to you. This requires the use of a different code. *Unicode* is a large character set capable of representing thousands of different characters using 8 or 16 bits of data.

CERTMIKE EXAM ESSENTIALS

▶ Binary data is the native format used by computer systems and is used to store values that can be represented as either 0 or 1. Decimal values are the base-10 numbers that we use in our everyday lives that use digits between 0 and 9.

▶ Hexadecimal values extend the number of possible values in a single digit to 16 by adding the values A–F as possibilities. Octal values limit the range of digits to those between 0 and 7.

▶ ASCII data representations are used to store the characters of standard English text in binary form. Unicode data representations can store English characters as well as characters used in other languages.

Practice Question 1

A developer is working on a new software program that will store data in memory about many different characteristics of customers of a bank. Each of these characteristics is best represented as a "yes" or "no" value.

What notational system would *best* store this type of data?

A. Hexadecimal
B. Decimal
C. Octal
D. Binary

Practice Question 2

Your company recently entered into a partnership with an organization based in Russia and you are helping an executive receive documents that must be translated from Russian into English. The documents contain Cyrillic characters, but those characters are not rendering properly on the screen.

What representational system is *best* used for this type of document?

A. ASCII
B. Binary
C. Unicode
D. Hexadecimal

Practice Question 1 Explanation

This question is asking us to identify the notational that would *best* meet the described need. This is a very common format for CompTIA exam questions, and you should be prepared to evaluate all of the possible answer choices and find the one that is better than all the others.

Let's evaluate these choices one at a time:

1. First, we have the possibility of using hexadecimal values. It would indeed be possible to store "yes" and "no" as hexadecimal values by using the hexadecimal value of 0 to represent "no" and 1 to represent "yes." However, this is wasteful because a single hexadecimal digit can be used to store up to 15 possible values and we only need the ability to store two possible values. So this isn't a great option.

2. Next, we are presented with the choice of storing the values in decimal form. As with hexadecimal, we could encode "no" as the decimal value 0 and "yes" as the decimal value 1, but that would be wasteful, so it is not the best option.

3. We could also use octal values to encode "no" as the octal value 0 and "yes" as the octal value 1, but that would also be wasteful, so it is not the best option.

4. The last option, binary, is the best one here. We can encode "yes" as the binary value 1 and "no" as the binary value 0 and use our data storage efficiently.

Correct Answer: D. Binary

Practice Question 2 Explanation

In this question, you're being asked to identify the best representational system to use when storing text data in a file. That allows us to narrow down our answer choices quickly. ASCII and Unicode are representational systems for text, whereas binary and hexadecimal are notational systems for storing data. We can, therefore, quickly eliminate binary and hexadecimal as answer choices.

When you take the Tech+ exam, watch for opportunities like this where you can immediately eliminate answer choices that are obviously wrong. This can help you focus your attention quickly and increase the odds that you will pick the correct answer.

Next, we must decide among the two remaining answers. ASCII only allows the storage of English characters, so it won't work very well in this scenario. We can, however, store the Cyrillic characters using a Unicode data representation, making Unicode our best option.

Remember, the use of non-English characters is a key indicator that Unicode is an appropriate choice!

Correct Answer: C. Unicode

## CHAPTER 3

Units of Measure

Objective 1.3: Compare and contrast common units of measure

Technologists throw around a lot of metrics and, as an IT professional, it's crucial that you understand the common measures used for storage, network throughput, and processing speed. You'll need to know how to compare these metrics and determine the largest, smallest, fastest, and slowest values.

In this chapter, you'll learn everything you need to know about Tech+ objective 1.3, including the following topics:

▶ Storage unit
▶ Throughput unit
▶ Processing speed

MEASURING DATA STORAGE

As you learned in Chapter 2, "Notational Systems," computers work with binary data, meaning data that is stored as simply 0s and 1s. Computers can easily use this binary format to store data on disk, keep it in memory, or send it over a network. Let's talk a little about how that actually works.

Bits and Bytes

Chapter 2 explained that the basic unit of storage in any computer system is the *bit*. A bit is a single value that can be either 1 or 0. The combination of 8 bits is known as a *byte*, and a byte can store a single character of text.

Many of the files that we store contains thousands, millions, billons, or even trillions of bytes! Instead of using extremely large numbers, we use larger units to help measure the size of stored data. You may already be familiar with this concept from the metric system; instead of referring to a distance as 1,000 meters, we can refer to that same distance as 1 kilometer. Data storage units use the same prefixes to denote multiples of bytes. Before you take the exam, you should be familiar with the standard multiples of bytes shown in Table 3.1.

TABLE 3.1 Data storage units

Unit	Number of bytes
Byte	1
Kilobyte (KB)	1,000
Megabyte (MB)	1,000,000
Gigabyte (GB)	1,000,000,000
Terabyte (TB)	1,000,000,000,000
Petabyte (PB)	1,000,000,000,000,000

EXAM TIP
You should be prepared to convert between these units. You may use the information in Table 3.1 and Table 3.2 to perform these conversions. For example, if you are presented with the fact that a file is 1.6 GB, you can use the table to convert that to 1,600 MB; 1,600,000 KB; or 1,600,000,000 bytes.

MEASURING DATA THROUGHPUT

We use bytes to measure how much data we have stored in memory, on a hard disk, or in another location where data is at rest. When data isn't at rest, it is in motion, being sent over a network. Networks don't store data, so it doesn't make sense to describe network capacity in terms of how much data a network can store. Networks move data around, so we measure network capacity in terms of the speed that a network can transfer data. This speed is a measure of how much data, measured in bits, that a network can move in a unit of time, such as seconds. That gives us the measure that we commonly use for network throughput: *bits per second*, or bps.

Notice that when we write bps, we use a lowercase b. When we measured storage capacity in kilobytes, megabytes, and so on, we used a capital B. That's an important difference because the lowercase b represents bits whereas the uppercase B represents bytes. Remember that 1 byte is equal to 8 bits. So if you wanted to see how many bytes a network could move per second, you have to divide the number of bits per second by 8. After you perform that division by 8, you get the less commonly used unit of *bytes per second*, or Bps.

Networks transmit data using a variety of methods, but they all rely on sending pulses that represent 1s and 0s. When there is a signal present, that represents a 1, whereas the absence of a signal represents 0. Wired networks accomplish this by using copper wires to transmit pulses of electricity. Wireless networks use radio waves to transmit radio signal pulses, and fiber-optic networks use strands of glass or plastic to transmit pulses of light.

Multiples of bps

Modern networks are able to move data very quickly, so we don't actually measure their speed in bits per second. Instead, we use multiples similar to those that we used for data storage, as shown in Table 3.2. Remember, these units are in bits per second, not bytes per second!

T A B L E   3 . 2   Data throughput units

Unit	Number of bits per second
bps	1
Kbps	1,000
Mbps	1,000,000
Gbps	1,000,000,000
Tbps	1,000,000,000,000

EXAM TIP

This material makes for easy exam question fodder. Expect to see at least one question asking you to compare values and/or units and select the largest or smallest value. When you see these questions, pay careful attention to the units and make sure that you're selecting a value that is appropriate for the question. If you're talking about storage, don't pick a throughput unit, and vice versa!

Your home Internet connection is probably measured in megabits per second, whereas your workplace's connection is likely measured in gigabits per second. You'd only see terabits per second on an extremely high-speed network inside a data center. We don't yet include petabits per second (Pbps) in this table, because currently no network is capable of transferring data at that speed.

NOTE

You'll often hear several different terms used to describe these measures of a network's capacity. Network speed, throughput, capacity, and bandwidth are all very similar terms. The difference between them is that network bandwidth and capacity refer to the amount of data that you are *supposed* to be able to send on a network and network throughout and speed refer to the amount that you are actually able to send on that network. They are all measured using these units of bits per second.

MEASURING PROCESSOR SPEED

We also need to measure how fast a computer can process data. Basically, that's describing how quickly the computer can think.

In Chapter 6, "Internal Computing Components," we'll discuss how the computer's central processing unit (CPU) is the central brain of a computer that does its thinking. CPUs have internal clocks that time how quickly they can perform a single mathematical operation. Now this isn't a clock like you or I might have in our home that ticks every second. Computers think extremely fast and their internal clocks tick billions of times per second. We measure the speed of a CPU based on how fast that clock ticks, and we count those ticks using a unit called *hertz*, where each hertz is a single tick.

If you think about the clock that you have in your home, you know that it ticks one time per second. That clock is a one-hertz clock; one tick per second is one hertz.

We measure computer clocks in multiples of hertz. Early personal computers measured clock speed in *megahertz (MHz)*, millions of ticks per second. Modern computer processors work in *gigahertz (GHz)*, billions of ticks per second. We call each of those ticks of the computer's clock a *cycle*.

That wraps up the three basic ways that we measure the speed and capacity of data, networks, and computers. We measure data storage on disks and in memory using bits and bytes. We measure network speed in bits per second. And we measure computer processing speed in hertz.

CERTMIKE EXAM ESSENTIALS

▶ The most basic unit of storage is the bit, which represents a single 0 or 1. We more commonly use bytes, which consist of 8 bits, and multiples of bytes including KB, MB, GB, TB, and PB.

▶ Network throughput is measured in the number of bits per second (bps) that the network can carry. Network speeds are measured in Kbps, Mbps, Gbps, and Tbps.

▶ Processor speed is measured in the number of cycles per second (hertz) that the processor completes. We commonly measure processor speed in MHz and GHz.

Practice Question 1

You are selecting a new computer for a user and are evaluating the speed of different processors. Which one of the following would be the highest processor speed?

A. 3.2 MHz
B. 3.2 Mbps
C. 3.2 PB
D. 3.2 GHz

Practice Question 2

You are looking at four files stored on a filesystem and would like to delete the largest file to free up space for other needs. Which one of the following files is the largest?

A. 16,000 GB
B. 900,000 KB
C. 1,000 MB
D. 1 TB

Practice Question 1 Explanation

This question boils down to understanding the different units used to measure processor speed. The first piece of information that you should call to mind is the fact that processor speed is measured in multiples of hertz, or cycles per second.

Based on this information, you can quickly eliminate two possible answer choices. 3.2 Mbps is a measure of network throughput, not one of processor speed. Similarly, 3.2 PB is a measure of data storage, not processor speed.

That leaves us with two possible answer choices: 3.2 MHz and 3.2 GHz. Both of these are indeed measures of processor speed, so we just need to know which unit is the largest of the two. 1 GHz is equal to 1,000 MHz, making 3.2 GHz the fastest processor speed listed here.

Correct Answer: D. 3.2 GHz

Practice Question 2 Explanation

This question is a little tricky because we're presented with file sizes in different units and asked to compare them. The best thing to do here is to first convert all of these file sizes to the same units. The smallest unit used in the question is kilobytes, so let's convert the four answer choices to KB.
That gives us:

▶ 16,000 GB = 16,000,000,000 KB

▶ 900,000 KB

▶ 1,000 MB = 1,000,000 KB

▶ 1 TB = 1,000,000,000 KB

With this information in hand, the comparison now becomes easy. 16,000,000,000 KB is the largest value, making our correct answer 16,000 GB.

If you face a question like this, where the units are all different and you have values with different numbers of zeros, the process we just outlined is the best approach. Convert all of the values to the same unit and then do the comparison.

You definitely should not just pick the largest unit. That's a common trap. Notice in this question that the answer choice with the largest unit (1 TB) was not the correct answer. There was another answer choice (16,000 GB) that is actually larger because 16,000 GB is 16 TB.

Correct Answer: A. 16,000 GB

## CHAPTER 4

Troubleshooting
Objective 1.4: Explain the troubleshooting methodology

As an IT professional, you'll often be called upon to troubleshoot issues that are causing problems for users or teams. Troubleshooting can be challenging because you may be trying to diagnose a problem that nobody else can figure out. But, personally, I find troubleshooting exhilarating! It's an opportunity to figure out a mystery and show off your IT skills. And when you solve the problem, you get to be the hero of the hour!

In this chapter, you'll learn everything you need to know about Tech+ objective 1.4, including the following topics:

▶ Identify the problem.
▶ Establish a theory of probable cause (question the obvious).
▶ Test the theory to determine the cause.
▶ Establish a plan of action to resolve the problem and implement the solution.
▶ Verify full system functionality and, if applicable, implement preventive measures.
▶ Document findings/lessons learned, actions, and outcomes.

TROUBLESHOOTING METHODOLOGY

Every troubleshooting situation is unique, but there are some basic steps that you can follow to conduct troubleshooting in an orderly manner that produces good results.

CompTIA endorses the six-step troubleshooting process shown in Figure 4.1. You should absolutely take the time to memorize the steps in this process.

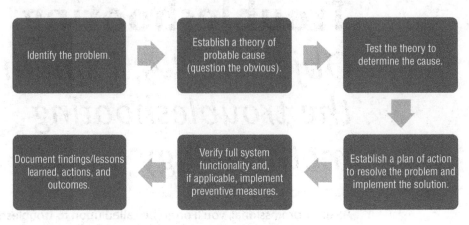

FIGURE 4.1 CompTIA's six-step troubleshooting methodology

Let's examine the process in more detail. We'll explain what occurs during each step and also walk through an example.

EXAM TIP

It is vital that you memorize the steps of the troubleshooting methodology shown in Figure 4.1. You will almost certainly find one or more questions on the exam asking you to evaluate a situation and identify the current step that a technician is following or the next step that they should take.

Identify the Problem

The first thing that you need to do is identify the problem. Talk to the end user and figure out what issues they're experiencing and identify the symptoms. For example, they might tell you that their network connection is slow or that they can't access a certain website. Gather as much information as you can and try to duplicate the problem. You'll want to replicate the user's experience so that you can help find the resolution. It's also a good idea during this phase to determine if anything has recently changed on the user's system. When you question the user, be sure to ask them whether they've recently installed any new software, changed any components of their system, or made any other technology changes.

> **TIP**
>
> When you visit a user, you might often find yourself bombarded with multiple problems. They might call you about their slow network connection but then say "While you're here, there's something else I need your help with." It's certainly fine to help users with all of their issues, but it's a good practice to tackle one problem at a time. By approaching multiple problems individually, you're increasing your likelihood of success.

Imagine that you're a desktop support technician and you are called to the desk of a user who is having trouble using a browser to access the Internet. When you first arrive, you should work to identify the problem. Here are some actions you might take:

- ▶ **Gather information** from the user and the system. Find out what the user is experiencing and examine the system's settings. You might learn that the user is seeing an error page no matter what website they try to visit.
- ▶ **Duplicate the problem** by trying to visit some websites yourself from the user's computer. You might also try visiting websites from other computers on the same network to identify whether the problem exists on only one system or whether it is network-wide.
- ▶ **Question the user** about any things they've tried to do to resolve the problem themselves. Have they tried restarting the computer or reseating the network cable?
- ▶ **Identify any symptoms** that might exist. Is this affecting only web traffic, or does the system appear to be completely disconnected from the network?
- ▶ **Determine if anything has changed.** Ask the user when they last were able to use the web and whether they or anyone else has installed any software or altered any settings since that last known good state.

The identification stage is crucial to the remainder of the troubleshooting process, as it ensures that you have all the information you need to evaluate the situation.

Establish a Theory of Probable Cause

Once you've identified the problem, it's time to conduct some research. If it's not a simple problem, you can go back to your own workspace and consult the references available to you. And yes, Googling things is absolutely fine! I often solve my own problems by searching on the Internet, so don't feel shy about doing that. Googling an error message often leads you directly to a page full of possible solutions. You should also visit the website for the vendor of the hardware or software involved in the problem. Vendors often have *knowledge bases* that you can search for troubleshooting advice. Your own organization also likely has an internal knowledge base that documents common issues found within the organization. Whatever information sources you use, verify that they are providing you with current, reliable information.

In the case of the user who can't access websites, you might consult the organization's knowledge base and discover that website connectivity issues are often the result of misconfigured servers, network outages, and incorrect domain names.

With this research under your belt, you can establish a theory of the probable cause. That's a fancy way of saying that you should make an educated guess about what's wrong. You don't have to be correct the first time; you're just trying to identify what you think is the most likely cause of the problem. When you do this, you should question obvious assumptions and consider multiple problem-solving approaches to help you find the best idea. If you have other team members assisting you, it's okay to take a *divide-and-conquer* approach, letting different team members pursue different theories.

In the case of the user who can't access the web, you might establish a theory of probable cause that the user's proxy settings are not correctly configured to use the organization's proxy servers. That's only one of many possibilities, however, so you'll next test that theory to see if it is correct.

Test the Theory to Determine the Cause

Once you have a solid theory, you'll want to test that theory to see if it's correct. This will help you determine the root cause of the incident. If your theory holds up, then you can move forward with solving the problem. If your theory doesn't work out, just return to the previous step and start testing a new theory.

To test your proxy server theory, you might examine the user's proxy settings and see if they match the organization's standard settings that you discovered in the knowledge base. If the settings are not properly configured, that validates your theory that they are the cause of the user's trouble, and you can move on to establish a plan of action to correct the problem.

Establish a Plan of Action to Resolve the Problem and Implement the Solution

After you determine the root cause of the incident, you can establish a plan of action to resolve the problem and identify any other effects that the problem may be having on this or other users. This may include altering system or network settings, installing or removing software, reconfiguring devices, replacing hardware, or performing many other possible steps.

If you discovered that the user's computer settings did not match the organization's standard proxy settings, you might then plan to reconfigure those settings to match the organization's standards. Before carrying out your plan, you should document the current settings so that you are able to undo any changes that you make if they are not successful.

If you're able to fix the problem yourself, you can implement the solution, or if you need help from other IT professionals, you may escalate the problem as needed. You might go through an iterative process of implementing several possible solutions. If that's the case, it's a good idea to completely implement and test one change and then undo that change if it didn't work before moving on to the next possibility. Making multiple changes at the same time increases the likelihood of new issues.

After documenting the user's current proxy settings, you may then change the settings to match the organization's standard settings.

Verify Functionality and, if Applicable, Implement Preventive Measures

Once you've implemented your solution, verify that the full system is functioning normally, and if it makes sense, put measures in place to prevent the problem from recurring for this user or affecting other users. You should test the new settings completely to ensure that not only have you fixed the problem, but also that your solution did not cause new issues.

For example, after changing the user's proxy settings, you should then attempt to visit a variety of internal and external websites to ensure that the changes were effective. If the user's system is not working properly, you will need to establish a new theory and repeat the troubleshooting process.

Document Findings/Lessons Learned, Actions, and Outcomes

Finally, the resolution of the problem isn't the last step in the process. You still have one more task to complete. Document your findings, lessons learned, actions, and outcomes. Documenting troubleshooting efforts isn't a very exciting part of our work, but it's important because it creates a record for other IT team members to follow if they experience similar issues. You're saving them the work of going through all the same troubleshooting steps that you just followed!

This may be as simple as updating the current incident details in your organization's incident tracking system. On the other hand, if you discovered new information during your troubleshooting that wasn't included in the knowledge base, this is a good time to document that information so that the next technician who encounters the problem may benefit from your discovery.

CERTMIKE EXAM ESSENTIALS

The CompTIA troubleshooting process consists of six steps:

1. Identify the problem.

2. Establish a theory of probable cause (question the obvious).

3. Test the theory to determine the cause.

4. Establish a plan of action to resolve the problem and implement the solution.

5. Verify full system functionality and, if applicable, implement preventive measures.

6. Document findings/lessons learned, actions, and outcomes.

Practice Question 1

You are working with a user who was experiencing an issue with displaying computer-aided design (CAD) graphics on their computer. You replaced the user's monitor and performed some tests that showed that the problem is resolved and the user has full system functionality. What should you do next?

A. Document your findings.
B. Close the ticket.
C. Conduct additional testing.
D. Escalate to senior technicians.

Practice Question 2

You are helping a user troubleshoot a problem where they cannot print to a new all-in-one device that was recently installed. You have researched the problem on the Internet and in your organization's knowledge base, and that research is pointing you at several possible issues. You are working to identify which issue is the most likely culprit. What step are you taking in the troubleshooting process?

A. Verify full system functionality.
B. Identify the problem.
C. Establish a plan of action to resolve the problem and implement the solution.
D. Establish a theory of probable cause.

Practice Question 1 Explanation

This is a straightforward question that is asking you to identify where you are in the troubleshooting process and determine the appropriate next step. If you consult the troubleshooting methodology in Figure 4.1, you'll discover that verifying full system functionality is the fifth step in the process.

There is no need for you to conduct any additional testing or escalate to a senior technician, as you have resolved the problem successfully.

However, you are also not ready to close the ticket because you have not yet documented your findings. You should complete documentation of findings/lessons learned, actions, and outcomes before closing out the case.

Correct Answer: A. Document your findings.

Practice Question 2 Explanation

This question is also testing your familiarity with the CompTIA troubleshooting methodology shown in Figure 4.1. In this case, you must determine where you are in the troubleshooting process.

The question indicates that you have researched the problem, but you have not yet figured out which issue is the likely problem. Researching the problem is part of step 2, establishing a theory of probable cause, but you have not yet completed that step by identifying a specific issue, so you are still in that step of the process.

You have already identified that the problem is that the user cannot print to the new device, so you know that the answer is not step 1, identify the problem. Therefore, you can eliminate that possibility.

You do not yet know which issue you are solving, so it would be premature to establish a plan of action to resolve the problem and implement a solution (step 4) or verify full system functionality (step 5). The next thing that you need to do is establish a theory of the probable cause (step 2).

Correct Answer: D. Establish a theory of probable cause.

Domain 2.0: Infrastructure

Infrastructure is the second domain of CompTIA's Tech+ exam. It covers the core infrastructure components in any IT environment: servers, endpoints, peripherals, networking, and storage. This domain has nine objectives:

2.1 **Explain common computing devices and their purposes**
2.2 **Explain the purpose of common internal computing components**
2.3 **Compare and contrast storage types**
2.4 **Given a scenario, install and configure common peripheral devices**
2.5 **Compare and contrast common types of input/output device interfaces**
2.6 **Compare and contrast virtualization and cloud technologies**
2.7 **Compare and contrast common Internet service types**
2.8 **Identify basic networking concepts**
2.9 **Explain the basic capabilities of a small wireless network**

Questions from this domain make up 24% of the questions on the Tech+ exam, so you should expect to see approximately 18 questions on your test covering the material in this part.

Domain 7.0: Infrastructure

## CHAPTER 5

Computing Devices

Objective 2.1: Explain common computing devices and their purposes

We use many different types of computing devices to help us get our work done, organize our lives, and even entertain ourselves. From laptops to mobile phones, it's not uncommon these days for each of us to have several devices that we use on a regular basis.

In this chapter, you'll learn everything you need to know about Tech+ objective 2.1, including the following topics:

- ▶ Smartphones
- ▶ Tablets
- ▶ E-readers
- ▶ Laptops
- ▶ Workstations
- ▶ Servers
- ▶ Gaming consoles
- ▶ Virtual reality systems
- ▶ Augmented reality systems
- ▶ Internet of Things (IoT)

COMPUTING DEVICE TYPES

In Chapter 1, "Computing Basics," you learned about the four basic operations performed by any computing device: input, storage, processing, and output. No matter what type of device you use, it performs all of these functions and those functions are coordinated by an operating system.

The *operating system* is software that normally comes preinstalled on a new computer and coordinates everything else that the computer does. When you start an app, the operating system manages the input and output devices, memory, and storage used by that app and ensures that different apps running at the same time don't interfere with each other.

Let's talk a little about the different types of computing devices that you may encounter while working in the world of information technology.

Desktop Computers

The standard *desktop computer* was once the mainstay of any office environment. Everyone had a computer on their desk and the reality was that the computer took up most of that desk! When I first started working at the National Security Agency in the late 1990s, I had two different computers: one for classified work and another for unclassified work. Those computers were so large that they took up an entire desk themselves—I had to have a second desk where I could actually work!

Today, desktop computers, such as the one shown in Figure 5.1, take up much less space, and they no longer dominate the office environment. Many people still have desktop computers because they are generally less expensive than more portable devices, but many users who travel or move around the office don't want to be tethered to their desks, so they choose other alternatives.

F I G U R E 5 . 1 Desktop computer system

Denis Rozhnovsky/Adobe Stock Photos

Workstations

Some users have special computing needs where they need enhanced graphics processing, computing power, or other capabilities. Instead of a normal desktop computer, they might use a specialized device called a *workstation* that provides high-performance computing at a user's desk. Video editors, graphic designers, and other people who work with computing-intensive applications use these devices.

Servers

There's one more type of nonportable computer that you should know about. *Servers* are powerful computers that carry out a dedicated function. Companies might use servers to share files internally, host a website, run a database, or perform many other functions. You'll learn more about server functions as you work your way through this book, but for now, just know that servers are powerful computers that typically reside in special data centers that are designed to house many servers in special racks, such as the ones shown in Figure 5.2.

FIGURE 5.2 Server racks in a data center

shock/Adobe Stock Photos

Mobile Devices

Today, more employees than ever find themselves working from locations other than the office. Whether they're traveling around the world meeting with customers or simply working from home, users and their managers prefer portable computing devices that can easily travel with users wherever they need to work.

Laptop Computers

Laptop computers (see Figure 5.3) are very similar to the desktop computers that used to sit in every cubicle and office but with the major benefit of being extremely portable. They package together all of the computer's components, including the display, keyboard, and trackpad, in a single device that can be easily moved from one location to another. Laptops also contain batteries, allowing them to be used for hours without connecting them to electricity. Today's laptop can be just as powerful as a modern desktop computer. The only disadvantage is that they typically cost more than desktop computers, and laptop users generally prefer to also have a full-sized monitor at their desk, increasing the total cost of their computing environment.

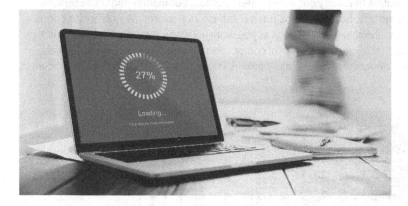

FIGURE 5.3 Laptop computer

Prostock-studio/Adobe Stock Photos

Smartphones

Most of us carry *smartphones* with us today, such as the one shown in Figure 5.4. These smartphones are also powerful computing devices. In fact, the smartphones we use today are far more powerful than the desktop computers that we used just a decade ago. Smartphones run their own specialized operating systems. iPhones run Apple's iOS operating system whereas most other devices run Google's Android operating system.

Tablets

Tablets fit in between smartphones and laptops in terms of both size and capabilities. Tablets, such as the one shown in Figure 5.5, have larger screens than a phone but lack the physical keyboard and processing power of a laptop device. Tablets are commonly used in environments where employees are walking around interacting with customers and need a device that is portable. They are also often used to power touchscreen kiosks, such as those found in a hotel lobby. E-readers are specialized tablets designed specifically for use in reading books and other digital content. They commonly use electronic ink (e-ink) technology to present text in a way that is easy to read.

FIGURE 5.4 Smartphone

artiemedvedev/Adobe Stock Photos

FIGURE 5.5 Tablet computer

jomaplaon/Adobe Stock Photos

Convertible laptops, such as the one shown in Figure 5.6, may be flipped around and used as either touchscreen tablets or normal laptops.

FIGURE 5.6 Convertible laptop being used as a tablet

santiago silver/Adobe Stock Photos

Wearable Devices

As computing technology continues to advance, it's finding its way into even smaller and more personal devices. *Wearable devices*, like the smartwatch shown in Figure 5.7, are at the forefront of this trend. These tiny yet powerful gadgets extend the functionality of computing to the body itself, allowing for an unprecedented level of integration into our daily lives.

Smartwatches are perhaps the most recognizable form of wearable technology. They serve not only as timepieces but also as fitness trackers, notification centers, and even as extensions of our smartphones. The smartwatch in Figure 5.7 is equipped with its own operating system, allowing it to run a variety of apps independently of a phone. While the small screen size can limit interaction, designers have overcome this by integrating voice control, touch gestures, and even contextual awareness into the user experience.

FIGURE 5.7 Smartwatch

juliars/Adobe Stock Photos

Beyond smartwatches, wearable devices include fitness bands, smart glasses, health monitors, and more. Each is designed with portability and constant wear in mind, often focusing on specialized functions that complement the capabilities of larger devices. They often connect to other computing devices, like smartphones or laptops, to sync data or leverage larger processing power and storage when necessary.

Gaming Consoles

You won't generally find *gaming consoles* in an office environment, but they are common on home networks. Gaming consoles, such as the one shown in Figure 5.8, actually contain very powerful computers that are optimized to deliver the graphics and audio capabilities necessary to run modern games.

In any large organization, you'll likely find a mix of these different types of computing device. Many users will have several devices. I have a desktop computer that I use regularly in my office, a laptop that travels around with me, a smartphone that I keep in my pocket, and a tablet that I use occasionally for reading or watching videos. Today's IT professional needs to understand the many different device types available to users and help them select devices that best meet their needs.

Virtual and Augmented Reality Systems

Virtual reality technology, such as the Apple Vision Pro shown in Figure 5.9, allows you to transport yourself into a different world. These headsets have built-in high-resolution displays targeted at each of your eyes, allowing them to display 3D and immersive content.

Augmented reality (AR) technology enhances the real world by overlaying digital information on top of it. Unlike virtual reality, which creates a fully immersive virtual environment, AR integrates digital content with the user's environment in real time.

AR applications can display information, 3D models, or animations over what the user sees in the real world, creating interactive experiences that blend the digital and physical worlds.

FIGURE 5.8 Gaming console

Nikolai Sorokin/Adobe Stock Photos

FIGURE 5.9 Apple Vision Pro virtual reality headset

Bruno/Adobe Systems Incorporated

INTERNET OF THINGS

It's not just laptops, desktops, and phones that contain computers these days. Virtually everything around us now contains an embedded computer and is connected to the Internet. These devices might automatically order groceries for our homes when we're running low, reduce our cooling and heating bills based on the weather forecast, or even manage our lawn sprinkler systems.

We use the term *Internet of Things (IoT)* to describe the way that we connect many everyday devices to the Internet. These devices commonly use wireless networking to make it easy to place them anywhere in our homes and connect back to web consoles or home automation systems that coordinate their activity.

Home IoT Devices

We can connect all sorts of different devices to an IoT network. Home appliances, such as refrigerators, stoves, and washing machines, can all connect to the Internet. Today's refrigerator can remind you to buy milk at the store or even have it delivered when you're running low. The washing machine might be able to reach out to your favorite e-commerce retailer and reorder detergent for you. It can also send you a text message to remind you to switch the load over to the dryer when it's finished.

Inside our homes, we also might have other home automation devices, including a smart thermostat, an Internet-connected security system with IP-enabled cameras, stream-ing media devices that connect to the Internet to deliver content, home assistants, smart deadbolts and door locks, video doorbells, exercise equipment, or even IoT vehicles that can obtain driving directions, report their maintenance status back to the dealer, or deliver entertainment content to passengers. Many IoT devices may be remotely controlled by smartphone apps.

Workplace IoT Devices

The Internet of Things also plays a role in the workplace, particularly in industrial settings. The many advances in technology that have sped up manufacturing, power plant moni-toring, wastewater treatment, and other industrial processes require the use of computers. *Industrial control systems (ICSs)* are the devices and systems that control industrial produc-tion and operation. They include systems that monitor electrical, gas, water, and other utility infrastructure and production operations, as well as the systems that control sewage processing and control, irrigation, and other processes.

IoT devices also play a role in modern healthcare. Virtually every medical device in a hospital is now connected to a network to improve patient care, and patients may even bring home insulin pumps, blood pressure monitors, and other devices that can report a patient's medical status back to their physician.

The Internet of Things is an awesomely powerful technology that reaches into almost every area of our lives, allowing us to take advantage of the power of modern computing to live better lives. As IT professionals, we're responsible for connecting these devices to the network, managing them, and ensuring that they have proper security controls in place to protect sensitive information.

CERTMIKE EXAM ESSENTIALS

▶ Desktop computers and workstations serve the computing needs of users who remain at a single location as they work. Laptops, tablets, and smartphones serve the needs of traveling users.

▶ Servers reside in data centers and provide a variety of services to users on the local network and/or the Internet.

▶ The Internet of Things connects everyday devices in both the home and the workplace to the network.

Practice Question 1

You are helping a user select a new computing device. The user is a video editor who requires a significant amount of computing power and will be using the device at a video-editing station. What type of device would best meet this need?

A. Workstation
B. Desktop computer
C. Laptop computer
D. Server

Practice Question 2

You are designing a check-in kiosk for a medical practice. You require the use of a touchscreen where users can register for their appointment. What type of computer would best meet this need?

A. Desktop
B. Laptop
C. Smartphone
D. Tablet

Practice Question 1 Explanation

We can take away a couple of important facts from this scenario. First, the user is working in a fixed location—at an editing station. There is no indication that they are mobile, so we can eliminate the need for a laptop computer.

Next, the user requires significant computing power. This would make us lean toward a more powerful computer than a desktop, such as a workstation or a server. However, since the user will be interacting with the computer directly, we would not want a server, which would reside in a data center. Therefore, a workstation is likely the best solution for this user.

Correct Answer: A. Workstation

Practice Question 2 Explanation

You should always select the computing device that best meets the requirements of a scenario while minimizing cost. In this case, there is a clear requirement for a touchscreen, eliminating the possibility of using a desktop computer.

While some laptops do have touchscreens, they are far more expensive than the other options, so we can eliminate that choice as well.

Smartphones and tablets are both lower-cost devices that have touchscreens, but a smartphone is likely too small to support a check-in kiosk, where users will want a larger screen. This makes a tablet computer the ideal choice.

Correct Answer: D. Tablet

## CHAPTER 6

Internal Computing Components

Objective 2.2: Explain the purpose of common internal computing components

We've covered the ways that you get data into and out of a computer system. Now let's take a look inside the computer itself and learn about the internal components of a computer.

In this chapter, you'll learn everything you need to know about Tech+ objective 2.2, including the following topics:

▶ **Motherboard/system board**
▶ **Firmware/BIOS**
▶ **RAM**
▶ **CPU**
▶ **Storage**
▶ **GPU**
▶ **Cooling**
▶ **NIC**

CPU

The central processing unit (CPU) is the brain of the computer, and it performs most of the processing that happens inside the computer. Different computers have different types of CPUs, and those CPUs may be manufactured by different companies. Figure 6.1 shows an example of a CPU.

FIGURE 6.1 Central processing unit (CPU)

Oleksandr Delyk/Adobe Stock Photos

The typical Windows computer contains a processor manufactured by one of two companies: Intel or AMD. These two companies create most of the processors used by laptop and desktop computers, and you'll generally be fine with either option. If you have a specialized use case with unique needs for computing power, you'll want to analyze the specifications of the available processors, but generally speaking, Windows runs fine on both Intel or AMD processors.

Mac devices also use processors made by two different companies: Intel and Apple itself. Until 2020, Mac computers used the same Intel processors found in many Windows computers. In 2020, Apple released their own M1 processor, and they offer many of their products with either processor installed.

Mobile devices, such as smartphones and tablets, also have CPUs, but they use a different type of CPU. ARM processors are designed specifically for these devices, and they are specially designed to use as little power as possible, extending the battery life of mobile devices.

CPU Performance

When you're measuring a CPU, there are a few characteristics you should consider:

- ▶ **Clock speed** is measured in gigahertz (GHz), and the faster the clock, the faster the computer can process data.
- ▶ CPUs are also measured in terms of their number of **processing cores**. Each core is a separate processing unit within the same chip. Having multiple cores allows a computer to perform more than one task at the same time. Modern computers may have eight or more cores and supercomputers may have thousands or millions of cores.

▶ We also measure CPUs in terms of how much memory they can manage at the same time. We measure this by describing the **number of bits** that may be in a memory address. 32-bit processors were common in years past, and they could manage up to 4 gigabytes of memory. That was plenty a decade ago, but modern computers can support much more than that because they use 64-bit processors. A 64-bit processor can manage 16 exabytes of memory. That's far more than any computer we will be using any time soon, so expect 64-bit processors to stick around for a while!

MOTHERBOARD

Inside the computer, the CPU lives on the *motherboard*, also known as the system board. This is a printed circuit board that connects the CPU to memory, interfaces, and other system components. Figure 6.2 shows a photograph of a motherboard. The CPU is located under the tall fan that appears on the back center of the motherboard.

FIGURE 6.2 Motherboard

vetkit/Adobe Stock Photos

FIRMWARE

When a computer starts up, it uses a very small program that's stored on the motherboard that has the basic job of getting the system up and running and loading the real operating system from disk. This operating system is stored as *firmware*, a type of software that is permanently written onto chips so that it may be accessed before any other software is loaded from disk. The chips that store firmware are also known as *read-only memory (ROM)*. There are two major options for the code stored in firmware:

▶ The *basic input/output system (BIOS)* is an older approach that has been largely phased out.

▶ The *Unified Extensible Firmware Interface (UEFI)* is a more modern approach that has largely replaced BIOS.

Modern computers are able to boot over the network, receiving software from a centralized server. This capability is known as the *Preboot Execution Environment (PXE)*.

MEMORY

The motherboard also contains slots where computer builders and technicians can insert memory chips known as dual in-line memory modules (DIMM). These memory chips contain the *random access memory (RAM)* that the computer uses to store software and data that it is actively using. The contents of memory are temporary and go away when the computer is turned off. This characteristic is known as *volatility*: volatile storage (such as RAM) is erased when the computer is turned off, whereas nonvolatile storage (such as a hard drive) retains its contents when turned off. Figure 6.3 shows an example of a DIMM.

FIGURE 6.3 Dual in-line memory module (DIMM)

Mauro Rodrigues/Adobe Stock Photos

DISK DRIVES

Data that we want to keep around must be stored on more permanent, nonvolatile storage and that's the role of disk drives. These drives may use magnetic media or solid-state storage. *Hard disk drives (HDDs)* are older and slower, but less expensive than *solid-state drives (SSDs)*, which are newer, faster, and more expensive than HDDs. We discuss disk drive types in more detail in Chapter 7, "Storage."

Figure 6.4 shows an example of a hard disk drive with its cover removed to reveal its inner workings.

Figure 6.5 shows an example of a smaller form solid-state drive.

FIGURE 6.4 Hard disk drive (HDD)

tuahlensa/Adobe Stock Photos

FIGURE 6.5 Solid-state drive (SSD)

pixelrobot/Adobe Stock Photos

NETWORK INTERFACE CARDS

Most computers also contain a *network interface card (NIC)*. The term NIC comes from the days that network interfaces were commonly expansion cards that were inserted into computers as they were built, such as the one shown in Figure 6.6. Today, expansion cards are still available that may be inserted directly into a computer or attached via a USB cable.

FIGURE 6.6 Network interface card (NIC)

Bacho Foto/Adobe Stock Photos

Modern NICs are often directly on the motherboard and provide the ability to connect to both wired and wireless networks. These NICs are known as *onboard* because they are "on the motherboard."

GPU

Some computers also contain specialized *graphics processing units (GPUs)*. These powerful processors are designed to perform the intensive calculations required to render complex graphics on the screen. They're used by graphic designers, video editors, and gamers to speed up processing. GPUs are also quite useful for data science, analytics, and blockchain applications that require a lot of math. GPUs are expensive, however, so you won't find them in every computer. They're a cost that's only necessary for specialized applications. Figure 6.7 shows an example of a GPU.

FIGURE 6.7 Graphics processing unit (GPU)

Maksym Yemelyanov/Adobe Stock Photos

POWER AND COOLING

The components of a computer system require a steady supply of power to operate. Specifically, they use a type of electric power called *direct current (DC)*. DC power is the type of power provided by batteries and is different from the *alternating current (AC)* power that is available in wall outlets. For this reason, computers must have *power supply units (PSUs)* that plug into the wall and convert the AC power supplied by electric utilities into the DC power used by computing components. Figure 6.8 shows a typical PSU that might be found in a desktop or server computer.

All of these components that we cram into a computer system generate a lot of heat. But computer components also don't like to be hot! Running electronic components in an overheated environment can result in errors and equipment failures, so computers and data centers contain cooling equipment that draws out the hot air and replaces it with cool air. Computers contain fans, and you can often hear those fans turn on when the computer is working hard. That whirring noise that you may hear is an actual fan inside the computer trying to cool it down. Data centers with many computers use massive air-conditioning systems to keep everything inside cool.

FIGURE 6.8 Computer power supply unit (PSU)

sergey makarenko/Adobe Stock Photos

CERTMIKE EXAM ESSENTIALS

▶ Computers perform everyday processing using the central processing unit (CPU). Graphics processing units (GPUs) supplement CPU capacity for complex mathematics.

▶ The motherboard holds the CPU, in addition to random access memory (RAM), read-only memory (ROM), and other computing components.

▶ Long-term storage is provided by hard disk drives (HDDs) and solid-state drives (SSDs). SSDs are faster and more expensive than HDDs.

Practice Question 1

You are upgrading an old computer and find that it is not able to support high-speed networking. What component of the computer should you consider upgrading?

A. NIC
B. CPU
C. GPU
D. RAM

Practice Question 2

You are helping to configure a new computer that will be used by an executive and are selecting a long-term storage option for the executive's files. Which one of the following options will provide the fastest possible long-term storage?

A. RAM
B. ROM
C. SSD
D. HDD

Practice Question 1 Explanation

Any of the upgrades listed here may have the effect of speeding up the computer, but this question is asking specifically about networking speed. The computer component that controls networking is the network interface card (NIC), and you should consider upgrading that card to support higher-speed networking.

The central processing unit (CPU) is the main processing hub of the computer where it executes instructions, and the graphics processing unit (GPU) provides supplementary computing capability in support of graphics, data science, and other applications that require complex mathematics. Random access memory (RAM) is used to store programs and data being actively used by the computer.

Correct Answer: A. NIC

Practice Question 2 Explanation

As you approach this question, you can eliminate options by examining the requirements. First, you are looking for an option that will allow the executive to store files for long-term use. Random access memory (RAM) is temporary working memory for the computer and does not store data long-term. Therefore, it is not suitable for this purpose. Similarly, read-only memory (ROM) is not suitable because users cannot write data to ROM.

That leaves us with the two types of drives commonly used in a computer system—hard disk drives (HDDs) and solid-state drives (SSDs). Of these, SSDs are often faster than HDDs, making an SSD the best option here.

Correct Answer: C. SSD

## CHAPTER 7

Storage
Objective 2.3:
Compare and contrast storage types

As we wrap up our look at the inner workings of a computer, let's take a deeper dive into the different types of storage used by computer systems. We've already discussed how computers need different types of storage for different purposes. There are two major categories of storage: volatile storage and nonvolatile storage.

In this chapter, you'll learn everything you need to know about the Tech+ objective 2.3, including the following topics:

▶ **Volatile versus nonvolatile**
▶ **Local storage**
▶ **Local network storage**
▶ **Cloud storage service**

VOLATILE STORAGE

Volatile storage is storage that is designed to be temporary. The most common example of volatile storage is the *random access memory (RAM)* that is on the computer's motherboard. RAM is very fast, but it's also relatively expensive. RAM contains all of the data that a computer is actively working with. However, it is volatile storage, so the contents of RAM are only there as long as the computer is turned on. If you turn the computer off, the contents of RAM are erased when you turn it back on again. A typical desktop or laptop computer might have 8–32 GB of RAM, but more powerful computers and servers may have hundreds of gigabytes of RAM.

You learned more about the different types of RAM in Chapter 6, "Internal Computing Components."

NONVOLATILE STORAGE

Nonvolatile storage is just a fancy way to say permanent storage. Nonvolatile storage comes in many different forms, but the common characteristic they share is that once you write something to nonvolatile storage, it stays there until you delete it, even if you turn off the power.

We measure nonvolatile storage drives in two ways. First, we measure the total storage capacity of the device in bytes and the different multiples of bytes that you learned about in Chapter 3, "Units of Measure." It's common for a typical computer to have hard drives or solid-state drives that can store 500 GB, 1 TB, or more data. Second, we measure the speed at which storage devices can store and retrieve data. We measure this using a unit called *input/output operations per second (IOPS)*.

Read-only memory (ROM) is an example of nonvolatile storage. We discussed ROM in Chapter 6.

Magnetic Hard Drives

Some nonvolatile storage is local to a computer system. We've already talked about the use of *magnetic hard disk drives (HDDs)*. Magnetic drives provide inexpensive storage that is relatively slow. Magnetic hard drives contain platters of magnetic material that spin around very quickly inside the computer where a head reads and writes magnetic charges to the disk. For this reason, magnetic hard drives are also commonly known as *spinning disk* drives. Figure 7.1 shows an example of a magnetic hard drive.

FIGURE 7.1 Magnetic hard disk drive (HDD)

tuahlensa/Adobe Stock Photos

Solid-State Drives

Solid-state drives (SSDs) are a modern replacement for magnetic drives. Instead of using spinning magnetic disks, they use stored electric charges and have no moving parts. This makes SSDs less likely to break and allows them to work more quickly than magnetic drives, but those benefits come with a cost: Solid-state drives are more expensive than magnetic drives. Figure 7.2 shows an example of a solid-state drive.

FIGURE 7.2 Solid-state drive (SDD)

pixelrobot/Adobe Stock Photos

External flash drives use the same technology as solid-state drives but in a removable form. Flash drives are fairly inexpensive, but they have limited storage capacity when compared to solid-state drives. Figure 7.3 shows an example of a flash drive with a USB interface.

FIGURE 7.3 USB flash drive

mercan1299/Adobe Stock Photos

Secure Digital (SD) cards are a proprietary format of flash drive and have the distinctive appearance shown in Figure 7.4. SD cards are primarily used as storage for cameras, tablet computers, and other portable devices due to their small size.

FIGURE 7.4 SD card

Luis Santos/Adobe Stock Photos

NONVOLATILE MEMORY EXPRESS

Nonvolatile Memory Express (NVMe) is a way to access high-speed storage media quickly and efficiently. It is a protocol for how data is transferred between the computer's main components and its storage. NVMe is designed to maximize the strengths of SSD storage, resulting in a system that can very quickly read and write data. This speed makes everything from starting the computer, to opening apps, to transferring files feel almost instantaneous.

Optical Drives

Optical drives use lasers to etch data onto a removable disc that may be stored separately from the computer system. These optical discs, such as the one shown in Figure 7.5, come in a variety of forms:

► *Compact discs (CDs)* were the original optical storage media, allowing the storage of up to 680 MB of data on a single disc.
► *Digital video discs (DVDs)* increase the density of storage, allowing the storage of up to 17 GB of data on a single disc.
► *Blu-ray discs (BDs)* have the highest capacity of any optical format, allowing the storage of up to 128 GB of data on a single disc.

FIGURE 7.5 Optical disc

dtuluu/Adobe Stock Photos

There are different types of each of these optical media:

▶ *Read-only* discs are recorded at the factory and users may not change the data stored on them.
▶ *Recordable* discs allow users to write data to them, but that data is then permanently stored on the disc and may not be erased or modified.
▶ *Rewritable* discs are erasable and may be reused after recording data on them.

Table 7.1 shows the common disc types.

TABLE 7.1 Common disc types

	Compact disc	Digital video disc	Blu-ray disc
Read-only	CD-ROM	DVD	BD-ROM
Recordable	CD-R	DVD-R	BD-R
Rewritable	CD-RW	DVD-RW	BD-RW

When optical drives read and write data to discs, they spin the disc rapidly in the drive and use a laser to read and write data. Therefore, optical drives, like HDDs, are examples of spinning disk media.

Enterprise Storage Services

Organizations generally don't want to manage large quantities of removable media or store data on drives attached to individual computers. Instead, they prefer to have centralized enterprise storage services that store data in a single location where it may be accessed by many different users.

Cloud Storage

Today, *cloud storage services* allow organizations to outsource storage, using services provided by a vendor who manages those storage resources and makes them available to users wherever they reside.

File Servers

Businesses that choose not to use cloud services may operate their own centralized storage services that meet the needs of their employees. They often do this by running a *file server*, which is just a computer with a lot of storage installed in it. The file server sits on the network and users may access it from their own computers.

Network attached storage (NAS) systems, are self-contained file servers that plug directly into a network to provide users with access to shared storage space. Figure 7.6 shows an example of a NAS device.

FIGURE 7.6 Network attached storage (NAS) array

300dpi/Adobe Stock Photos

File servers and other enterprise storage services make use of technology called *Redundant Arrays of Inexpensive Disks (RAID)* to protect against disk failures. The general idea behind RAID technology is that the server or NAS array writes the same data to multiple disks so that if a single disk fails, the data may still be retrieved.

CERTMIKE EXAM ESSENTIALS

▶ Volatile storage, such as RAM, retains its contents only while a device is powered on. Nonvolatile storage such as HDDs, SSDs, and flash drives retain contents permanently, until the data is intentionally deleted or overwritten.

▶ Hard drives may be either magnetic hard disk drives (HDDs), which use spinning disks, or solid-state drives (SSDs), which have no moving parts.

▶ Optical media may be used to store data on removable disks. Common optical media formats include CDs, DVDs, and Blu-ray discs.

Practice Question 1

You are operating a computer system that will work in close proximity to a medical device that uses strong magnetic fields to image body parts. What type of storage is most likely to be damaged by the presence of these magnetic fields?

A. HDD

B. CD

C. SSD

D. DVD

Practice Question 2

Which one of the following storage options is an example of volatile storage?

A. NAS

B. Flash

C. BD-RW

D. RAM

Practice Question 1 Explanation

To answer this question, you need to know which storage media use magnetic fields to store data. Magnetic hard disk drives (HDDs) do this and would likely be damaged by the medical devices.

Solid-state drives (SSDs) use electricity, rather than magnetism, to store data and would be less likely to be damaged.

Compact discs (CDs) and digital video discs (DVDs) store data in optical form, which would not be damaged by the presence of a magnetic field.

Correct Answer: A. HDD

Practice Question 2 Explanation

Volatile storage is storage that loses its data when it is powered off. Random access memory (RAM) is temporary storage used by a computer to store data that is currently in use and it does lose its data when powered off. Therefore, RAM is an example of volatile storage.

Network attached storage (NAS), flash drives, and Blu-ray discs all retain data when power is removed. All three of these are examples of nonvolatile storage.

Correct Answer: D. RAM

## CHAPTER 8

Installing Peripherals

Objective 2.4: Given a scenario, install and configure common peripheral devices

Users depend on a wide variety of peripherals to support their work with desktop computers, laptops, tablets, and other devices. From entering data with keyboards, mice, and scanners to generating paper documents with a printer, peripherals play an important role in making computers useful in an office environment.

In this chapter, you'll learn everything you need to know about Tech+ objective 2.4, including the following topics:

▶ Devices
▶ Installation types

PERIPHERAL TYPES

Peripherals are the devices that we connect to our computers that play a supporting role. We each use many different peripherals in our daily work. Let's explore some of the common peripherals you might find in an office environment.

Keyboards and Mice

Keyboards and mice are peripheral devices that allow you to provide input to a computer system. The keyboard allows you to enter text and numeric data, and the *mouse* allows you to move objects around and work within a graphical user interface (GUI). Keyboards and mice are pretty much mandatory for desktop computers. They're often built into laptops, but many laptop users prefer to have external keyboards and mice on their desks because these full-sized devices are easier to use than the smaller devices built into laptops. Figure 8.1 shows an example of a typical keyboard (on the left) and mouse (on the right).

FIGURE 8.1 Keyboard and mouse

Leo Lintang/Adobe Stock Photos

Display

Displays are also pretty much mandatory for a computer to be useful to its users. The typical display is a *monitor* that allows the user to see what the computer is doing while they interact with the computer, such as the one shown in Figure 8.2. Servers generally don't have displays connected to them, but laptop and desktop computers must use displays to be useful to people. As with keyboards and mice, laptops also have built-in displays, but users often have larger monitors on their desks for when they're using their laptops in the office. Touchscreen displays are also quite popular because they allow users to interact directly with the display without using the keyboard or mouse.

Depending on business requirements, computers may use something other than a traditional display to show their output. For example, computers may be attached to *smart televisions* or *projectors* for displaying content to large audiences.

Speakers

Speakers (see Figure 8.3) produce sound and are also commonly connected to computer systems so that users may hear the sound created by or streamed through the computer. In busy office environments, users often prefer to use *headsets* instead of speakers for privacy and to avoid annoying their officemates.

Printers and Scanners

Printers, such as the one shown in Figure 8.4, produce paper output and are either directly connected to an individual computer or are connected to the network to serve many people.

Scanners, such as the one shown in Figure 8.5, take paper and create digital documents in PDF form or using other image formats so that they may be stored electronically. Printing and scanning functionality is often combined in multifunction devices (MFDs).

FIGURE 8.2 Typical computer display

Maxim Basinski/Adobe Stock Photos

FIGURE 8.3 Computer speakers

Artem Merzlenko/Adobe Stock Photos

FIGURE 8.4 Typical desktop printer

Sergey Peterman/Adobe Stock Photos

FIGURE 8.5 Typical desktop scanner

Song_about_summer/Adobe Stock Photos

Web Cameras

Web cameras, such as the one shown in Figure 8.6, allow users to capture still images and video. They're pretty much essential today for participation in videoconferences. Laptops and smartphones usually have a built-in camera, whereas desktops require an external camera (which may be built into a monitor).

FIGURE 8.6 Web camera used to capture still images and video

Dan74/Adobe Stock Photos

External Hard Drives

Users with large storage needs may use *external hard drives* in addition to the internal storage contained within their computer. These drives may be easily moved between computers.

> **EXAM TIP**
>
> As you prepare for the Tech+ exam, be sure to understand the purpose of each of these peripheral types and whether they are used for input, output, and/or storage. Keyboards, mice, cameras, and scanners are used for input. Printers, displays, and speakers are used for output. External hard drives are used for storage. Touchscreens are a special case that can be used for *both* input and output.

That's an overview of the most common types of peripheral devices used with modern computers. You'll find many more specialized devices in almost any business environment, and IT professionals spend a lot of their time configuring and troubleshooting peripherals.

Uninterruptible Power Supply

Uninterruptible power supplies (UPSs) play an important role in providing fault-tolerant power to systems. These devices, such as the one shown in Figure 8.7, have large batteries that are capable of keeping equipment running in the face of a brief power outage. UPS batteries typically only last for minutes, so longer-term outages require alternative sources of power, such as those offered by a diesel-powered generator.

FIGURE 8.7 Uninterruptible power supply

Destina/Adobe Stock Photos

INSTALLING AND CONFIGURING PERIPHERALS

IT professionals are often asked to install peripherals for use by individual employees or by the entire office. The process for installing and configuring these devices varies quite a bit and can be simple or quite challenging.

The simplest devices use a technology called *plug-and-play (PnP)* to make it easy for users to install them on their own. Just like the name implies, you simply plug these devices into the computer and the operating system automatically configures them to work properly.

Other devices, particularly specialized or outdated devices, may require manual installation. The most important part of this is finding and installing a *driver* for that device and your operating system. The driver is a small piece of software that tells the operating system how to interact with the peripheral. You can usually find them on the peripheral manufacturer's website. Once you download the correct driver, you may select it when configuring the new peripheral through a computer's operating system.

Devices that are shared by an entire office, such as a large printer, typically don't connect to a single computer. Instead, they connect directly to the network and then may be accessed and managed over an Internet Protocol (IP) network connection. These devices typically have web-based interfaces that allow administrators to configure, manage, and monitor the device remotely. You simply connect to the web-based interface using the web browser on a computer that is connected to the same network and then the device will guide you through the configuration process.

CERTMIKE EXAM ESSENTIALS

▶ Keyboards and mice provide users with the ability to provide input to a computer. Computers show users output on a display.

▶ Scanners allow users to create digital copies of paper records, whereas printers allow the creation of paper output from digital content.

▶ Plug-and-play (PnP) devices attempt to configure themselves automatically when connected to a computer system. Devices that do not support PnP often require specialized software drivers.

Practice Question 1

You recently received a new external hard drive for your computer that attaches via a USB cable. On the hard drive's package, you read that it is a PnP device. What is the first step that you will need to take to install the drive?

A. Download and install a driver.

B. Identify the drive's model number.

C. Connect the USB cable.

D. Configure the I/O settings.

Practice Question 2

You are installing a large printer that will be shared by many people in your office. What is the most common way of connecting this type of device?

A. Ethernet cable

B. USB cable

C. FireWire cable

D. SATA

Practice Question 1 Explanation

The key to answering this question is noticing that the device uses plug-and-play (PnP) technology. This means that the device should configure itself automatically when it is connected to the computer. There should be no need to take any other steps, such as finding the device's model number, downloading or installing a driver, or performing any special configuration tasks. Instead, the PnP technology should automatically configure the device and make it ready for use as soon as it is connected to the computer with a USB cable.

Correct Answer: C. Connect the USB cable.

Practice Question 2 Explanation

This question asks you to pull together a few pieces of information. You learned in this chapter that shared printers are most often connected directly to the network and accessed by users via the shared device's IP address. Network connections are made using Ethernet cables. Therefore, the correct answer here is that you should use an Ethernet cable to connect the printer to the network, where it may be accessed by any user.

It is possible to connect a printer to a single computer using a USB cable, but this printer would then be available only to users of that computer, unless it is shared. If the user of that computer wanted to share the printer with others, they would need to leave their computer powered on all day and configure it as a print server. That is a much more cumbersome process than simply connecting the printer directly to the network.

Serial ATA (SATA) connections are used for storage devices, not printers. FireWire is an older standard that used to directly connect peripherals to a single computer and not to connect networked devices to an Ethernet network.

Correct Answer: A. Ethernet cable.

## CHAPTER 9

Input/Output Device Interfaces

Objective 2.5: Compare and contrast common types of input/output device interfaces

IT professionals are responsible for an almost overwhelming series of cables and connectors. As you work with users to connect their devices to networks, peripherals, and graphic displays, you'll need to know how to select the appropriate interface for a given situation and then use a cable with the correct connectors.

In this chapter, you'll learn everything you need to know about Tech+ objective 2.5, including the following topics:

▶ **Networking**
▶ **Peripheral devices**
▶ **Display ports**
▶ **Display technology**

NETWORK INTERFACES

The computers that we use are powerful, but they become even more powerful when they're connected to each other. That's the role of a *network*: connecting computer systems together, whether it's within an office or to the global Internet. Networks allow us to send email messages around the world, stream video, print to a printer down the hall, and perform many other important tasks.

We have two basic options for connecting computers, mobile devices, and other network-connected components to our networks: wired networks and wireless networks.

Wired Networks

Wired network connections function by connecting a cable called an Ethernet cable from a computer to an Ethernet network jack in the wall, such as the one shown in Figure 9.1. Behind that wall plate there are more cables running back to switches and other network devices that make the network function.

FIGURE 9.1 Wall plate containing four Ethernet network jacks

RJ-45 Connectors

The Ethernet cables that we use for wired networks have plugs at the end that look like the one shown in Figure 9.2. This is called an *RJ-45* connector and it's an industry standard. RJ is an acronym for "registered jack" and the RJ-45 connector is the 45th standard in that series.

You'll sometimes hear the RJ-45 connector referred to as an 8-pin connector. That's because it has eight copper pins on the end. If you were to cut an Ethernet cable open, you'd find that there are actually eight copper wires inside. Each one of those wires connects to one of the pins on the connector.

RJ-45 connectors are installed onto network cables using special tools called crimpers. An example of a crimper appears in Figure 9.3. Technicians can check that a cable is working properly using a specialized cable tester, such as the one shown in Figure 9.4.

Small form-factor pluggable (SFP) modules, such as those shown in Figure 9.5, are used for connecting fiber-optic cables to network devices. These modules plug into a network switch or router to link it with the network's fiber-optic system. They are used for high-speed data transmissions and are essential for network setups that cover large distances or require fast transfer rates that traditional copper cables can't handle.

FIGURE 9.2 RJ-45 network connector

titelio/Adobe Stock Photos

FIGURE 9.3 Network crimper

Ivan/Adobe Stock Photos

Wireless Networks

Wired networks have the advantage of offering very high-speed connections, but they come with the major inconvenience of requiring physical cables between devices. For that reason, we often rely on *wireless networks* to make life more convenient.

Wi-Fi networks create powerful wireless LANs (WLANs) that allow us to use smartphones, laptops, and other networked devices anywhere in our home or office. You'll also hear Wi-Fi networks referred to as 802.11x networks because they are based on the 802.11x standard. We'll talk more about Wi-Fi networking in Chapter 15, "Wireless Networks."

FIGURE 9.4 Cable tester

KPixMining/Adobe Stock Photos

FIGURE 9.5 Small form-factor pluggable (SFP) interface

Климов Максим/Adobe Stock Photos

You've probably also used a couple of other wireless networking technologies. *Bluetooth* networks are what we call *personal area networks (PANs)*. They're usually created by a computer or smartphone, and they're designed to support a single person. The main use of Bluetooth networks is to create wireless connections between a computer and its peripherals.

Bluetooth allows us to use wireless headsets and connect our phones to our cars for hands-free access. The range of a Bluetooth network is around 30 feet, or 10 meters, and they use *radio frequency (RF)* communications.

Near-field communication (NFC) technology allows extremely short-range wireless connections. For two devices to communicate using NFC, they need to be no more than a few inches apart. NFC technology is often used for wireless payments and building access control systems.

> **EXAM TIP**
>
> Be sure that you know the uses and distances associated with the various wireless networking options and be prepared to select the one that's appropriate for a given scenario!

Bluetooth and NFC networks aren't general-purpose networks that connect many computers together, but they're very useful for short-range applications.

PERIPHERAL INTERFACES

Peripheral devices are the ancillary components, such as printers, scanners, keyboards, and mice, that we connect to computer systems. You'll learned about the different types of peripherals in Chapter 8, "Installing Peripherals." For now, you need to know that there are many different kinds of connectors and cables used to connect peripheral devices to computer systems. As you get ready for the exam, you should be able to recognize each one of these connectors.

USB

The first set of connectors work with many different kinds of devices. The most common of these is the *Universal Serial Bus (USB)* connector. USB connectors come in three different variations: USB-A, USB-B, and USB-C. Those connectors each come in different sizes to make things more complicated.

Figure 9.6 shows you the common types of USB connectors that you might come across. You'll want to be able to recognize them so that you can select an appropriate cable for any situation that you face.

Lightning

The *Lightning* connector is a specialized connector that was designed by Apple for use with mobile devices. It uses the connector shown in Figure 9.7 to connect and charge Apple mobile devices. However, the Lightning connector is now being phased out in favor of the standard USB-C.

FIGURE 9.6 USB connectors

FIGURE 9.7 Lightning connectors

Serial ATA

The *serial ATA (SATA)* connector is used to connect hard drives, optical drives, and other storage devices for high-speed data transfer. The SATA standard is typically used for devices that reside inside a computer system, whereas external storage devices can use the *external SATA (eSATA)* connector for the same purpose. Figure 9.8 shows the SATA and eSATA connectors.

FIGURE 9.8 SATA and eSATA connectors

DISPLAY PORTS

We use a whole set of display port connectors to work specifically with video displays, projectors, and other graphics devices.

VGA

Older displays use *Video Graphics Array (VGA) connectors*, such as the one shown in Figure 9.9. They can only support very low-resolution displays that run at 640×480 resolution, so you won't find them in use on modern equipment, but you should be able to recognize VGA connectors on the exam.

FIGURE 9.9 VGA connector

DVI

Digital Visual Interface (DVI) connectors, such as the ones shown in Figure 9.10, are also an older standard that you still may find out there. These connectors support high-definition video up to 1080p resolution.

FIGURE 9.10 DVI connectors

EXAM TIP
The various connector types are an alphabet soup that can be very confusing! Be sure that you understand which connectors are used for video and which are used for other types of peripherals as you prepare for the Tech+ exam.

HDMI

High-Definition Multimedia Interface (HDMI) connectors are commonly used to connect home audio and video equipment and to connect computers to televisions and many monitors. The unique thing about HDMI is that it can carry both audio and video on the same wire. HDMI supports high-resolution video, up to 5K and beyond. You can see an example of an HDMI connector in Figure 9.11.

FIGURE 9.11   HDMI connector

DisplayPort

DisplayPort (DP) connectors also support very high-resolution video, including 5K and greater resolution. They are also capable of carrying audio along with the video signal. Figure 9.12 shows this connector.

FIGURE 9.12   DisplayPort connector

USB and Thunderbolt

Modern monitors also may be connected to computers using USB-C connections. USB-C connections can also run at the maximum resolutions available today and have the added benefit of sending video, audio, and power over the same cable when used with the *Thunderbolt* standard.

Thunderbolt is a hardware interface standard designed by Intel that allows both data and power to be sent over a single wire. Thunderbolt uses some familiar connectors. Modern Thunderbolt connections (Thunderbolt 3 and 4) use USB-C connectors.

Wireless Display Technology

Users may also want to wirelessly display content on other devices and they have two technologies available to assist with this. First, *screen mirroring* allows you to duplicate your computer's display on another screen. This is useful when giving presentations.

Casting is a technology that allows you to transmit multimedia content from one device to another. This is commonly used to stream video from a phone onto a large monitor.

CERTMIKE EXAM ESSENTIALS

▶ Users may connect to wired networks using Ethernet cables that follow the 8-pin RJ-45 standard. These cables may be built using network crimpers and tested using cable testers.

▶ Radio frequency (RF) connections include Wi-Fi, which provides wireless networking connections that cover a large area, such as a building or outdoor area. Bluetooth connections are used for peripherals with a range of approximately 30 feet. Near-field communication (NFC) connections are used for short-range connections, such as contactless payment.

▶ Peripherals may be connected to computers using USB, Lightning, eSATA, or wireless connections.

▶ Graphic displays may be connected to computers using VGA, DVI, HDMI, DisplayPort, USB-C, and Thunderbolt connections.

▶ Screen mirroring allows you to duplicate your computer's display on another screen. Casting allows you to transmit multimedia content from one device to another.

Practice Question 1

You are preparing to connect a user's desktop computer to a new monitor that they just purchased. Which one of the following connectors would *not* be a suitable option for this task?

A. HDMI

B. USB-C

C. SATA

D. DP

Practice Question 2

You are assisting a user with connecting a wireless headset to their laptop computer. Which one of the following connection types would be most appropriate for this scenario?

A. Bluetooth

B. USB-A

C. USB-C

D. NFC

Practice Question 1 Explanation

Many different types of connectors are used to connect displays to computers and other devices. These include High-Definition Multimedia Interface (HDMI) connectors and DisplayPort (DP) connectors, which are cable types used exclusively for audiovisual content.

Universal Serial Bus (USB) connectors are used for many different types of peripherals. The USB-C connector may be used to connect monitors and provide very high-resolution connections that combine video, audio, and power over a single cable.

Serial ATA (SATA) connectors are used to connect storage devices inside a computer and would not be used to connect a display.

Correct Answer: C. SATA

Practice Question 2 Explanation

Bluetooth is a wireless connection protocol that is specifically designed for connecting peripherals to devices with a range of approximately 30 feet. That makes it an ideal option for this scenario.

While USB connections are very commonly used to connect peripherals, they require a cable, and this scenario specifically requested a wireless connection. Therefore, USB-A or USB-C connections would not be appropriate.

Near-field communication (NFC) connections have much shorter range than Bluetooth and are most commonly used for brief connections, such as those used to enter a building using a proximity card or to complete a payment using a contactless payment system.

Correct Answer: A. Bluetooth

## CHAPTER 10

Virtualization and Cloud Technologies

Objective 2.6: Compare and contrast virtualization and cloud technologies

The world of enterprise computing has changed dramatically over the years, and the advent of virtualization is one of those transformative changes and is the driving force behind cloud computing infrastructure.

In this chapter, you'll learn everything you need to know about the Tech+ objective 2.6:

▶ Virtualization
▶ Cloud concepts
▶ Deployment models

VIRTUALIZATION

It was only a few decades ago that enterprise computing was confined to the world of the data center and its mainframe. Dozens of computing professionals carefully tended to this very valuable resource that served as the organization's electronic nerve center.

Then, in the 1980s and 1990s, the enterprise IT landscape shifted dramatically. We moved away from the world of monolithic mainframes to a new environment of client/server computing. This shift brought tremendous benefits. First, it put computing power right on the desktop, allowing users to perform many actions directly on their machines without requiring mainframe access. Centralized computing improved as well by allowing the use of dedicated servers for specific functions. It became much easier to maintain data centers with discrete servers than tending to a cranky mainframe.

Virtual Servers

Over the past decade, we've seen another shift in the computing landscape. The client/server model served us well, but it also resulted in wasted resources. Data center managers realized that most of the time, many of their servers were sitting idle waiting for a future burst in activity. That's not very efficient. Around that same time virtualization technology became available that allows many different *virtual servers* to make use of the same underlying hardware. This shared hardware platform makes it easy to shift memory, storage, and processing power to wherever it's needed at the time. *Virtualization* platforms like VMware and Microsoft Hyper-V make this possible.

Hypervisors

At a high level, virtualization platforms involve the use of a host machine that has physical hardware. That hardware then hosts several virtual guest machines that run *guest operating systems* of their own. The host machine runs special software known as a *hypervisor* to manage the guest virtual machines. The hypervisor basically tricks each guest into thinking that it is running on its own hardware when, in reality, the guest is running on the shared hardware of the host machine. The operating system on each guest machine has no idea that it is virtualized, so software on that guest machine can function in the same way as it would on a physical server.

There are two different types of hypervisors:

▶ In a *Type 1 hypervisor*, also known as a bare-metal hypervisor, the hypervisor runs directly on top of the hardware and then hosts guest operating systems on top of that. This is the most common form of virtualization found in data centers.

▶ In a *Type 2 hypervisor*, the physical machine actually runs an operating system of its own and the hypervisor runs as a program on top of that operating system. This type of virtualization is commonly used on personal computers. Common Type 2 hypervisors include VirtualBox and Parallels.

In an enterprise technology environment, you'll often encounter Type 1 hypervisors. If your organization runs its own data centers, those data centers will probably use a Type 1 hypervisor to run many different virtual machines (VMs) on the same hardware. If you use *infrastructure as a service (IaaS)* providers to run your servers, you'll also be using machines that run on a Type 1 hypervisor, but you won't see the hypervisor yourself. In the case of cloud services, the cloud service provider is responsible for managing the hypervisor.

CLOUD COMPUTING

Cloud computing is the delivery of computing services to users over a network. Or, more formally, the National Institute of Standards and Technology (NIST) defines cloud computing as follows:

> A model for enabling ubiquitous, convenient, on-demand network access to a shared pool of configurable computing resources (e.g., networks, servers, storage, applications, and services) that can be rapidly provisioned and released with minimal management effort or service provider interaction.

Drivers for Cloud Computing

Organizations choose the cloud for some or all of their IT workloads for a variety of reasons.

First, the cloud offers *on-demand* self-service computing. This means that technologists can access cloud resources almost immediately when they need them to do their job. That's an incredible increase in agility for individual contributors and, by extension, the organization. Before the era of on-demand computing, a technologist who wanted to try out a new idea might have to spec out the servers required to implement the idea, gain funding approval, order the hardware, wait for it to arrive, physically install it, and configure an operating system before getting down to work. That might have taken weeks, whereas today the same tasks can be accomplished in the cloud in a matter of seconds. On-demand self-service computing is a true game changer.

Cloud solutions also provide *scalability*. This means that, as the demand on a service increases, customers can easily increase the capacity available to them. This can occur in two different ways:

- ▶ *Horizontal scaling* refers to adding more servers to your pool. If you run a website that supports 2,000 concurrent users with two servers, you might add a new server every time your typical usage increases by another 1,000 users. Cloud computing makes this quite easy, as you can just replicate your existing server with a few clicks.
- ▶ *Vertical scaling* refers to increasing the capacity of your existing servers. For example, you might change the number of CPU cores or the amount of memory assigned to a server. In the physical world, this means opening up a server and adding physical hardware. In the cloud, you can just click a few buttons and add memory or compute capacity.

The cloud also offers rapid *elasticity*. Elasticity is a concept that is closely related to scalability. It refers to both increasing and decreasing capacity as short-term needs fluctuate. If your website starts to experience a burst in activity, elasticity enables you to automatically add servers until that capacity is met and then remove those servers when the capacity is no longer needed.

The cloud offers broad network access. If you have the ability to access the Internet, you can connect to public cloud solutions from wherever you are—in the office, at a coffee shop, or on the road.

Finally, the cloud offers *measured service* as one of its defining characteristics. This means that almost everything you do in the cloud is metered. Cloud providers measure the number of seconds you use a virtual server, the amount of disk space you consume, the number of function calls you make, and many other measures. This allows them to charge you for precisely the services you use—no more and no less. The measured service model is a little intimidating when you first encounter it, but it provides cloud customers with the ability to manage their utilization effectively and achieve the economic benefits of the cloud.

CLOUD SERVICE CONCEPTS

Cloud services come in a variety of concepts. This section discusses the four major service concepts of cloud computing that you'll need to know for the Tech+ exam: software as a service (SaaS), infrastructure as a service (IaaS), platform as a service (PaaS), and desktop as a service (DaaS).

Software as a Service (SaaS)

In a *software as a service (SaaS)* model, the public cloud provider delivers an entire application to its customers. Customers don't need to worry about processing, storage, networking, or any of the infrastructure details of the cloud service. The vendor writes the application, configures the servers, and basically gets everything running for customers, who then simply use the service. Very often these services are accessed through a standard web browser, so very little, if any, configuration is required on the customer's end.

Common examples of SaaS applications include email delivered by Google Workspace or Microsoft 365, and storage services that facilitate collaboration and synchronization across devices, such as Box and Dropbox. SaaS applications can also be very specialized, such as credit card processing services and travel and expense reporting management.

Infrastructure as a Service (IaaS)

Customers of *infrastructure as a service (IaaS)* vendors purchase basic computing resources from vendors and piece them together to create customized IT solutions. For example, IaaS vendors might provide compute capacity, data storage, and other basic infrastructure building blocks. The three major vendors in the IaaS space are Amazon Web Services (AWS), Microsoft Azure, and Google Cloud Platform.

Platform as a Service (PaaS)

In the third tier of public cloud computing, *platform as a service (PaaS)*, vendors provide customers with a platform where they can run their own application code without worrying about server configuration. This is a middle ground between IaaS and SaaS. Users don't need to worry about managing servers, but they are still running their own code.

Desktop as a Service (DaaS)

As companies turn to telecommuting and other remote work arrangements, the demand increases for technologies that allow those users to easily interact with enterprise systems from their homes and other locations.

Desktop as a service (DaaS) solutions take the power of virtualization and apply it to desktop technology. Users can use any system of their choice to access a desktop environment that is running on a remote server. This might be a DaaS solution running in the company's own data center or a cloud-based DaaS product, such as Amazon's WorkSpaces.

CLOUD DEPLOYMENT MODELS

When deploying cloud services, organizations have three primary choices: on-premises private cloud computing, public cloud computing, and hybrid cloud computing.

On-Premises/Private Cloud

In the *private cloud* approach, the organization builds and runs its own cloud infrastructure or pays another organization to do so on its behalf. Organizations using the private cloud model want to gain the flexibility, scalability, agility, and cost effectiveness of the cloud but do not want to share computing resources with other organizations. These private clouds may be operated in the organization's own on-premises data center or in a facility owned and/or operated by a partner.

Public Cloud

The *public cloud* uses a different approach: the *multitenancy* model. In this approach, cloud providers build massive infrastructures in their data centers and then make those resources available to all comers. The same physical hardware may be running workloads for many different customers at the same time.

Multitenancy simply means that many different customers share use of the same computing resources. The physical servers that support your workloads might be the same as the physical servers supporting your neighbor's workloads.

In an ideal world, an individual customer should never see the impact of multitenancy. Servers should appear completely independent of each other and enforce the principle of *isolation*. From a security perspective, one customer should never be able to see data belonging to another customer. From a performance perspective, the actions that one customer takes should never impact the actions of another customer. Preserving isolation is the core crucial security task of a cloud service provider.

Of course, sometimes this concept breaks down. If customers do suddenly have simultaneous demands for resources that exceed the total capacity of the environment, performance degrades. This causes slowdowns and outages. Preventing this situation is one of the key operational tasks of a cloud service provider, and they work hard to manage workload allocation to prevent this from happening.

Hybrid Cloud

Organizations adopting a *hybrid cloud* approach use a combination of public and private cloud computing. In this model, they can use the public cloud for some computing workloads, but they also operate their own private cloud for some workloads, often because of data sensitivity concerns.

EXAM TIP

As you prepare for the Tech+ exam, be ready to review a scenario that describes a cloud service and then select the appropriate cloud service concept or deployment model described in that scenario.

CERTMIKE EXAM ESSENTIALS

▶ Virtualization technology allows multiple virtual servers to share the same physical hardware. When virtualization is used, a hypervisor is responsible for managing access to the physical hardware.

▶ Type 1 hypervisors are used in enterprise data centers. These "bare-metal" hypervisors run directly on physical hardware and do not require a host operating system.

▶ Type 2 hypervisors generally run on personal computers and require the presence of a host operating system. They are typically used to allow users to run software that requires a different operating system or to create a test or development environment.

▶ Cloud services come in four service concepts: software as a service (SaaS), platform as a service (PaaS), infrastructure as a service (IaaS), and desktop as a service (DaaS).

▶ Cloud customers can choose from three deployment models. Public cloud offerings use shared hardware for many customers in a multitenant approach. Private cloud offerings dedicate hardware to a single customer and may be run on-premises. Hybrid cloud offerings mix resources from two or more deployment models.

Practice Question 1

You are assisting a user who prefers to normally use a MacBook but occasionally needs to run software that is only available for Windows. You want to meet this user's needs while keeping costs under control. What would be the best solution to this problem?

A. Deploy a Type 1 hypervisor.
B. Deploy a Type 2 hypervisor.
C. Switch the user to a Windows laptop.
D. Provide the user with both Mac and Windows laptops.

Practice Question 2

Your organization is shifting a series of workloads from an on-premises data center to the cloud. You are working with a vendor that allows you to start up virtual server instances as needed, and then you configure those servers to meet your business requirements. Which cloud service category does this describe?

A. PaaS
B. SaaS
C. DaaS
D. IaaS

Practice Question 1 Explanation

Any one of these solutions could provide the user with the ability to run the Windows program. However, most of the options fail to meet other requirements.

Switching the user from a MacBook to a Windows laptop does not meet the requirement that the user prefers to use a MacBook.

Providing the user with two separate laptops would meet the software requirements, but would be both inconvenient for the user (who would have to carry around two laptops!) and expensive for the organization.

Using a hypervisor to provide a virtualized Windows environment that the user may access is the best solution here. A Type 2 hypervisor is inexpensive and could run on the user's laptop. A Type 1 hypervisor requires specialized hardware that would run in a data center. Therefore, a Type 2 hypervisor is the best choice to meet this need.

Correct Answer: B. Deploy a Type 2 hypervisor.

Practice Question 2 Explanation

This is an example of an infrastructure as a service (IaaS) cloud offering because the service provider is offering you virtual server instances (a core infrastructure component), and then you are configuring those server instances to meet the needs of your organization.

In a software as a service (SaaS) approach, the provider would sell you a complete application that runs in the cloud, and you would not configure any of the underlying infrastructure yourself.

In a platform as a service (PaaS) approach, the provider would allow you to run your own application code on a platform that they manage. You still would not manage any of the underlying infrastructure.

Finally, in a desktop as a service (DaaS) offering, the cloud provider offers end-user productivity desktops that users can use in place of personal computers. That is not the situation described in this scenario.

Correct Answer: D. IaaS

## CHAPTER 11

Internet Service Types

Objective 2.7: Compare and contrast common Internet service types

The internal networks built by organizations connect the computers and other devices in that organization to each other. They may serve a single building or a campus, or even connect together buildings in different geographic locations. However, these networks become most powerful when they are connected to the Internet, allowing access to any connected device around the world. Organizations connect their networks to the Internet by contracting with an Internet service provider (ISP), and those ISPs provide different types of service that should be familiar to all IT professionals.

In this chapter, you'll learn everything you need to know about Tech+ objective 2.7, including the following topics:

▶ Fiber optic
▶ Cable
▶ DSL
▶ Wireless

SERVICE TYPES

We have various technology options available to us for connecting our LANs to the global Internet. We purchase an Internet connection from an *Internet service provider (ISP)*, but the service may be delivered to us over a variety of types of connections.

These are important to understand because the type of connection that we have will determine the speed of our Internet connection.

All of the connections that we use today are known as *broadband* connections. These are always-on Internet connections that run at much greater speeds than the old dial-up modems that we used decades ago. However, not all broadband connections are equal. Some are much faster than others.

> **EXAM TIP**
>
> Questions related to this objective will likely be straightforward. You should expect to see a question where you are asked to identify the best possible service type in a situation. When you see questions like this, remember that more than one option may be a possible solution and that you should evaluate which of those possibilities *best* meets the needs of the organization.

Dial-Up Modems

When we used dial-up modems, our computers placed telephone calls over standard copper telephone lines. When the computer on the other end answered, the computers transmitted data by making sounds, just as if you and I were speaking to each other on the telephone. This was incredibly slow and just didn't work that well for anything other than text.

I remember when I got my first dial-up modem in the 1980s and it had a speed of a whopping 300 bits per second. Now remember, it takes 8 bits to make a byte, right? And a byte is a single character. So that 300-bits-per-second modem would send and receive about 38 characters per second. At that speed, you could see the characters appearing on your screen one at a time. I could literally read faster than my computer could receive data!

Fortunately, we don't use these slow connections anymore. Today's Internet connection speeds are measured in megabits or gigabits per second. They're literally a million or even a billion times faster than my old modem!

Digital Subscriber Line (DSL)

One of the oldest technologies still in use today is the *digital subscriber line (DSL)* connection. DSL is the modern equivalent of that old dial-up modem, except it's much faster and offers an always-on connection. DSL connections do use a special DSL modem, but there's no "dialing up." The Internet is always there and ready for use. DSL works over copper telephone lines, and the technology it uses is able to achieve speeds measured in megabits per second. These days you'll still find DSL technology in some homes and small businesses, but it is not commonly used because it typically offers very low speeds, in the ballpark of 10 Mbps.

Cable

Cable television lines run through much of the developed world. These connections use the coaxial cable that you're probably used to seeing coming out of the back of a television or cable box. Just like DSL connections, cable Internet connections use a modem to convert the digital signals of a computer network to the analog signals that travel on copper wires. Cable modems can achieve very high speeds of 1 Gbps and beyond, with many different service offerings available suitable for homes or businesses.

Fiber Optic

The fastest connections available today come over *fiber-optic* cables. These cables are strands of glass that run between locations on a fiber-optic network. Fiber-optic networks use lasers to transmit data using pulses of light that can travel over the glass at extremely high speeds. The potential speed here is almost limitless. With perfect technology, you could theoretically send signals on fiber-optic cables at speeds approaching the speed of light! ISPs providing fiber-optic service today routinely offer multi-gigabit connections.

Wireless Connections

Sometimes a wired network connection just won't work for us. If we're moving around in a vehicle or on foot, we obviously can't drag a cable around with us. If we're in a remote location, there may not be any ISPs available to us. In those cases, we can use wireless connections to meet our needs.

Cellular

For mobile users, the best option is usually *cellular* service. Modern 5G wireless networks are capable of speeds up to 20 gigabits per second and are available in major metropolitan areas. Slower 4G networks are more widely available and offer speeds of around 14 megabits per second, which is still pretty respectable. This service is usually inexpensive and available through normal cellular providers.

Radio Frequency

Home users in remote locations may make use of fixed wireless services. These services are point-to-point services that use *radio frequency (RF)* communications. You'll need an antenna on your building that points directly at an antenna run by your ISP, so you'll need to be in an area where this service is provided.

Satellite

In very remote locations, *satellite* Internet connections provide service almost anywhere on the planet. For many years, satellite connections were very expensive and very slow, but that's changing. The new Starlink service offered by Elon Musk's company is deploying satellite service offering 100 megabit speed at a reasonable price.

Satellites are also used to provide *Global Positioning System (GPS)* service. While this is not an Internet connection type, it is a widely used service that can help devices pinpoint their exact location by using signals from multiple satellites.

CERTMIKE EXAM ESSENTIALS

▶ Fiber-optic connections offer the fastest possible Internet connections and should be the primary choice for high-bandwidth applications. However, fiber-optic connections are not available in all areas.

▶ Cable and DSL connection options offer slower, but reliable, wired connections in most populated areas.

▶ Wireless connections, such as cellular, satellite, and radio frequency (RF) service, are useful for supporting temporary locations and in areas where wired connectivity is not available.

Practice Question 1

You are helping your organization develop a connection to a new office location that is in a major metropolitan area. The users in that location will be working on computer-aided design (CAD) tasks that have very high bandwidth requirements. Which one of the following Internet service types provides the highest bandwidth?

A. Fiber optic
B. Cable
C. DSL
D. Satellite

Practice Question 2

You are supporting a team of scientists who will be traveling to a remote mountain area on a research expedition. They will need Internet service for emergency communications and to send back small quantities of research data during their trip. What type of connection would best meet their needs?

A. Cellular
B. Satellite
C. DSL
D. RF

Practice Question 1 Explanation

All of these connection types are possibilities for connecting an office located in an urban environment, but fiber-optic connections are the fastest possible connection type, so they would be the best option for an office that requires significant bandwidth.

Cable and DSL connections may also function in this environment, but they provide lower speeds than fiber. Satellite connections are also slower than fiber and may be difficult to implement in an urban area where the view of the sky may be obscured.

Correct Answer: A. Fiber optic

Practice Question 2 Explanation

Here we have a scenario where users are traveling in a remote location, making a wired connection impossible. Therefore, we can immediately rule out DSL as a possibility because DSL service requires wired telephone service to operate.

Cellular and radio frequency (RF) service are also not good options for this scenario. While they are wireless service types, they are only available near populated areas and it is extremely unlikely they will be available in a remote mountain area.

Satellite service is generally slow and expensive, but it is available almost anywhere on Earth. That makes it the best (and most likely only) option for this scenario.

Correct Answer: B. Satellite

## CHAPTER 12

TCP/IP Networking
Objective 2.8: Identify basic networking concepts

The computers that we use are powerful, but they become even more powerful when they're connected to each other. That's the role of a network: connecting computer systems together, whether it's within an office or to the global Internet. Networks allow us to send email messages around the world, stream video, print to a printer down the hall, and perform many other important tasks.

In this chapter, you'll learn everything you need to know about the first portion of Tech+ objective 2.8, including the following topics:

▶ **Basics of network communication**
▶ **Network identifiers**
▶ **Networking models**
▶ **Local area network (LAN)**
▶ **Wide area network (WAN)**

The remaining portions of objective 2.8 are covered in Chapter 13, "Application Protocols," and Chapter 14, "Network Devices."

NETWORK TYPES

The networks that we have in our homes and offices are called in Chapter 13 is "Application Protocols," *local area networks (LANs)*. LANs connect devices together that are in the same building so that they can talk to each other and to servers, printers, and other devices located in the office.

LANs are then connected to *wide area networks (WANs)*. WANs connect together offices in different locations and also connect us to the Internet. When our LAN is connected to a WAN, it allows us to become part of the global Internet and communicate with anyone we'd like.

Wi-Fi networks create powerful wireless LANs that allow us to use smartphones, laptops, and other networked devices anywhere in our home or office. We'll talk more about Wi-Fi networking in Chapter 15, "Wireless Networks."

You've probably also used a couple of other wireless networking technologies. *Bluetooth* networks are what we call *personal area networks (PANs)*. They're usually created by a computer or smartphone, and they're designed to support a single person. The main use of Bluetooth networks is to create wireless connections between a computer and its peripherals. Bluetooth allows us to use wireless headsets and connect our phones to our cars for hands-free access. The range of a Bluetooth network is around 30 feet, or 10 meters.

Near-field communication (NFC) technology allows extremely short-range wireless connections. For two devices to communicate using NFC, they need to be no more than a few inches apart. NFC technology is often used for wireless payments and building access control systems.

Bluetooth and NFC networks aren't general-purpose networks that connect many computers together, but they're very useful for short-range applications. These are examples of *peer-to-peer networks*.

CLIENT/SERVER MODEL

The *client/server model* of networking is a centralized approach where a server provides resources and services to client devices. Clients, such as computers or mobile devices, request information or services from the server, which then responds to these requests. This model is fundamental to much of the Internet and many local networks, enabling functionality like email, file sharing, and web browsing.

For example, consider a simple website. The company hosting the website operates a web server that contains all of the web content and answers user requests. The user accesses the website using a web browser and that browser is responsible for presenting the data to the end user. In this example, the web server is the server and the user's system is the client.

TCP/IP NETWORKING

Now that you understand a little about the types of network connections, let's talk about how data flows on a network. To do that, we need to dive into a protocol that you've probably heard about but might not be familiar with yet. It's called *TCP/IP*. You might have heard people refer to TCP/IP networking because it's the protocol that runs the Internet and basically every LAN on the planet.

The acronym TCP/IP has two parts to it. The first part is the *Transmission Control Protocol (TCP)* and the second part is the *Internet Protocol (IP)*. Each of these protocols plays a vital role in making sure that data gets from point A to point B.

Internet Protocol

IP is responsible for routing information over the network. Even though we call it the Internet Protocol, IP is used both on the Internet and on your local area network.

IP assigns each computer on the network its own address, called an *IP address*. We'll talk more about those addresses later in this chapter. For now, just know that IP addresses uniquely identify computers on a network and they are the way that computers identify each other.

When data travels on a TCP/IP network, the Internet Protocol breaks it up into small pieces called *packets*. Each packet is a few kilobytes of data. If you're sending a large file consisting of many megabytes or gigabytes, it will be divided up into thousands of smaller packets that are sent over the network.

The reason that we break data up into packets like this is to make our networks more reliable. If we tried to stuff megabytes into a single transmission and that transmission failed for some reason, we'd have to do the whole thing over again. If we break that up into thousands of smaller packets and one of those packets fails, we only need to retransmit that single small packet.

Larger packets would also clog up our networks. Think about a city street. When we have lots of small cars moving through the streets, traffic flows pretty smoothly. Now imagine we had a miles-long freight train try to drive down a city street. That would clog up traffic for miles around and nobody else would be able to use the road until the train left the city. That would leave us with a lot of unhappy computer users!

The Internet Protocol's job is to manage all of this work. We can just send a large file and IP will handle breaking it up into packets and then putting those packets back together again on the other side.

Transmission Control Protocol

The Transmission Control Protocol (TCP) is also part of the TCP/IP suite of protocols. TCP is responsible for setting up connections between systems and tracking the packets that are sent. If a packet is lost or damaged along the way, it's TCP's job to request that the sender transmit a new packet to replace the one that didn't arrive correctly.

Internet Control Message Protocol

The *Internet Control Message Protocol (ICMP)* is the housekeeping protocol of the Internet. It is part of the TCP/IP suite and it's designed to allow networked devices and systems to communicate with each other about the operation of the network. For example, ICMP may be used to detect whether remote systems are live on the network, to discover the network path between two systems, and to report issues with network devices.

Now there's a lot of other stuff involved in getting TCP/IP up and running on a network, but fortunately, you won't need to know about those for the Tech+ exam.

NETWORK ADDRESSING

We've talked a bit about network addressing already, but let's dive into it a little deeper. First, you need to know that each computer has two different addresses: the IP address that we already talked about and another address called a *media access control (MAC)* address.

IP Addresses

Just like telephones use phone numbers and postal mail uses street addresses, the Internet needs an addressing scheme to ensure that data reaches its intended destination. The addresses that are used by the Internet Protocol are known as IP addresses.

In most cases, IP addresses are written in what's known as the dotted quad notation of IPv4. This means that they are four numbers, separated by periods. Each number may range between 0 and 255. For example, you might have a computer that uses the IP address 10.15.100.240.

> **NOTE**
>
> The dotted quad notation is used by IPv4, the most common protocol in use today. IPv6, the next generation of addresses, uses eight groups of four hexadecimal digits—for example, fae0:2660:a0a1:2efe:c84b:4c44:3467:a1ed is an IPv6 address.

That number 255 might sound familiar to you from our discussion of the binary numbering system back in Chapter 2, "Notational Systems." Can you guess why each one of the pieces of an IP address may have values ranging from 0 to 255?

That's right! It's because each number is represented using 1 byte, or 8 binary bits. The entire IP address consists of 32 bits, or 4 bytes.

A system's IP address uniquely identifies it on a network. If the system is directly connected to the Internet, the IP address it uses must not be used by any other system in the world, just as your mobile phone number is not used elsewhere in the world.

Systems that are connected to private networks, such as the one in your home or office, may use private IP addresses that are reusable on other networks. Your router or firewall takes care of translating those addresses to public IP addresses when you communicate over the Internet.

There are two IP addresses involved in every network communication:

▶ The *source address* indicates the system sending information.
▶ The *destination address* indicates the system receiving information.

As two systems communicate back and forth, the source and destination addresses will swap places, depending on who sends each packet. For example, examine the communication between a user with IP address 10.12.0.1 and a web server with IP address 10.51.1.2.

When the user is sending data to the web server, the source address is the user's IP address, and the destination server is the web server's IP address, as shown in Figure 12.1.

When the web server replies and sends data back to the user, the direction switches and the web server's IP address is the source address, and the user's IP address becomes the destination address, as shown in Figure 12.2.

Source: 10.12.0.1
Destination: 10.51.1.2

FIGURE 12.1 Communication from a user to a web server

Destination: 10.12.0.1
Source: 10.51.1.2

FIGURE 12.2 Communication from a web server to a user

IP addresses may be assigned in two ways:

▶ You can assign an IP address **statically**. This means that you go into the system's settings and manually specify its IP address. You'll be responsible for ensuring that you choose a unique address that fits within the range for that network.

▶ You can assign an IP address **dynamically** by using the *Dynamic Host Configuration Protocol (DHCP)*. DHCP allows you to configure a pool of IP addresses, and then DHCP will automatically assign those addresses to systems as they join the network. Typically, servers are configured with static IP addresses and end-user devices are configured with dynamically changing IP addresses.

If a system is not configured with a static IP address, it reaches out on the network searching for a DHCP server that can supply it with a dynamic address. If the system is unable to find a DHCP server, it assigns itself an address using *Automatic Private IP Addressing (APIPA)*. APIPA addresses all begin with 169.254. If you see one of these addresses in use on your network, it means that something has likely gone wrong, as the system with that address was unable to obtain a valid IP address. In all but the smallest networks, addresses should be assigned by a DHCP server instead of being left to APIPA to assign.

Identifying Valid IPv4 Addresses

One of the things that you may be asked to do on the exam is to identify which IP addresses are valid for a host on a network. If you see a question like this, you should approach it using a process of elimination. Let's walk through a few simple rules that you can follow to eliminate invalid IP addresses.

No octet in an IP address should ever be larger than 255.   If you see a number greater than 255 in an IP address, that is not a valid address and you can immediately eliminate it as a possibility.

IP addresses starting with the number 127 are reserved for use as loopback addresses.   These addresses always reference the local system and are not valid as addresses on a network. The most common loopback address is 127.0.0.1 in IPv4 and 0:0:0:0:0:0:0:1 in IPv6. When it's used in communications, it's the equivalent of telling a system to talk to itself. You should never see an address beginning with 127 as a host address for this reason.

The first number in an IP address should never be higher than 223.   While you can have values up to 255 in any octet, numbers higher than 223 in the first octet are reserved for special uses and shouldn't be assigned to systems. Addresses with first numbers between 224 and 239 are called *multicast addresses*, and they are used for sending messages to many systems at the same time and should never be assigned to an individual system. Addresses beginning with values between 240 and 255 are reserved for experimental use and, again, should not be found on individual systems.

MAC Addresses

I mentioned earlier that each computer on a network has two different addresses. The IP address is the one used to address network packets, and it's the one that we'll refer to most often. But computers also have media access control (MAC) addresses. MAC addresses are how computers communicate with their immediate neighbors on a network. Systems that are directly connected to each other use these addresses to transfer data. MAC addresses are assigned to a computer's network interface by the manufacturer and generally never change. IP addresses change frequently because they're usually assigned by the local network. If a computer moves from one network to another, its MAC address will remain the same but its IP address will change.

MAC addresses are written in hexadecimal notation, which you learned about in Chapter 2. This means that we can have MAC addresses consisting of the digits 0–9 and the letters A–F. Each MAC address is 12 hexadecimal digits. The first six digits identify the manufacturer of the device, and the next six digits are a unique identifier assigned by the manufacturer. MAC addresses are assigned to one device at the factory and should never be reused.

Here's an example of a MAC address:

```
14:9d:99:7f:3a:67
```

In this address, `14:9d:99` is the portion of the address that identifies the manufacturer of the device and `7f:3a:67` is the portion that uniquely identifies the device.

Address Lookup

As networks transmit data back and forth, computers and network devices often need to look up and translate between different types of addresses. They use special protocols to perform these lookups.

Domain Name System

Computers use IP addresses to communicate over the network. but those addresses are very difficult for people to remember. Just imagine if you had to memorize the IP address of every web server that you needed to access! The *Domain Name System (DNS)* allows people to use easily recognizable names in place of IP addresses.

DNS servers translate the names that you're more familiar with, such as www `.certmike.com`, into the IP addresses that computers use to communicate, such as `54.174.107.98`. DNS is responsible for translating the *uniform resource locator (URL)* addresses that we commonly use for websites to the IP addresses associated with the servers supporting those sites.

> **NOTE**
>
> All of this terminology may be a little confusing. A domain name is a top-level name that may be registered by a company, organization, or individual. For example, `https://www.certmike.com` and `comptia.org` are both domain names. A URL is the address of a specific web page or other resource hosted on that domain. For example, `www.comptia.org/certifica-tions/it-fundamentals` is a URL.

Every time you connect to a network, that network provides your computer with the IP address of a local *DNS server* that it can use to look up IP addresses. Then, whenever you type in the domain name of a website in your browser, your computer sends a request to the local DNS server asking it for the IP address associated with that name.

If the server knows the answer to your question, it simply responds to the request with the IP address, and then your web browser can go ahead and connect to the website using its IP address. If the local DNS server doesn't know the answer to your question, it contacts other DNS servers to determine the correct answer and then responds to you.

DNS is a hierarchical system, and organizations who own domain names designate DNS servers that are the responsible sources of information about their domain name. When a local DNS server needs to perform a lookup, it asks a series of questions that eventually lead it to the definitive answer from the DNS server that is responsible for a domain.

Address Resolution Protocol (ARP)

Network devices also often need to translate between the IP addresses used on the Internet and the MAC addresses used on local networks. That's the job of the *Address Resolution Protocol (ARP)*. You don't need to know much about ARP for the Tech+ exam. Just remember that it's used to look up the MAC address associated with an IP address.

NETWORK PORTS AND APPLICATIONS

IP addresses can uniquely identify each system on a network, but those systems might be responsible for running many different applications. That's where network ports come into play.

Network ports are particular locations on a system associated with a specific application. Imagine that each computer on the network is an apartment building and each application is an individual apartment. The IP address on the computer is like the street address on the apartment building, but once you arrive at the building, you need specific instructions to get to the right apartment. The network port is like the apartment number, guiding traffic to the correct application.

Network ports are represented using a number ranging from 0 to 65,535. Different ranges of ports are used in different ways.

▶ Ports between 0 and 1,023 are called *well-known ports*. These are reserved for common applications and assigned by Internet authorities. Using well-known ports ensures that everyone on the Internet will know how to find common services on a system, such as web servers, email servers, and other commonly used applications. For example, web servers use the well-known port 80, whereas secure web servers use port 443 by default.

▶ Ports between 1,024 and 49,151 are known as *registered ports*. Application vendors can register their applications to use these ports. For example, Microsoft reserved port 1433 for SQL Server database connections, while Oracle registered port 1521 for its own databases use.

▶ Ports above 49,151 are set aside as *dynamic ports* that applications can use on a temporary basis.

EXAM TIP

Be sure that you are able to identify valid host IP addresses when you take the exam. Remember these three rules:

▶ No value in an IPv4 address should ever be higher than 255.
▶ The first value in an IPv4 address should never be 127.
▶ The first value in an IPv4 address should never be higher than 223.

CERTMIKE EXAM ESSENTIALS

▶ Each computer on a network has two different addresses: an IP address to identify it on the Internet and a MAC address to identify it on the local network.

▶ A system's IP address uniquely identifies it on a network. IPv4 addresses use the dotted quad notation of four integers ranging from 0 to 255 separated by periods. IPv6 addresses use eight groups of four hexadecimal digits separated by colons.

▶ The Domain Name System (DNS) translates URLs and other domain names to IP addresses. The Address Resolution Protocol (ARP) looks up the MAC address for an IP address.

▶ Network ports are particular logical locations on a system associated with specific applications. Port numbers range from 0 to 65,535.

Practice Question 1

You are assigning a host address to a new system on a network using a static IP address assignment. Which one of the following is a valid IP address?

A. 12.274.16.4
B. 127.19.6.200
C. 194.243.129.144
D. 240.1.15.2

Practice Question 2

Which one of the following characters should never appear in a MAC address?

A. 0
B. 9
C. . (Period)
D. F

Practice Question 1 Explanation

Let's walk through our three rules of valid IP addresses and handle this question by the process of elimination. We'll rule out any invalid IP addresses and then be left with the one valid address. First, no value in an IP address should ever be higher than 255. That eliminates our first option because it contains the value 274.

Second, the first value in a host address should never be 127. That eliminates the second option.

And finally, the first value in a host address should never be higher than 223. That eliminates the last option, which contains 243 as an octet value. That leaves us with one valid address: 194.243.129.144.

You should be prepared to answer questions like these when you take the Tech+ exam. If you see a question like this, be sure to read it carefully. Depending on how it's phrased, it may be asking you to identify which one of a set of addresses is valid or which one of a set of addresses is invalid. Don't get tricked by assuming what the question is asking before you read the entire question.

Correct Answer: C. 194.243.129.144

Practice Question 2 Explanation

The underlying fact that you need to know to answer this question is that MAC addresses are written using hexadecimal notation. Hexadecimal notation allows the use of numeric digits and the alphabetic characters A, B, C, D, E, and F.

Looking at this question, the characters 0, 9, and F are all valid. The period should never be used in a MAC address. Periods are used to separate the octets of an IPv4 address. MAC addresses use colons (:) to separate different pieces of the address, as do IPv6 addresses.

Correct Answer: C. . (Period)

## CHAPTER 13

Application Protocols
Objective 2.8: Identify basic networking concepts

You've already learned about the roles that the Transmission Control Protocol (TCP) and the Internet Protocol (IP) play in routing traffic from one destination to another on the Internet. TCP and IP are used in combination with other protocols that are specific to the activity that the user is conducting.

In this chapter, you'll learn everything you need to know about the second portion of Tech+ objective 2.8, including the following topics:

► **Basic network services**
► **Secure web browsing**
► **File transfer**
► **Email**

The remaining portions of objective 2.8 are covered in Chapter 12, "TCP/IP Networking," and Chapter 14, "Network Devices."

APPLICATION PROTOCOLS

There are different protocols for websites, email, file transfers, and other applications. As you prepare for the Tech+ exam, you'll need to be familiar with a few of these protocols.

> **EXAM TIP**
>
> There are two main types of questions that you should be prepared for related to application protocols. You should be able to identify the appropriate application protocol for use in a given situation, and you should be able to identify secure alternatives for insecure protocols.

Websites

The *Hypertext Transfer Protocol (HTTP)* is the protocol used for websites. When you load up your web browser and type in a URL, the web browser opens a TCP/IP connection to the web server that contains the content for that site. The server then uses HTTP to send you all the elements of the web page: text, graphics, ads, and anything else on the page. Your web browser then reassembles all of that content into a website that you can view.

There is one important catch to HTTP: It's not secure. When you connect to a website using HTTP, your information is unencrypted, and anyone watching your network connection can see what you're doing online.

The fix for this is an updated version of HTTP that builds in security. The *Hypertext Transfer Protocol Secure (HTTPS)* adds encryption to web connections to prevent eavesdroppers from seeing what you're doing on a website.

EXAM TIP

Eavesdropping is a significant confidentiality concern for data in transit and the use of encryption (such as HTTPS) is a strong control to protect against this risk. Keep this in mind as you take the Tech+ exam!

Email

A whole series of protocols are used to support email messages. You'll need to be familiar with these for the exam as well.

Before we get into the specifics of email protocols, we need to first discuss how email works. If I send you an email message, my computer takes that message and sends it to my email server. When my email server gets the message, it looks to see whether you have an account on my mail server. If you do, it places the email in your inbox. If you don't, it looks up the correct email server for your address and transfers the message to that server where it is placed in your inbox. That transfer, sending the message from one server to another, uses a protocol called the *Simple Mail Transfer Protocol (SMTP)*.

When you go to check your email, your email client reaches out to your email server and requests your messages. That connection can take place using three different protocols:

- ▶ If you're using a web-based email client, such as Gmail, your connection takes place over the web, so it uses HTTPS for both sending and receiving messages.
- ▶ If you're using a traditional email client, such as Microsoft Outlook, your email client connects to the mail server and retrieves messages using either the *Post Office Protocol (POP3)* or the *Internet Message Access Protocol (IMAP)*.

POP3 and IMAP share a similar purpose, but they work in different ways. POP3 is an older protocol that takes new messages waiting for you on the server and downloads them to your computer. Once they're downloaded, they are deleted from the server and you won't be able to download them again. Your email lives only on your computer.

IMAP, on the other hand, uses a more modern approach where all of the emails remain on the server and your mail client just accesses them each time you connect. This allows you to access your email wherever you are, from any device. Traditional email clients use POP3 or IMAP only to receive messages. They use SMTP to send messages to your mail server for delivery.

All of these email protocols have both secure and insecure versions. The secure versions add encryption to the older, insecure versions of the protocol. These secure protocols include POP3 Secure (POP3S), SMTP Secure (SMTPS), POP3 over TLS (Transport Layer Security), and IMAP Secure (IMAPS).

File Transfer and Administrative Connections

Finally, you should be familiar with a series of protocols that are used to transfer files between clients and servers and connect to remote systems. The original protocol used for this purpose is the *File Transfer Protocol (FTP)*. As with many older protocols, the FTP protocol does not include any security features. Two newer versions of the protocol, the *Secure File Transfer Protocol (SFTP)* and the *File Transfer Protocol Secure (FTPS)*, add encryption to enhance the security of file transfers.

You may make an administrative connection to a remote server using a command-line interface. The *Secure Shell (SSH)* protocol and tool provide this functionality. SSH is built into most common operating systems.

> **EXAM TIP**
>
> Make sure that you're familiar with all of these protocols and their purposes as you prepare for the Tech+ exam.

CERTMIKE EXAM ESSENTIALS

▶ Websites are written in the Hypertext Markup Language (HTML). The HTML files that make up a website are sent to users through the Hypertext Transfer Protocol (HTTP) and its secure alternative, the Hypertext Transfer Protocol Secure (HTTPS).

▶ Email is transferred from the sender to the mail server and between mail servers using the Simple Mail Transfer Protocol (SMTP). Users access their mail using HTTPS, the Internet Message Access Protocol (IMAP), or the Post Office Protocol (POP3). IMAP and POP3 have secure alternatives, known as IMAPS and POP3 over TLS, respectively.

▶ Files may be transferred between systems using the File Transfer Protocol (FTP). FTP is insecure and it is better to use the Secure File Transfer Protocol (SFTP) or the File Transfer Protocol Secure (FTPS). Administrative connections may be made to remote servers using the Secure Shell (SSH) protocol.

Practice Question 1

You are helping a user who needs to send sensitive information to a website. What protocol would be most appropriate for this situation?

A. HTTP

B. FTP

C. HTTPS

D. SMTP

Practice Question 2

You create an email message and send it to your email server. Before it can reach its destination, the message must pass between several email servers. What protocol is most likely used for this communication between email servers?

A. IMAP

B. IMAPS

C. POP3

D. SMTP

Practice Question 1 Explanation

The first thing we should notice about this question is that the communication is between a user and a web server. This means that we should be using some version of the Hypertext Transfer Protocol (HTTP). For this reason, we can immediately eliminate the File Transfer Protocol (FTP), which is used to transfer files between systems, and the Simple Mail Transfer Protocol (SMTP), which is used for forwarding email messages.

Next, we should notice that the user is sending sensitive information. Sensitive information should always be sent using a secure protocol because those secure protocols encrypt data to protect it from prying eyes. Therefore, we should use the HTTP Secure (HTTPS) protocol for this communication instead of the insecure and unencrypted HTTP.

Correct Answer: C. HTTPS

Practice Question 2 Explanation

Messages are forwarded between mail servers using the Simple Mail Transfer Protocol (SMTP) or the secure version of that protocol (SMTPS). SMTPS is not an option here, so we should choose SMTP as the correct answer.

The other protocols listed here—the Internet Message Access Protocol (IMAP), IMAP Secure (IMAPS), and the Post Office Protocol (POP3)—are all used to transfer messages from the mail server to the intended recipient. They are not used to transfer messages between mail servers.

Correct Answer: D. SMTP

## CHAPTER 14

Network Devices

Objective 2.8: Identify basic networking concepts

Networks are more than just cables. They also rely on a series of specialized network devices that help the network carry data to its destination. These devices are the unsung heroes of modern information technology. They're often locked away in basements and closets, quietly playing a crucial role in keeping our networks running. In this chapter, we discuss some of these devices and the roles that they play on our networks.

In this chapter, you'll learn everything you need to know about the third portion of Tech+ objective 2.8, including the following topics:

▶ **Networking devices**
▶ **Modem**
▶ **Router**
▶ **Switch**
▶ **Access point**
▶ **Firewall**

The remaining portions of objective 2.8 are covered in Chapter 12, "TCP/IP Networking," and Chapter 13, "Application Protocols."

MODEMS

Modems provide a bridge between the analog and digital worlds, offering digital systems the ability to communicate over older transmission technologies. The word *modem* is an abbreviated form of two words that describe the functions of the device: modulator and demodulator. A modem converts a signal from digital form to an analog form, such as audio, electrical impulses, light pulses, or whatever is required by the transmission media. This is called *modulation*. On the other end of the connection, a modem converts that analog transmission back to digital form, a process called *demodulation*.

The earliest modems were used to connect computers to telephone lines that were designed to carry audio signals. They literally enabled computers to "speak" to each other over telephone lines.

Today, in home and small office environments, digital subscriber line (DSL) communications use modems to carry high-speed Internet over telephone lines, and cable modems such as the one shown in Figure 14.1 perform a similar task to allow the use of cable television infrastructure for data signals. You learned about these Internet service types in Chapter 11, "Internet Service Types."

FIGURE 14.1   Cable modem

jeremy/Adobe Stock Photos

SWITCHES

Switches are at the front lines of networking. In Chapter 12, you learned that each of the network jacks in the wall of your office has cables running out of the back of it up into the ceiling. Those cables travel to a nearby technology closet, where they plug into a switch.

Switches, such as the ones shown in Figure 14.2, connect all of the devices on a local area network and make sure that the right data gets to the right device. They work using MAC addresses to send traffic that they receive to the correct port on the switch, traveling back through the appropriate wire to the computer at the other end of the right wall jack.

FIGURE 14.2 Network switches

Shock / Adobe Stock

EXAM TIP

Remember that switches are the devices that connect normal end-user devices to the network. In the case of a wired network connection, the cable connects from the device to the switch. Later in this chapter, you'll learn how wireless access points connect wireless devices to a switch over a wired connection between the access point and the switch.

ROUTERS

Routers are the core of the modern network. All of the switches in an organization connect back to a router that manages the traffic between an organization's switches and the Internet. I mentioned earlier that switches send traffic around the local network segment using MAC addresses. Routers carry traffic between those local networks and the Internet and do so using IP addresses.

FIREWALLS

Firewalls provide security for the network. They sit between two or more networks and monitor all the connection attempts that try to cross between those networks. Figure 14.3

shows an example of how a firewall might be used to separate three networks: an internal network, the Internet, and a special network known as the *screened subnet* or *demilitarized zone (DMZ)* that contains publicly accessible servers.

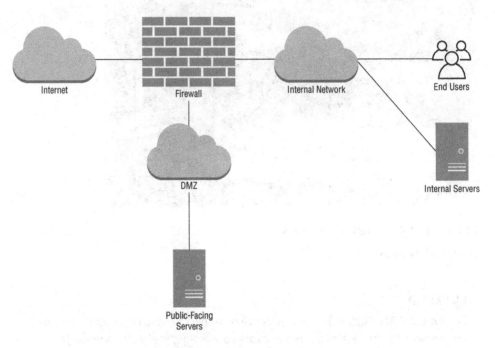

Internet

Firewall

Internal Network

End Users

DMZ

Internal Servers

Public-Facing
Servers

FIGURE 14.3 Network firewall deployment

Firewalls contain a set of rules describing the types of connections that are allowed to cross from one network to the other, and they strictly enforce that policy. Any connection attempts that aren't specifically allowed by a firewall rule are blocked from crossing between the networks. The most common example of a firewall is a border firewall that sits between an organization's internal network and the Internet. Any Internet connections that aren't covered by a firewall rule are automatically blocked, protecting the network from attack.

EXAM TIP

You won't need to know how to configure firewalls (or any other network device) on the Tech+ exam. When you review this material, you should focus on the roles of different network devices and be ready to answer questions about what type of network device would be used in a scenario.

ACCESS POINTS

Home and business networks use *wireless access points*, such as the larger of the two devices shown in Figure 14.4, to connect wireless devices to the building's wired network. These access points contain powerful antennas, transmitters, and receivers that allow them to broadcast Wi-Fi signals over large areas. They are also connected with a cable to a traditional wired network. Wireless devices in the area can then communicate with the access point to connect to other networks.

FIGURE 14.4 Wireless access point

Quality Stock Arts/Adobe Stock Photos

You'll learn more about wireless networking in Chapter 15, "Wireless Networks."

CERTMIKE EXAM ESSENTIALS

▶ Modems are used to convert between analog and digital signals. Today, they are commonly used for cable and DSL Internet connections.

▶ Routers and switches are the devices that form the backbone of the modern network. Networked devices connect to a switch via a network cable or to a wireless access point via a Wi-Fi connection. Switches connect to each other and to routers. Routers send traffic between switches on the internal network and the Internet.

▶ Firewalls are security devices that restrict the traffic that may enter and leave a network.

Practice Question 1

You are concerned about the ability of outside individuals to access your internal network and would like to use a network device to restrict this access. Which one of the following devices would *best* meet this need?

A. Firewall
B. Router
C. Switch
D. Access point

Practice Question 2

You are helping a user troubleshoot the network connection on their desktop computer. You examine the computer and it seems to be functioning normally. When you examine the network card, you determine that the cable is plugged in correctly but the link light is not on, indicating that there is a problem with the connection to the next network device. What type of network device should you check next?

A. Router
B. Access point
C. Switch
D. Firewall

Practice Question 1 Explanation

Looking at this question, you should be able to immediately eliminate two of the answer choices. Switches are components of an internal network. They are not connected to external networks and would not be used to control access into a network. Wireless access points are also internal network components used to connect wireless devices to the wired network. We can eliminate both of these options as possible correct answer choices.

That leaves us with two devices that do connect to external networks: firewalls and routers. The reality is that both firewalls and routers have the potential to fulfill this requirement. They both have filtering capabilities that can block unwanted external traffic. To answer this question correctly, focus on the word *best* that appears in the final sentence. We're not asking which device *can* meet this need—we're asking which can *best* meet this need. While routers do have limited filtering capability, they are not designed for this purpose. Firewalls, on the other hand, are designed specifically to restrict network traffic, making a firewall the best solution to this problem.

Correct Answer: A. Firewall

Practice Question 2 Explanation

There is a lot of detail in this question, but the most important fact that you can pick out to get started on your answer is that you are looking for the network device that is directly connected to a desktop computer. End-user computing devices connect to switches over a wired network connection or wireless access points over a Wi-Fi connection. They do not normally connect directly to a router or firewall.

Next, we notice in the question that the connection uses a network cable. This tells us that the connection is a wired connection and that it would use a switch, rather than an access point, because access points are only used on wireless networks.

Correct Answer: C. Switch

## CHAPTER 15

Wireless Networks

Objective 2.9: Explain the basic capabilities of a small wireless network

Wireless networking is everywhere. We use wireless networks to provide network access to our smartphones, tablets, and laptop computers and to a wide variety of other devices, including televisions, thermostats, and home automation systems. As the use of wireless networks continues to increase, the security of those networks becomes of critical importance.

In this chapter, you'll learn everything you need to know about Tech+ objective 2.9, including the following topics:

▶ 802.11/n/ac/ax
▶ Older versus newer standards
▶ Band options

WIRELESS NETWORKING

The most common wireless standard in use today is *Wi-Fi* technology. Wi-Fi is a set of standards created by the Institute of Electrical and Electronics Engineers (IEEE) and describes the technical details of how wireless devices communicate with each other and wireless access points. The use of a standard is absolutely essential because without a standard, wireless devices wouldn't speak the same language. Standardization is what allows any Wi-Fi device to work with any Wi-Fi network around the world.

Wi-Fi works by replacing the wires and cables of wired networks with radio transmitters and receivers. Every device that supports Wi-Fi contains a radio transceiver that is capable of communicating on one or more standard Wi-Fi bands. From smartphones to laptops and video game consoles to Internet-connected smoke detectors, each device contains a small chip and antenna used to transmit and receive Wi-Fi signals.

Most Wi-Fi networks are also connected to wired networks that are, in turn, connected to the Internet. This allows wireless devices to communicate with wired devices and systems located anywhere on the Internet.

Home and business networks use wireless access points to perform that connection. Enterprise networks may use sophisticated, ceiling-mounted access points, such as the one you saw in Figure 14.4. Small office/home office (SOHO) networks may use tabletop access points, such as the one shown in Figure 15.1. Both types of access points contain powerful antennas, transmitters, and receivers that allow them to broadcast Wi-Fi signals over large areas. They are also connected with a cable to a traditional wired network. Wireless devices in the area can then communicate with the access point to connect to other networks.

FIGURE 15.1 SOHO wireless access point

mkos83/Adobe Stock Photos

Wireless Networking Standards

The *IEEE 802.11* standard is the base standard for all Wi-Fi networks in use today. There are different versions of this standard that describe different versions of Wi-Fi networking and they're differentiated by the letter(s) that appear after 802.11. The two major differences among the standards are the maximum speed that each is able to achieve and the radio frequency bands they use.

Band Options

Wireless networks using the 2.4 GHz frequency range are able to reach a longer distance than networks that use other frequencies, but they have slower speeds. Those running in the higher 5 GHz frequency range offer higher speeds but cover reduced distances. The newest 6 GHz frequency range, like the 5 GHz, provides even higher speeds and is less prone to interference but will have a similar or slightly reduced coverage area compared to 5 GHz.

Choosing your frequency range requires thinking through this trade-off between speed and distance. If you want to use a 5 GHz or 6 GHz network, you'll need to have more wireless access points because each access point covers a smaller area.

> **NOTE**
>
> When selecting wireless networking frequencies, be sure to consider device compatibility. You'll want to ensure that every device that must connect to your network is compatible with at least one of the frequencies that you offer.

802.11 Standards

The earliest version of Wi-Fi, 802.11, was released in 1997 and allowed communications up to 2 megabits per second (Mbps) using the 2.4 GHz frequency range. Modern Wi-Fi networks operate at much higher speeds. *802.11n* brought a tremendous boost in bandwidth to 600 Mbps in 2009 by using special antennas known as multiple input-multiple output (MIMO) antennas. 802.11n networks run at both 2.4 and 5.0 GHz. The *802.11ac* standard allows communication at speeds over 1 Gbps using the 5.0 GHz band. The 802.11ax standard operates at both 5.0 and 6.0 GHz and provides speeds of up to 5.4 Gbps. When run at the 5.0 GHz band, 802.11ax is also known as Wi-Fi 6. When run at the 6.0 GHz band, it is known as Wi-Fi 6E.

Table 15.1 provides a summary of these facts.

> **EXAM TIP**
>
> Memorize the information in Table 15.1. This is absolutely crucial information for the exam. Yes, it's a boring list of numbers, but you shouldn't be surprised to find at least one question asking you about frequency ranges and/or speeds of different Wi-Fi standards on the Tech+ exam.

TABLE 15.1 Wireless standard frequencies and speed

Standard	Frequency range	Maximum speed
802.11n	2.4 or 5.0 GHz	600 Mbps
802.11ac	5.0 GHz	1 Gbps
802.11ax	5.0 or 6.0 GHz	5.4 Gbps

WIRELESS SIGNAL PROPAGATION

Wi-Fi signals are radio transmissions and, as such, they can be picked up by anyone with a suitable antenna and receiver. Unlike wired networks, wireless signals can travel out in many different directions. This introduces new security concerns as network administrators must carefully protect against eavesdropping attacks.

The radio waves that carry wireless network traffic are affected by many different factors as they travel across an area. Building materials, antenna placement, power levels, and many other characteristics can alter the flow, or propagation, of wireless signals. When conditions weaken radio signals, we call that situation *attenuation*. Attenuation limits the range of wireless networks.

Wireless Antennas

There are many different types of wireless antennas that may be used. While many organizations use the simple antennas built into wireless access points, other options are available. There are two basic categories of antennas:

▶ *Omnidirectional antennas* are the basic antennas used with wireless access points. They transmit radio waves in a donut-shaped pattern. The short, stubby, pole-like antennas attached to wireless access points are examples of omnidirectional antennas. The wireless access point in Figure 15.1 uses an omnidirectional antenna.

▶ *Directional antennas* allow network administrators to point a wireless signal in a specific direction, such as when creating a point-to-point network between buildings. This greatly increases the range of the network by focusing power in a single direction.

802.11ac networks include a new technology known as *beamforming*. With beamforming, the access point uses multiple antennas that look like simple omnidirectional antennas to detect the location of a device connecting to the access point and then steer the signal in the direction of the device. You can think of beamforming as a virtual directional antenna that can shift as needed based on device location.

Wireless Device Placement

Placing antennas and access points in a facility is a highly specialized area of networking. Many different characteristics of a building will affect wireless signal propagation, and engineers must take those into account to prevent dead spots while also ensuring that physically adjacent access points don't interfere with each other.

While it is possible to sketch out diagrams and place access points based on a theoretical design, the best way to place wireless access points is to conduct a *site survey* that uses specialized hardware and software to measure signal strength and provide optimal wireless signal coverage.

These surveys often produce a heat map that graphically illustrates areas of strong coverage and those that require improvement. They also may identify areas where electromagnetic interference is causing disruptions to your wireless network.

Interference

The Wi-Fi standard supports the use of different frequencies within the standard 2.4, 5.0 and 6.0 GHz bands. The frequencies available in each band are known as *wireless channels*. You can often improve your wireless coverage by adjusting the channels that you use in your building to avoid overlap with the channels used by other nearby businesses.

You also may find that other devices in the area, such as radio transmitters, baby monitors, and even microwave ovens can be sources of *electromagnetic interference (EMI)*. If you're experiencing wireless signal issues, it's helpful to track down and remove possible sources of electromagnetic interference while you troubleshoot.

Network engineers also have the ability to manipulate the power levels transmitted by each access point to tweak coverage and prevent interference. These power levels may be manually adjusted or automatically managed by wireless controllers.

CERTMIKE EXAM ESSENTIALS

▶ Wireless networks vary in terms of the frequency ranges that they use and their maximum bandwidth. You should memorize the frequency ranges and speeds associated with each of the 802.11 standards.

▶ You can often improve your wireless coverage by adjusting the channels that you use in your building to avoid overlap with the channels used by other nearby businesses.

▶ If you're experiencing wireless signal issues, it's helpful to track down and remove possible sources of electromagnetic interference while you troubleshoot.

Practice Question 1

Which Wi-Fi band option offers the highest possible transmission speed?

A. 2.4 GHz

B. 5.0 GHz

C. 6.0 GHz

D. 8.6 GHz

Practice Question 2

Which one of the following wireless standards would allow you to achieve the highest speed connection using the 2.4 GHz frequency range?

A. 802.11ac

B. 802.11ax

C. 802.11g

D. 802.11n

Practice Question 1 Explanation

The 6.0 GHz band offers the highest possible transmission speed because it is part of the newer Wi-Fi 6E standard, which provides more bandwidth and less interference than the 2.4 GHz and 5.0 GHz bands. The 2.4 GHz band is widely used but is more prone to interference and generally offers slower speeds due to its lower frequency and greater range. The 5.0 GHz band offers faster speeds than 2.4 GHz because it has more channels and less interference, but it still does not match the 6.0 GHz in speed or bandwidth. The 8.6 GHz option does not exist as a standard Wi-Fi band; Wi-Fi technologies currently use the 2.4 GHz, 5.0 GHz, and 6.0 GHz bands.

Correct Answer: C. 6.0 GHz

Practice Question 2 Explanation

This question requires that you have the information from Table 15.1 memorized. Consulting that table helps you quickly identify the correct answer.

The fastest Wi-Fi network standard is 802.11ac, operating at speeds up to 1 Gbps. However, you also need to note that 802.11ac runs at 5.0 GHz, not 2.4 GHz, so it doesn't meet the requirements of the question. The same is true for 802.11ax. The fastest option for a 2.4 GHz Wi-Fi network is the 802.11n standard, operating at 600 Mbps.

The other Wi-Fi standard here, 802.11g, is an older standard that runs at a maximum speed of 54 Mbps.

Correct Answer: D. 802.11n

Domain 3.0: Applications and Software

Applications and Software is the third domain of CompTIA's Tech+ exam. In this domain, you'll learn about the role of the operating system and how it mediates access between different types of applications and the computer's hardware. This domain has five objectives:

3.1 Identify components of an OS

3.2 Explain the purpose of operating systems

3.3 Explain the purpose and proper use of software

3.4 Given a scenario, configure and use web browser features

3.5 Identify common uses of artificial intelligence (AI)

Questions from this domain make up 18% of the questions on the Tech+ exam, so you should expect to see approximately 14 questions on your test covering the material in this part.

## CHAPTER 16

Filesystems
Objective 3.1: Identify components of an OS

Filesystems provide the operating system (and its users!) with a method to organize all of the data that is stored on disk to make it easy to find files and open them with the appropriate application. As you prepare for the Tech+ exam, you'll need to be familiar with the features of common filesystems.

In this chapter, you'll learn everything you need to know about the first set of sub-topics for Tech+ objective 3.1:

▶ **Filesystem characteristics**
▶ **File management**
▶ **Interfaces**

The remainder of objective 3.1 is covered in Chapter 17, "Services and Processes," and Chapter 18, "Drivers, Utilities, and Interfaces."

FILES AND FILESYSTEMS

Earlier in this book, you learned how computers store data on magnetic and solid-state drives using magnetic or electrical charges to represent values of 0 and 1. We also talked about how one of the operating system's jobs is to make sense of all those binary values and organize them into the files that we use every day. The *filesystem* is the technology that defines how that data is stored, and the operating system is responsible for managing the filesystem on a disk.

Files and Folders

The most important task performed by the filesystem is remembering where the bits comprising a file are stored on the disk and organizing those files into *folders* (also known as *directories*) that help us manage where our files are stored. These directories are hierarchical. That just means that we can put folders inside other folders to help us organize our files.

For example, Figure 16.1 shows a folder structure on a Mac. Inside the My Documents folder, there are subfolders for Math, Science, and History. Inside the Science folder is a Word document containing a report called Unravelling the Mystery.

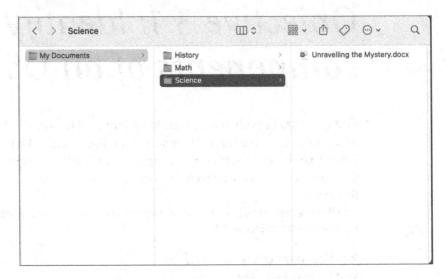

FIGURE 16.1 Directory structure

All filesystems provide you with the ability to organize files hierarchically. We can also set *permissions* on our files to control who can access them and whether they can read, write, edit, or execute each file. Figure 16.2 shows the detailed properties of that file. In the bottom section of that window, you'll notice a Sharing & Permissions section that details who has what access rights to the file. In this case, my account (mchapple) has read and write access to the file. This file is also set so that anyone in a group called staff or, in fact, everyone using this computer, has the ability to read this file. If this file contained any sensitive information, I could change that setting to limit access to the file to just me.

These examples show how you can access files through the Mac operating system's *graphical user interface (GUI)*. This approach allows users to interactively use the mouse/trackpad and keyboard to navigate through the filesystem. Other operating systems, such as Windows and Linux, provide similar capabilities.

In addition to the GUI, all modern operating systems provide *command-line interface (CLI)* access to the filesystem. This approach, also known as *console* or *terminal* access, allows users to navigate through the filesystem using text-based commands, such as those shown in Figure 16.3.

When you access filesystems through a command-line interface, you are able to see file attributes and properties more directly. For example, Figure 16.4 shows the permission settings for the Unravelling the Mystery file in text form. These permissions are the same as those seen through the GUI in Figure 16.2.

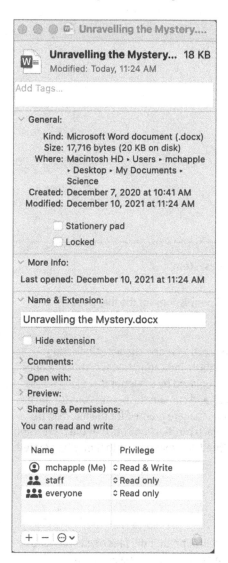

FIGURE 16.2 File permission settings

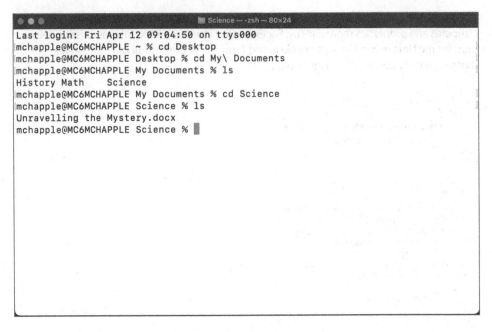

FIGURE 16.3 Command-line access to the filesystem

The highlighted text contains the attributes and permissions for the file:

`-rw-r--r--`

You can read this string in four sections. The first section is one character indicating whether the object is a directory. In this case, it is a dash, indicating that the attribute does not apply. If it were a directory, the dash would be replaced by the letter d.

The next three sections are three characters each and contain the permissions for the file. The letters that are present indicate the permissions that are granted for the file: read (r), write (w), and execute (x), in that order. Dashes in each position indicate that the permission is not granted. The three sections correspond to three different groups that may be granted permissions:

▶ The file owner
▶ Members of the file's group
▶ Everyone with access to the system

The first of these groups contains the text `rw-` indicating that the file's owner has read and write permissions, but not execute permission on the file. This makes sense, as this is a Word document and not an executable file. The second of these groups contains the text `r--`, indicating that members of the file's group may read but not write or execute the file. The third group also contains `r--`, indicating that everyone else on the system also may read but not write or execute the file.

```
● ● ●                  ▓ Science — -zsh — 80×24
mchapple@MC6MCHAPPLE Science % ls -al
total 40
drwxr-xr-x  3 mchapple  staff     96 Apr 12 09:22 .
drwxr-xr-x  5 mchapple  staff    160 Apr 12 09:22 ..
-rw-r--r--  1 mchapple  staff  17716 Apr 12 09:22 Unravelling the Mystery.docx
mchapple@MC6MCHAPPLE Science % ▮
```

FIGURE 16.4 File attributes at the command line

Filenames and Extensions

Every file has both a name and an *extension*. The name is whatever the user chooses to name the file. The extension tells the operating system and users what type of file we have and what application to use to open that file. In Figure 16.2, we have a Microsoft Word document, so it has the extension .docx, which is the standard format for Word documents. So, the full name of this file on disk is Unravelling the Mystery.docx.

Other file types use different extensions. For example:

- ▶ Microsoft Excel spreadsheets are saved with the .xlsx extension.
- ▶ Microsoft PowerPoint presentations are saved with the .pptx extension.
- ▶ Adobe Acrobat documents are saved with the .pdf extension.
- ▶ Java archive files are saved with the .jar extension.
- ▶ Python programs are saved with the .py extension.

One of the roles of the operating system is to keep track of which programs should be used to open files with each extension.

Some operating systems use special reserved file extensions for *executable files*, files that should be run as applications instead of opened with another application. For example, Windows systems commonly use the .exe extension for executable files, instructing the operating system to treat the file as an application. Similarly, the Android mobile operating system uses the .apk extension for mobile apps stored as Android packages.

> **EXAM TIP**
> Filesystems associated with Macintosh and Linux/Unix systems do not depend on file extensions to determine whether a file is executable. Instead, they track a special attribute for each file that indicates whether it is an application.

When you name files on disk, you can generally use any name that you'd like. However, filesystems do have some naming restrictions that prevent you from using some special characters in filenames because they cause undesirable results if the filesystem uses them for other purposes. These reserved characters include /, \, *, <, >, ", |, ?, and :. While every filesystem might not prohibit all of these characters, it's a good idea to avoid them just to be safe.

FILESYSTEM FEATURES

Let's talk now about some of the key features of filesystems. We've already talked about one of those core features: permissions and the role that they play in limiting access to files. We can set permissions on files to allow different users and groups of users the ability to read, write, delete, and modify files. There are two other key features that you'll need to understand for the Tech+ exam: compression and encryption.

Compression

Compression is a feature provided by some filesystems that reduces the amount of space taken up on disk by a file. Many of our documents contain a lot of repetitive data. For example, Figure 16.5 shows the properties of a file containing the full text of William Shakespeare's play *MacBeth* in HTML format for viewing in a web browser. It takes up 196 kilobytes on the disk.

FIGURE 16.5 Uncompressed *MacBeth* script

Figure 16.6 shows a compressed version of the file. After compression, the file type changes from HTML text to a ZIP archive and the file shrinks to a much smaller size, 56 kilobytes. That's less than a third of the size of the original file, saving space on the disk. Compression works by replacing duplicate chunks of data in a document with smaller values. For example, the word *strange* appears 16 times in *MacBeth*. The compressed file only needs to store the full word one time and can then be replaced with a smaller placeholder value everywhere else that it appears.

FIGURE 16.6 Compressed *MacBeth* script

Encryption

Encryption is an important security feature of filesystems. It is a technology that makes it impossible for someone to read a file unless they have the necessary decryption key. Many filesystems can apply encryption to files, folders, and entire disks automatically, making it easy for users to add security to their data. You'll learn more about encryption in Chapter 39, "Encryption."

EXAM TIP

Encryption is an excellent control to protect information stored on a laptop from compromise in the event the laptop is lost or stolen.

CERTMIKE EXAM ESSENTIALS

▶ Filesystems organize files into folders or directories to provide users with a way to sort and locate files in a logical manner.

▶ Compression reduces the amount of space taken up on disk by a file.

▶ Encryption is a technology that makes it impossible for someone to read a file unless they have the necessary decryption key.

▶ File permissions control who can access files and whether they can read, write, edit, or execute each file.

Practice Question 1

Which one of the following operating systems requires that specific file extensions be used to indicate that a file is executable?

A. macOS
B. Windows
C. Linux
D. UNIX

Practice Question 2

Which one of the following filesystem features adds security to a file that prevents others from reading it?

A. Compression
B. GUI
C. Encryption
D. Folders

Practice Question 1 Explanation

Of the operating systems covered by the Tech+ curriculum, only Windows and Android require the use of specific file extensions for executables. Windows commonly uses the .exe extension and Android uses the .apk extension.

Filesystems based on the UNIX standard, including Linux, UNIX, and macOS, do not require specific file extensions. A file with any name may be marked as executable in those operating systems.

Correct Answer: B. Windows

Practice Question 2 Explanation

Encryption enhances security by scrambling the contents of a file, making it unreadable without the correct decryption key, thus protecting sensitive information from unauthorized access.

Compression reduces the file size but does not prevent others from accessing the file's contents.

A graphical user interface (GUI) improves user interaction but does not directly contribute to file security.

Organizing files into folders helps with file management but does not secure the files from being accessed by others.

Correct Answer: C. Encryption

## CHAPTER 17

Services and Processes

Objective 3.1: Identify components of an OS

Operating systems bear responsibility for executing applications and managing interactions between different pieces of software running on a computer. Each time an application executes, it runs as a process. Some processes are configured as services. These services have special privileges to execute in the background.

In this chapter, you'll learn everything you need to know about the second set of subtopics for Tech+ objective 3.1:

▶ **Services**
▶ **Processes**

The remainder of objective 3.1 is covered in Chapter 16, "Filesystems," and Chapter 18, "Drivers, Utilities, and Interfaces."

APPLICATIONS

You use a wide variety of software applications every day, ranging from productivity applications like word processors and spreadsheets to communications tools like web browsers.

Each of these applications is stored as one or more files on the hard drive, accessible to the operating system. Applications are stored in a special type of file known as an *executable* file, meaning that it is a program that the operating system should run, or execute, rather than a file containing data that you'd want to read.

As discussed in Chapter 19, "Operating Systems," some operating systems require that these executable files have specific extensions for the operating system to recognize that they are executable. On Windows systems, executable files often end with the `.exe` extension. On Android devices, executable files must be stored in Android packages with the .apk extension. Linux, UNIX, and Mac operating systems also have executable files, but they do not require any specific extensions for those files to execute. Instead, they allow users to set an attribute on a file indicating that it is executable.

PROCESSES

Every application that is running on a computer system runs as a *process*. A process is simply an instance of an executable application that is actively in use. Processes are stored in memory and have access to the CPU, memory, and disk to carry out their work. Some applications may use multiple processes to run more efficiently. For example, web browsers like Google Chrome use a separate process for each tab that you have open. This allows the browsers to load multiple web pages at the same time and keep separate resources allocated for each page.

> **EXAM TIP**
> Remember that a process is an instance of an application that is actively running on an operating system.

Operating systems provide utilities that help you monitor the processes that are in active use at any time. Figure 17.1 shows the Activity Monitor utility running on a Mac as part of the macOS operating system. Each line in this tool represents a single process, and there are dozens of processes running on this computer. You can see a bunch of processes associated with Google Chrome as well as processes for Microsoft Teams, Safari, Google Drive, and other applications running on my computer. You can also see the percentage of CPU time being used by each process and all processes combined. That's helpful information when you're troubleshooting performance issues.

Windows Task Manager provides you with similar information for a Windows system, as shown in Figure 17.2. Using these tools, you can not only monitor performance but also kill troublesome processes that are misbehaving and consuming more resources than expected.

SERVICES

If you examine the Activity Monitor in Figure 17.1, you'll notice that there were many processes running on this computer, which is a normal user's MacBook. If you look at the processes running on your computer, you'll see the same thing. You'll recognize some processes that are running the applications that you have open, but you'll also see some other processes that you don't recognize. These are services that are part of the operating system.

Process Name	% CPU	CPU Time
Skitch Helper	48.4	2:01.24
Google Chrome Helper (Renderer)	26.4	22:56.58
Google Chrome Helper (GPU)	14.1	1:56:24.29
RStudio	5.5	3:42:30.21
Google Chrome Helper (Renderer)	5.4	11:33.18
Google Chrome	3.7	3:21:00.71
VTDecoderXPCService	3.6	5:14.72
zoom.us	3.3	11:53:34.33
Google Chrome Helper	3.1	2:40:23.43
LogiTune Helper (GPU)	2.7	12:22:25.45
Google Chrome Helper (Renderer)	2.0	1:26.36
Google Chrome Helper (Renderer)	1.8	47:53.16
Google Chrome Helper (Renderer)	1.5	36:29.09
LogiTune Helper (Renderer)	1.4	146:08:57.63
Skitch	1.3	24:30.39
Activity Monitor	1.2	14:52.22
Microsoft Teams Helper (GPU)	0.9	3:06.56
Acrobat Pro DC	0.9	5:44.80

System:	13.08%	CPU LOAD
User:	19.45%	
Idle:	67.47%	

FIGURE 17.1 Activity Monitor on a Mac

Services are processes that run in the background, mostly invisible to the end user. They manage networking, disk access, memory, and many of the other tasks performed by the operating system. If you didn't go looking for them, you'd never know that they were there! These processes do show up in operating system performance monitoring utilities because you can use the information about them that appears in those tools to help with trouble-shooting performance problems.

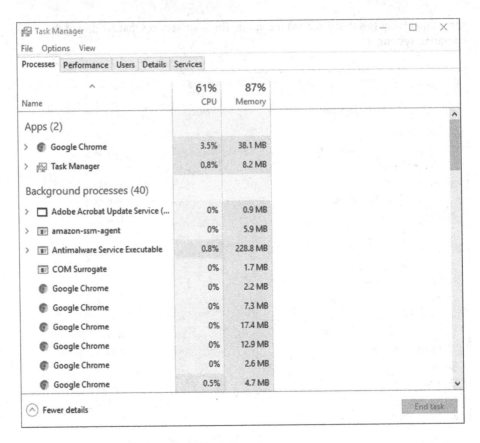

FIGURE 17.2 Windows Task Manager

CERTMIKE EXAM ESSENTIALS

▶ Applications are software programs stored on a computer in executable files. Executable files on Windows systems often have names ending with the `.exe` extension whereas Android applications have names ending with `.apk`. Linux, UNIX, and Mac operating systems do not require any specific file extension for executables.

▶ Each time an application executes on a computer, it creates one or more new processes. The process is the instance of that application.

▶ Some processes run automatically in the background to perform operating system and related tasks. These processes are called services, and they are normally invisible to end users.

Practice Question 1

You are working with a new desktop publishing application on a Windows system. The application is stored on your hard drive and you just double-clicked it to launch it. What term best describes what you created when you launched the application?

A. Service
B. File
C. Patch
D. Process

Practice Question 2

You would like to examine the different processes currently running on a Windows system. What utility would best assist you with this task?

A. Activity Monitor
B. Process Evaluator
C. Process Manager
D. Task Manager

Practice Question 1 Explanation

When you launch an application on a Windows system (or any other computer, for that matter), you create a new process on the system that is associated with that particular application launch. The process is created using an executable file, but the act of launching an application does not *create* a new file.

User applications run as processes that are visible to the user. Services are background processes that run invisibly and do not require any user intervention. Patches are updates to applications and the operating system that may be applied to fix bugs, correct security vulnerabilities, or add new features.

Correct Answer: D. Process

Practice Question 2 Explanation

Windows provides the Task Manager utility to allow users to view and manage the processes running on a Windows system. macOS provides the Activity Monitor utility for a similar purpose.

Process Evaluator and Process Manager are not the names of Windows or Mac utilities. They are simply made-up distractors designed to sound like the names of actual tools.

When you review the answer choices on the Tech+ exam, be careful to keep an eye out for sneaky tricks like the ones used in this question. If you read the question quickly, you might be tempted to answer Activity Monitor if you did not notice that the question asked about Windows systems.

Correct Answer: D. Task Manager

## CHAPTER 18

Drivers, Utilities, and Interfaces

Objective 3.1: Identify components of an OS

The operating system (OS) requires some internal components to help administrators manage the way it works and ensure compatibility with different hardware and applications. Drivers, utilities, and interfaces play an important role in the world of IT.

In this chapter, you'll learn everything you need to know about the third set of subtopics for Tech+ objective 3.1:

▶ **System applications and utilities**
▶ **Drivers**
▶ **Interfaces**

The remainder of objective 3.1 is covered in Chapter 16, "Filesystems," and Chapter 17, "Services and Processes."

DRIVERS

Drivers are software components that tell the operating system how to interact with a particular piece of hardware. They are pieces of software that allow Windows, Mac, and Linux systems to all use the same printers, monitors, and other peripherals.

Your operating system comes preinstalled with hundreds or thousands of commonly used drivers. These drivers allow you to set up many pieces of hardware with plug-and-play technology, where the hardware can easily start working without much, if any, configuration on your part. It's the responsibility of each hardware manufacturer to create drivers for all the operating systems they wish to support and then make those drivers available to their customers. This is another reason that it is important to keep current with operating system updates.

In cases where you have a piece of hardware that doesn't just start working with plug-and-play functionality, you'll need to find the correct driver. Visit the website of that hardware's manufacturer and find the driver that matches the exact model of hardware that you're installing and your operating system version. It's important to have the correct operating system and model because your hardware may either behave strangely or not function at all if you use the wrong driver.

INTERFACES

The operating system also provides two different interfaces to users. You're already familiar with the *graphic user interfaces (GUIs)* that load when you start up your Windows or Mac system. GUIs are the most common way that people interact with computers. You can point-and-click with your mouse and access all of the operating system's functionality. Figure 18.1 shows an example of the GUI on a Mac system, and Figure 18.2 shows the GUI on a Windows system.

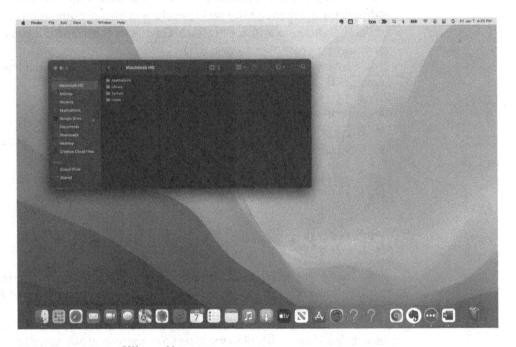

FIGURE 18.1 GUI on a Mac

As you learned in Chapter 16, operating systems also provide another interface known as a console or command-line access. This is a text-based interface that allows you to type commands that you'd like the computer to execute. You can use this console access to launch applications, navigate the filesystem, or modify running processes. Using the console does require that you understand the commands used by the computer and it is technically complex, but skilled system administrators and power users often find the console a much easier way to quickly handle administrative tasks.

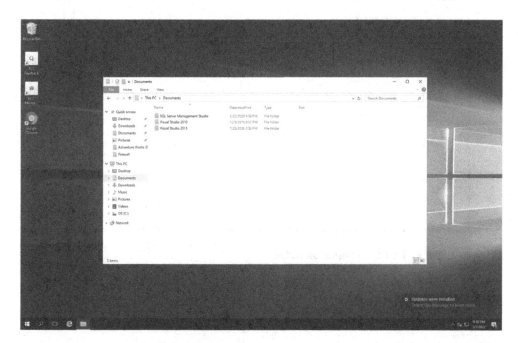

FIGURE 18.2 GUI on a Windows system

You access the console using different command-line interfaces (CLIs). On a Mac you use an application called *Terminal* to type commands into the console. You can see an example of Terminal in Figure 18.3.

Windows systems provide two console utilities. The *Command Prompt*, the tool most commonly used by end users, is automatically installed on all Windows systems. It's shown in Figure 18.4.

PowerShell is an advanced shell with scripting capabilities that is a favorite of system administrators and others who want to access advanced capabilities of the operating system.

SYSTEM APPLICATIONS AND UTILITIES

Operating systems also come with a number of system applications and *utilities* designed to help make using them easier. In Chapter 17, you saw Activity Monitor on the Mac and the Windows Task Manager.

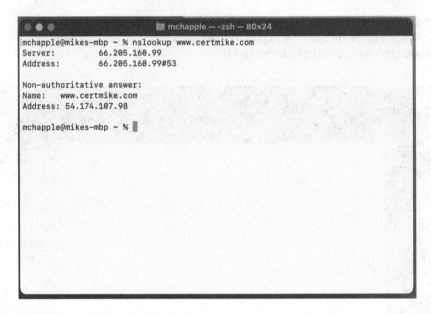

FIGURE 18.3 Terminal on a Mac

```
Command Prompt                                                    —    □    ×
Microsoft Windows [Version 10.0.14393]
(c) 2016 Microsoft Corporation. All rights reserved.

C:\Users\mchapple>dir
 Volume in drive C is OS
 Volume Serial Number is C621-9DC9

 Directory of C:\Users\mchapple

12/10/2021  07:52 PM    <DIR>          .
12/10/2021  07:52 PM    <DIR>          ..
07/06/2021  02:32 PM       101,834,752 AdventureWorksDW2019 (1).bak
07/06/2021  02:31 PM       101,834,752 AdventureWorksDW2019.bak
01/07/2022  09:35 PM    <DIR>          Contacts
01/07/2022  09:35 PM    <DIR>          Desktop
01/07/2022  09:35 PM    <DIR>          Documents
01/07/2022  09:35 PM    <DIR>          Downloads
01/07/2022  09:35 PM    <DIR>          Favorites
01/07/2022  09:35 PM    <DIR>          Links
01/07/2022  09:35 PM    <DIR>          Music
01/07/2022  09:35 PM    <DIR>          Pictures
01/07/2022  09:35 PM    <DIR>          Saved Games
01/07/2022  09:35 PM    <DIR>          Searches
01/07/2022  09:35 PM    <DIR>          Videos
               2 File(s)    203,669,504 bytes
              13 Dir(s)  73,634,742,272 bytes free

C:\Users\mchapple>_
```

FIGURE 18.4 Command Prompt on a Windows system

You may also need to schedule tasks to run on a system at a specific time. You can use the Task Scheduler utility on Windows systems or the Automator utility on macOS for this purpose.

Those are some examples of utilities, but there are many others. Different utilities allow you to use accessibility features of the operating system designed for the vision and hearing impaired, manage disks, and fine-tune many other aspects of the operating system. They're very useful to learn as you deepen your understanding of operating systems.

CERTMIKE EXAM ESSENTIALS

▶ Drivers provide operating systems with the ability to interact with hardware from different vendors. Each driver is specific to a hardware device and operating system combination.

▶ Graphic user interfaces (GUIs) allow users to interact with a computer through a point-and-click interface. Command-line interfaces (CLIs) allow users to interact with the computer using text commands.

▶ System applications and utilities perform a variety of tasks for the operating system, including disk management, process management, and accessibility.

Practice Question 1

You would like to enter commands into a Mac system using a text-based interface. What utility would assist you with this work?

A. PowerShell

B. Command Prompt

C. GUI

D. Terminal

Practice Question 2

You are having difficulty getting a new printer to work with a computer system in your office. You connected the printer via USB cable, but it does not appear to be working properly. Text prints in a garbled mess and printer options are not available. What component should you attempt to update?

A. Driver

B. Print Manager

C. Operating system

D. Application

Practice Question 1 Explanation

Mac systems provide two different user interfaces: a graphical user interface (GUI) and a text-based command-line interface (CLI) called Terminal. The GUI is a point-and-click interface, so it would not be appropriate for your situation. Terminal, however, is the perfect match to your needs.

The Command Prompt and PowerShell also provide text-based interfaces to a computer system, but they are designed for Windows systems and are not available on macOS.

Correct Answer: D. Terminal

Practice Question 2 Explanation

Since you are installing a new printer, it is unlikely that the issue is with the operating system or application. It is far more likely that this is an issue with the compatibility between this printer and the operating system. Therefore, the best solution would be to locate an updated print driver designed to work with this printer and operating system combination.

Correct Answer: A. Driver

## CHAPTER 19

Operating Systems

Objective 3.2: Explain the purpose of operating systems

The operating system is at the heart of the modern computer. Whether you use Microsoft Windows, Apple macOS, or a version of Linux, the operating system plays the same important role on every computer. It serves as an essential interface between you and the computer, translating your keystrokes to bits and bytes and displaying output on the screen. It's the interface between applications and hardware, providing software with the memory, storage, and network access that it needs to carry out its work.

In this chapter, you'll learn everything you need to know about Tech+ objective 3.2, including:

▶ **Interface between applications and hardware**
▶ **Disk management**
▶ **Task and process management**
▶ **Application management**
▶ **Device management**
▶ **Access control**
▶ **OS Types**

OPERATING SYSTEM ROLES

The *operating system (OS)* serves as a layer of *abstraction*. This just means that it hides the details of the hardware from different software applications. The creators of a new web browser don't need to design that browser to work with every possible hardware configuration imaginable. Instead, they design it to work with common operating systems, and then it's the operating system's job to serve as an interface for interactions between applications and the hardware.

Let's dive a little deeper into the many different roles handled by the operating system.

Disk Management

The operating system is responsible for *disk management*. As you learned in Chapter 7, "Storage," hard drives are just massive storage devices that contain billions of individual locations where you can store values of 0 and 1. There's no natural organization to a hard drive. You can think of it as an enormous empty warehouse.

The operating system brings order to the empty warehouse of a hard drive. Just like you'd create aisles and install shelving in a warehouse, the operating system builds a folder structure on disk that helps you organize your files. It also then has to remember where all of the bits making up each one of those files are stored on the disk. Then when you want to read that file from disk, the operating system finds the right bits and puts them back together in your file.

Memory Management

Memory works in a way that is very similar to disks. It's just a large storage location as well and the operating system performs *memory management* tasks to organize the contents of that memory. It's also responsible for making sure that different applications only have access to the memory areas reserved for their use. It would be a big security issue if one application was able to access memory spaces reserved for another application.

Task and Process Management

When you're using your computer, you're normally running many different pieces of software at the same time. You might be using a web browser, working on a Word document, and listening to music all at once. You also might have other software running in the background, synchronizing your files to the cloud, scanning for security issues, and performing many other tasks. Each instance of these applications that's actively running on a computer is called a *process*, and the operating system manages those processes to make sure that they each get their fair share of access to the CPU when they need to perform some processing.

Operating systems are also responsible for performing *task scheduling*. This allows administrators to configure a computer to execute an action at a specific time in the future, either once or on a repeating basis. For example, an administrator might configure a script to run once a day to generate a daily report of system activity. Figure 19.1 shows the Task Scheduler tool that is part of the Windows 11 operating system.

Application Management

IT professionals sometimes need to intervene when a process goes haywire. If an application crashes and won't respond to user input, every operating system provides a mechanism to manually *kill* that process, ending the task and allowing the user to restart it and get things up and running again. This work of *application management* is another of the major roles of the operating system.

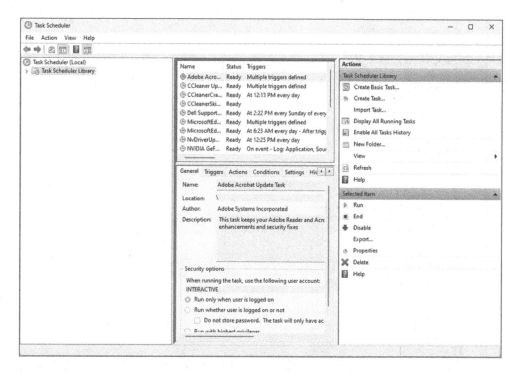

FIGURE 19.1 Task Scheduler on a Windows 11 system

Device Management

In Chapter 8, "Installing Peripherals," you learned about some of the different peripheral devices that you might use with a computer. That's another one of the operating system's jobs: *device management*. The operating system is responsible for running the *drivers* that tell the computer how to interact with different devices, interpreting the data received from devices, and sending data to them as appropriate. The Device Manager tool in Windows 11, shown in Figure 19.2, allows users and administrators to manage connected hardware.

Access Control

Finally, the operating system also plays an important role in the world of cybersecurity. It performs access control tasks. These include making sure that only authorized users gain access to a computer system and that those users can't access data that exceeds their assigned permissions.

FIGURE 19.2 Device Manager on a Windows 11 system

OPERATING SYSTEM TYPES

You should now have a good understanding of the role that the operating system plays in the world of computing. It's a critically important interface between users, software, and all the hardware components of a device. You also know that there are different operating system options out there, and you may have used some different operating systems yourself. Maybe you've used a mix of Microsoft Windows, Linux, and Apple operating systems. The next thing that you need to understand is that there are different types of operating systems for different uses.

Desktop/Workstation Operating Systems

The one that you're probably the most familiar with are the desktop, laptop, and workstation operating systems that run on most of the computers that we interact with on a daily basis. The two most common workstation operating systems are Microsoft Windows and Apple's macOS. If you're using Apple laptop and desktop computers, you'll run macOS on them. If you're using any other brand of computer, you're most likely running Microsoft Windows.

There are other operating systems for laptops and desktops, but they're just not all that common. For example, you can run variants of the Linux operating system on a laptop or desktop computer if you'd like, but many people choose not to do that because they want the convenience of being able to run consumer software that is usually only available for the Windows and Mac platforms.

Another operating system that we're seeing more frequently these days is Chrome OS and a free variant of Chrome OS called Chromium. These operating systems, built around Google's Chrome browser, are designed to run on very inexpensive minimal computers called *thin clients*. Chromebooks and other thin clients are meant to be a cheap way to get onto the web and use software as a service applications. They're very popular in schools and other environments where you want inexpensive access to computing.

Mobile Operating Systems

Mobile operating systems run mobile devices, such as smartphones and tablets. In the mobile operating system space, there are three major players. Apple's iOS runs on iPhones and iPadOS runs on iPads. Google's Android operating system supports a wide variety of mobile devices. Microsoft once made a mobile version of Windows but stopped supporting Windows phones a few years back and now makes a version of the desktop Windows operating system that runs on tablets.

Server Operating Systems

Servers also need operating systems, and they run operating systems that are similar in function to those that support desktop and laptop computers, but they are engineered to support the file sharing, web hosting, and other functions specific to servers. The two major server operating systems are Microsoft Windows Server and the many different distributions of the Linux operating system.

Embedded Operating Systems

As we continue to develop the Internet of Things (IoT), many common household, office, and industrial devices are basically small computers with a specific purpose. These devices also need operating systems to be able to interact with users, communicate on the network, and carry out their intended function. The operating systems that run on these devices are called *embedded operating systems*. These embedded operating systems are very small and have limited functionality when compared with their desktop and server cousins because they're designed to run on hardware with limited memory and processing power. Many embedded operating systems are capable of being stored in *firmware* so that the IoT device doesn't require a hard drive.

You'll likely encounter all of these different types of operating systems during your career in information technology, so you should be familiar with the options available and the use cases they serve.

CERTMIKE EXAM ESSENTIALS

▶ Operating systems serve as an interface between applications and hardware, abstracting the details of the hardware from the application.

▶ The operating system serves in several roles: disk management, memory management, process management and scheduling, application management, device management, and access control.

▶ Different operating systems provide support for desktops, laptops, workstations, mobile devices, servers, and embedded devices.

Practice Question 1

You are assisting a manager who oversees a team of telephone sales representatives. The manager maintains a spreadsheet on their computer that tracks sales and would like to email a copy of that spreadsheet to the team every morning at 9 a.m. They would like to automate this to save time. What operating system role can best assist with this task?

A. Memory management

B. Disk management

C. Process management

D. Task scheduling

Practice Question 2

You are working with the floor supervisor in a factory to troubleshoot a series of sensors that help track the manufacturing process. These are small devices that gather information on temperature, humidity, and motion. What type of operating system do they most likely run?

A. Mobile operating system

B. Embedded operating system

C. Desktop operating system

D. Workstation operating system

Practice Question 1 Explanation

Automating this report would be an excellent way for the sales manager to save time. Any time you encounter a situation where someone is performing repetitive actions that require little thought or insight, you should consider the possibility of automating that work.

This type of automation may be accomplished by using task scheduling. You can work with the manager to design a script that creates and sends the required report and then schedule that task to run every morning at 9 a.m.

Memory management, disk management, and process management are all operating system roles, but they are concerned with managing the real-time operations of the computer, rather than scheduling automated tasks.

Correct Answer: D. Task scheduling

Practice Question 2 Explanation

This is a perfect example of an Internet of Things (IoT) deployment where many sensors are distributed throughout the factory to gather information that may be used for real-time or after-the-fact analysis. These small devices have simple tasks to perform and only need a very lightweight, power-efficient operating system. The best choice for this type of environment is an embedded operating system that may be stored in the device's firmware.

While it would be possible to create sensors that could run more robust operating systems, such as mobile, desktop, or server operating systems, the hardware required to do so would likely increase the cost and physical size of the sensor with no real added benefit.

Correct Answer: B. Embedded operating system

## CHAPTER 20

Software Types
Objective 3.3: Explain the purpose and proper use of software

Software is what makes computers powerful. We can use a wide variety of applications on our computers to transform them into the tools that we need to get our jobs done. Some of these applications are very common. Almost everyone uses web browsers, word processors, and spreadsheets to get their work done. Other software provides specialized technology for software developers, designers, and others requiring special tools for their needs.

In this chapter, you'll learn everything you need to know about Tech+ objective 3.3:

▶ **Productivity software**
▶ **Collaboration software**
▶ **Instant messaging software**
▶ **Web-browsing software**
▶ **Remote support software**

SOFTWARE

Over the past four chapters, you've read a lot about the operating system and how it helps you interact with the hardware in your computer. The operating system and its components are one example of *software*—a set of instructions that tell the computer what to do. There are also many other kinds of software that help us meet our needs for productivity and collaboration. You'll need to know about each of these when you take the Tech+ exam.

Productivity Software

Productivity software is the common software that we all use to get our work done on a daily basis. Administrators typically install the same productivity software on every system they control because basically everyone needs it.

Word processing software, such as Microsoft Word, Google Docs, and Apple Pages, allows us to create and edit written documents and share them with one another. If you're creating text, whether it's a short note, a business report, or even an entire book, word processing software is the right tool for the job. Figure 20.1 shows a draft of this chapter being written in Microsoft Word.

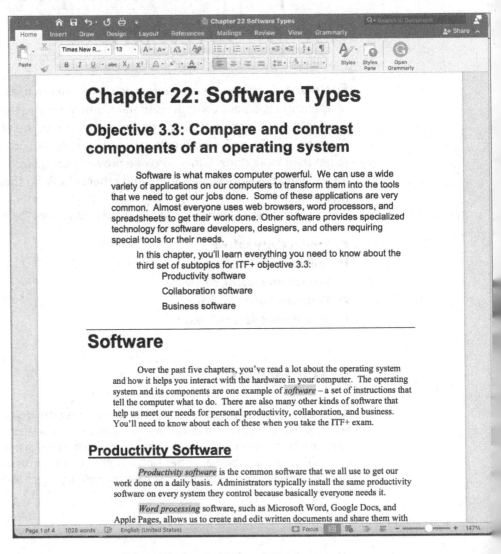

FIGURE 20.1   Editing a chapter in Microsoft Word

Spreadsheets, such as Microsoft Excel, Google Sheets, and Apple Numbers, allow us to easily create documents that are mostly made up of numbers organized into tables. We can use spreadsheets to quickly sort data and perform calculations. Spreadsheets also allow us to quickly create charts that display our numeric data visually. You can see an example of a Google Sheets spreadsheet being used to create a pie chart from a table of data in Figure 20.2.

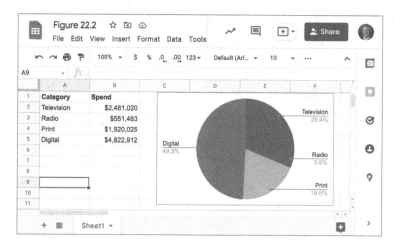

FIGURE 20.2 Creating a pie chart in Google Sheets

Presentation software, such as Microsoft PowerPoint, Google Slides, and Apple Keynote, provides us with the ability to quickly create visual slides that we can use to share information with others. We often display these presentations to our audience using large monitors or projectors. Figure 20.3 shows an example of a slide deck created in Keynote.

Web browsers, such as Google Chrome, Microsoft Edge, and Apple Safari, allow us to access the Internet, retrieving web pages from remote web servers and interacting with them. Figure 20.4 shows the use of Google Chrome to access the CompTIA website.

Visual diagramming software, such as Microsoft Visio and Lucid Software's Lucidchart, allows us to quickly create diagrams that we can then use in word processing documents, presentations, web pages, or other materials. Figure 20.5 shows the use of Lucidchart to create a network diagram.

EXAM TIP

You will almost certainly find at least one question on your Tech+ exam from this objective. There are quite a few different types of software listed here, so you should be familiar with each of them, and you should be able to identify and explain the appropriate type of software to meet a given need.

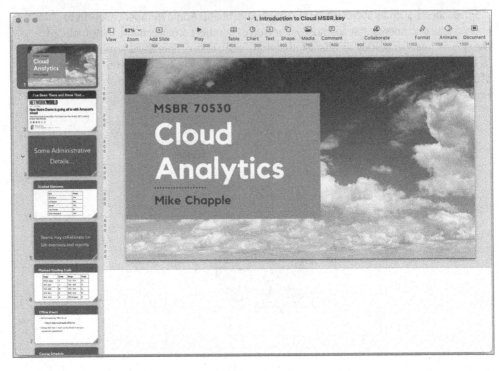

FIGURE 20.3 Editing a slide deck in Apple Keynote

Collaboration Software

Collaboration software is the software that allows us to interact with our teammates, customers, and business partners on a regular basis.

Email clients are one of the most common pieces of collaboration software. While many of us access email through a web browser, programs like Microsoft Outlook allow us to manage our email using separate software.

Conferencing software, such as Zoom, Skype, and Microsoft Teams, allows us to have audio and video conferences that can save on travel by taking the place of in-person meetings. Conferencing software also often has instant messaging features that allow us to exchange text messages with our colleagues without having a live meeting. Figure 20.6 shows a video conference in progress using conferencing software.

Many organizations also use *online workspaces*, such as Microsoft Teams, to communicate with each other through message boards and shared documents. Figure 20.7 shows the Microsoft Teams workspace used to manage the files associated with the creation of a new book.

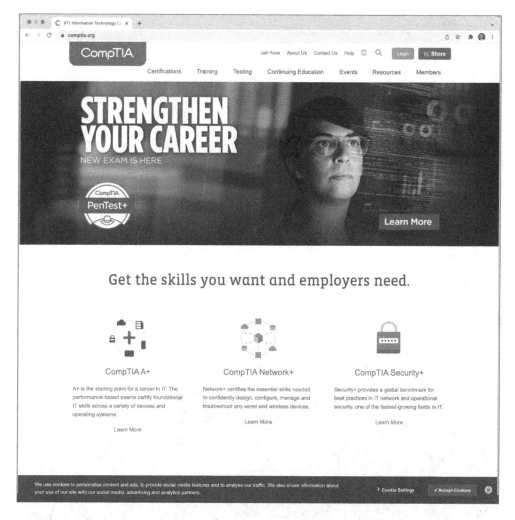

FIGURE 20.4 Accessing `comptia.org` using Google Chrome

Instant Messaging Software

Instant messaging software provides a way for individuals and teams to communicate in real time through text. These applications are essential for quick communications, often replacing the need for emails or phone calls for immediate, less formal interactions. Examples of popular instant messaging software are WhatsApp, Slack, and Telegram. They offer various features like group chats, file sharing, and voice or video calls, enhancing workplace communication effectiveness. This type of software is particularly useful in environments where teams need to stay connected and exchange information quickly and efficiently.

FIGURE 20.5 Creating a network diagram in Lucidchart

FIGURE 20.6 Conferencing software hosting a video meeting

master1305/Adobe Stock Photos

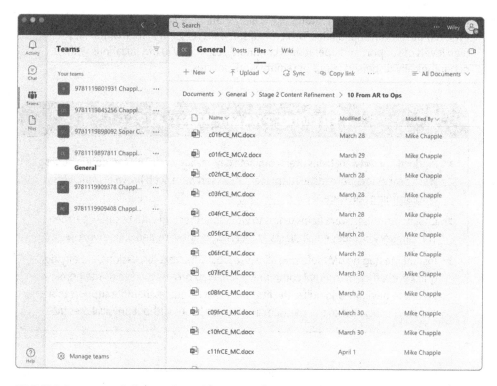

FIGURE 20.7 Collaborating with Microsoft Teams

Web Browsing Software

Web browsers are applications designed to retrieve, present, and traverse information resources on the World Wide Web. Notable examples include Google Chrome, Mozilla Firefox, and Apple Safari. These tools interpret the HTML coding of web pages to display the content in a user-friendly format. Features such as tabbed browsing, bookmarks, and private browsing enhance user experience. Additionally, security features like phishing and malware protection are crucial for safe Internet navigation. You'll learn more about web browsers in Chapter 21, "Web Browsers."

Remote Support Software

Remote support software allows IT professionals and helpdesk technicians to provide assistance by accessing a client's computer remotely. This is particularly valuable for troubleshooting, software installations, and updates without needing physical access to the device. Prominent tools in this category include TeamViewer, AnyDesk, and Microsoft

Remote Desktop. They offer features like screen sharing, remote control, file transfer, and even remote reboot capabilities. This type of software is essential for maintaining high levels of support and operational continuity, especially in organizations with geographically dispersed teams or remote work policies.

CERTMIKE EXAM ESSENTIALS

▶ Productivity software helps users complete day-to-day work. This category includes word processors, spreadsheets, presentation software, web browsers, and visual diagramming software.

▶ Collaboration software helps teams to work together and with business partners. This category includes email clients, conferencing software, and online workspaces.

▶ Instant Messaging (IM) software allows for real-time text discussions, enhancing quick and efficient internal communication. Web browsers serve as the primary means to navigate and utilize the Internet's vast resources. Remote support tools enable IT specialists to troubleshoot and resolve issues without physical presence.

Practice Question 1

You recently conducted a survey of your customers and would like to use a software package to create some quick charts of the results to share with your team. Which one of the following approaches would best meet your needs?

A. Spreadsheet

B. Database

C. Flat file

D. Accounting software

Practice Question 2

You lead a team that is working on a complex software migration effort where you have many different individuals following complicated schedules to complete their work. You would like to use a software package to allow the team to communicate in real time as they work. Which one of the following software packages would best meet your needs?

A. Spreadsheet software

B. Presentation software

C. Visual diagramming software

D. Instant messaging software

Practice Question 1 Explanation

This question is asking us to choose the best option from among several possibilities. Looking at the choices here, accounting software is clearly inappropriate because it is used to track an organization's finances and there is no financial data involved in this scenario.

Any of the other options could conceivably be used to store the data. However, storing the data in a flat file would not allow us to create charts, as a flat file simply contains data with no embellishment or formatting.

That leaves us with two options that would support the creation of charts—a spreadsheet or a database. Both of these software packages could meet the needs of this scenario, but notice that the scenario specifies that we would like to create some "quick charts." That leads us toward selecting a spreadsheet as the best option because we can load the data into a spreadsheet and quickly produce some charts in a matter of minutes. Using a database would require setting it up and configuring it. While that would give us a more permanent mechanism for storing the data in an organized and accessible form, it is overkill for this scenario.

Correct Answer: A. Spreadsheet

Practice Question 2 Explanation

This is another question where you are being asked to select the *best* option from among a set of feasible choices. You could definitely use a spreadsheet to track information about a project, and it's also possible that you could use the diagrams created by visual diagramming software as a project communication tool. It's even conceivable that you would use a presentation to communicate information about the project. While any of these tools may be useful in communicating about a project, none is designed for the purpose.

Instant messaging software, on the other hand, is specifically designed to meet this use case and includes features designed to facilitate real-time communication. That makes it the best solution in this scenario.

Correct Answer: D. Instant messaging software

## CHAPTER 21

Web Browsers

Objective 3.4: Given a scenario, configure and use web browser features

These days, the applications that we use most frequently are our web browsers. Whether we're accessing data in the cloud for work, watching streaming media, or just surfing the web, the web browser is our portal to the Internet.

In this chapter, you'll learn everything you need to know about Tech+ objective 3.4:

▶ **Private browsing**
▶ **Browser add-ons/extensions**
▶ **Caching/clearing cache**
▶ **Pop-up blockers**
▶ **Compatible browser for application(s)**
▶ **Profile synchronization**
▶ **Organizing features**
▶ **Default search engine**
▶ **Password management**
▶ **Accessibility**
▶ **Appearance**

HOW THE WEB WORKS

Web browsers are the software that we use to access websites. They understand the *Hypertext Transfer Protocol (HTTP)* and help us view web pages. They reach out to the web servers containing the information we'd like to view and then open an HTTP, or a secure HTTPS, connection to that server and transfer the web content to our computer, where the browser displays it to us.

EXAM TIP

HTTP does not use encryption, so it is extremely vulnerable to eavesdropping attacks. It should never be used to transfer sensitive information, and in fact, it's a good idea to avoid it entirely if possible!

Figure 21.1 shows how this process works. When an end user wants to visit a website, they open a web browser on their computer and type the URL of that site into the address bar in their browser. The browser then determines the appropriate web server that hosts the web page the user wants to view and sends an HTTP GET request to that web server. The web server processes the request, determines what content the user should see, and sends the web page back to the user. The web content returned to the user is written in the *Hypertext Markup Language (HTML)* and the user's web browser reads this HTML and converts it into the web page that the user sees in their browser.

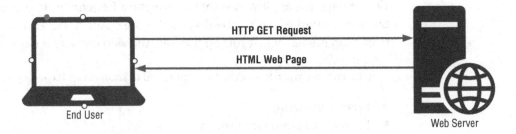

FIGURE 21.1 Retrieving a web page

For the most part, modern web applications should be compatible with all modern browsers. However, you may encounter a web application that doesn't work in a particular browser. If you see strange behavior on the web, a good troubleshooting step is to try opening the site in a different browser and see if that makes a difference. Web applications that commonly experience browser compatibility issues often advertise a list of browsers that will work properly with their sites.

CONFIGURING WEB BROWSERS

Because we use web browsers so frequently, it's important that IT professionals understand how to configure and use them. Let's talk about a few of the important settings that you can modify on a web browser.

EXAM TIP

The examples in this chapter show the configuration process for Google Chrome, but other browsers are similar. You won't be asked to actually configure these settings using any specific browser on the Tech+ exam, but you should be familiar with the various types of settings that you might alter.

Web Caches

Web browsers *cache* content. That means that they keep copies of content that we've viewed previously to make loading pages in the future move more quickly. That cache is saved on disk, and it does contain information about the web pages we've visited. If you want to delete that information, you can manually clear your cache.

In Google Chrome, you do so by clicking the icon with three dots in the upper-right corner of the browser, selecting More Tools, and then clicking Clear Browsing Data. You'll then get the pop-up window shown in Figure 21.2 asking you what you'd like to clear. Let's look more carefully at these settings.

FIGURE 21.2 Clearing browsing data in Chrome

The first thing you can do is specify the time range from which you'd like to clear data. The default is just to clear information for the sites that you've visited in the last hour, but you can change that to whatever period of time you'd like or all time.

After you specify the time period that you'd like to clear, you next specify the types of data that you'd like to clear. Your first option is to clear your browsing history. This is the list of sites that you've visited that autocomplete as you're typing URLs into the browser window. If you visited a site that you don't want other people to see when you start typing a URL, this is the setting to clear.

You can also specify to clear cookies and other site data. This is the authentication information that's saved on your computer for later use. If you've ever logged into a website and then came back later and were still logged in, that's because the website left a cookie on your browser that identifies you. If you clear your cookies, you'll be logged out of all of those websites.

And then the last thing you can clear are cached images and files. This deletes all of the saved files in your cache. It removes that information from your computer so that other users can't see it, and it's also a useful step when you're troubleshooting issues with a website.

Private Browsing

Speaking of visiting websites confidentially, browsers also offer *private browsing* modes. When you're using private mode, your browser won't save information about the sites that you visit in your browsing history or cache. It's important to understand that this doesn't mean the website won't know who you are—the site will still see your IP address. It just means that information about the site won't be saved on your computer.

In Chrome, private browsing is called incognito mode and you activate it by opening up an incognito window. Just select the File menu and then choose New Incognito Window to activate it. Chrome will open the new browser window shown in Figure 21.3 that advises you that you are in incognito mode.

Browser Add-Ons/Extensions

Browser add-ons, or browser extensions, are extra software that you download to run in your web browser. Extensions help you with scheduling meetings, managing files, and performing many other tasks.

In Chrome, you can click the puzzle piece icon to access information about the extensions you're currently using. You'll see the pop-up window shown in Figure 21.4. In this window, you can add and remove extensions and also enable and disable them without removing them permanently.

Pop-up Blockers

Many websites open pop-up windows that contain information or advertisements, and users often find these pop-ups annoying. Because of this, web browsers allow you to disable pop-up windows.

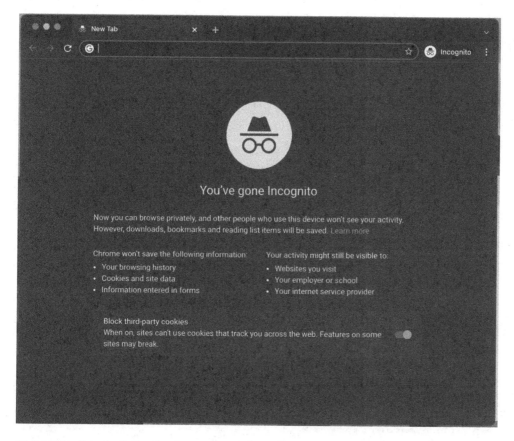

FIGURE 21.3 Activating incognito mode in Chrome

In Chrome's Settings, go to Security And Privacy, click Site Settings, and then choose Pop-ups And Redirects. Just like with script blocking, you can use the settings shown in Figure 21.5 to either allow or block pop-ups for all sites or set exceptions for specific sites.

Organizing Features

Web browser organizing features enhance user experience and efficiency. *Bookmarks* allow users to save and manage their favorite websites quickly. They can be organized into folders, enabling users to categorize their Internet resources based on topics, projects, or any other personal or professional categorization scheme. This helps in creating a structured and quick navigation process across frequently accessed web resources. Additionally, modern browsers support syncing bookmarks across devices, ensuring that a user's favorite sites are always at hand, whether they're working from a laptop, phone, or tablet.

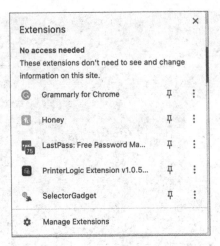

FIGURE 21.4 Managing browser extensions in Chrome

← Pop-ups and redirects   🔍 Search

Sites might send pop-ups to show ads, or use redirects to lead you to websites you may not want to visit

Default behavior

Sites automatically follow this setting when you visit them

○ ☑ Sites can send pop-ups and use redirects

◉ ☒ Don't allow sites to send pop-ups or use redirects

Customized behaviors

Sites listed below follow a custom setting instead of the default

Not allowed to send pop-ups or use redirects   Add

    No sites added

Allowed to send pop-ups and use redirects   Add

    No sites added

FIGURE 21.5 Disabling pop-ups and redirects in Chrome

Profiles help users maintain separate browsing environments within the same browser application. This is particularly useful for separating work from personal browsing, managing different roles or projects, or even maintaining distinct settings and extensions for various online activities. Each profile can have its unique set of bookmarks, saved passwords, history, and custom settings, which can be synced across devices if the user chooses. *Profile synchronization* enhances the flexibility and personalization of the browsing experience, allowing users to switch seamlessly between contexts or roles while maintaining an organized and tailored browsing environment. This compartmentalization boosts productivity and enhances security and privacy by segregating data and activities.

Password Management

Web browsers offer integrated *password management* systems that store and retrieve login credentials automatically. These systems typically prompt users to save passwords the first time they log into a new website. Once saved, the browser will autofill these credentials when the user returns to the site, eliminating the need to remember and manually enter passwords for each visit. This feature not only saves time but also encourages users to employ more complex passwords, as they do not need to remember them for every login session.

However, while convenient, relying solely on a browser's built-in password manager may not always be the most secure option. To enhance security, most browsers now offer additional layers of protection such as password encryption, requiring a main password to access the saved login information. This main password is the only one the user needs to remember, and it protects all other stored credentials. Some browsers also integrate with third-party password managers, which can offer more robust security features like two-factor authentication, secure password generation, and cross-platform compatibility. These tools ensure that even if one device is compromised, the integrity of a user's entire password library isn't necessarily breached.

Many browsers now also feature security checks that analyze saved passwords for potential exposure in data breaches or suggest changes if passwords are weak or reused across multiple sites. This proactive approach secures individual accounts and enhances overall web security by encouraging stronger, more unique passwords.

Default Search Engine

Browsers allow users to set a *default search engine* that determines which service their browser will use to process queries entered in the address bar or search box. This choice can significantly impact the relevance of search results, the speed of information retrieval, and browsing privacy. Most browsers offer a selection of major search engines from which users can choose, including options that prioritize user privacy or provide enhanced search capabilities specific to certain types of content.

Figure 21.6 shows the default search engine setting in Google Chrome.

Browser Appearance

Users can also customize the appearance of the web browser. They can modify the visual aspects of their browser interface according to their preferences or needs. These options typically include themes that change the color scheme and background of the browser, adjustable font sizes and styles for better readability, and the ability to alter the layout of toolbars and buttons to improve navigability.

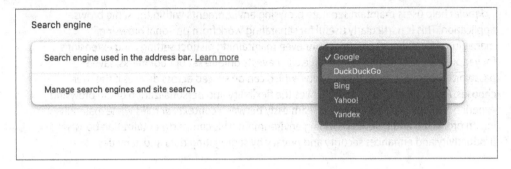

FIGURE 21.6 Setting the default search engine in Chrome

Figure 21.7 shows the browser appearance settings in Google Chrome.

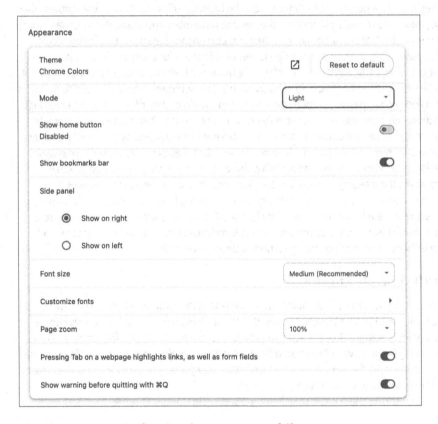

FIGURE 21.7 Configuring the appearance of Chrome

Accessibility

Accessibility features in web browsers are crucial for ensuring that all users, including those with disabilities, can navigate the Internet effectively and comfortably. Modern browsers are equipped with a variety of tools designed to enhance the accessibility of web content. These tools include options for increasing text size for better readability, customizing font styles and colors to address visual impairments, and implementing high-contrast themes that make content easier to view for users with limited vision.

In addition to visual modifications, browsers support screen readers and voice navigation to assist users with severe visual impairments or those who prefer auditory learning. Keyboard navigation enhancements are another critical accessibility feature, allowing users who cannot use a traditional mouse to navigate efficiently through web pages using keyboard shortcuts. Browsers can also be configured to ignore or override certain Cascading Style Sheets (CSS) styles that can make web content difficult to access for some users, such as disabling animations or reducing motion.

Figure 21.8 shows the accessibility features in Google Chrome.

Accessibility

Live Caption
Automatically creates captions for audio and video

Caption preferences
Customize caption size and style for Live Caption. Some apps and sites will also use this setting.

Show a quick highlight on the focused object

Navigate pages with a text cursor
To turn caret browsing on or off, use the shortcut F7

Get image descriptions from Google
If an image doesn't have a useful description, Chrome will try to provide one for you. To create descriptions, images are sent to Google.

Swipe between pages
Select the More Gestures tab, then turn on Swipe between pages to navigate back and forward

Add accessibility features
Open Chrome Web Store

FIGURE 21.8 Configuring accessibility features in Chrome

CERTMIKE EXAM ESSENTIALS

▶ Users access websites by using web browsers that reach out to web servers using HTTP or the more secure HTTPS to retrieve web pages written in HTML.

▶ Users and administrators may configure a variety of security and privacy settings to customize their web browsing experience. These include clearing caches, enabling private browsing, managing browser add-ons, and disabling pop-ups.

▶ Web browsers include built-in password managers to help users remember strong, unique passwords for each website they visit. They also support integration with third-party password managers.

▶ Bookmarks, profiles, appearance settings, and accessibility features allow users to customize the appearance and functionality of a web browser to meet their unique needs and preferences.

Practice Question 1

You are helping a user configure their web browser. They have two different roles in the organization and would like to be able to maintain different browser settings for each role. Which one of the following browser features would help you meet this need?

A. Profiles
B. Private browsing mode
C. Bookmarks
D. Pop-up blocker

Practice Question 2

You are assisting a blind user who is having difficulty configuring a web browser to meet their needs. What type of settings are most likely to meet this user's needs?

A. Privacy
B. Accessibility
C. Appearance
D. Bookmarks

Practice Question 1 Explanation

Profiles allow users to maintain distinct settings, extensions, and browsing histories for different aspects of their lives, such as separate roles at work. This feature is ideal for someone who needs to switch between different configurations without merging data or preferences between them.

Private browsing mode is designed for temporary and secure browsing sessions that do not save history or cookies permanently, but it does not allow for the customization of settings or extensions across sessions.

Bookmarks help in saving frequently visited websites but do not support the separation of browser settings or history.

Pop-up blockers enhance browsing security by blocking unsolicited pop-ups but do not manage different user settings or profiles.

Correct Answer: A. Profiles

Practice Question 2 Explanation

Accessibility settings in a web browser are specifically designed to enhance usability for users with disabilities, including those who are blind. These settings can modify the browser's behavior and appearance to better suit their needs, such as enabling screen readers, adjusting text size, or altering color contrasts to facilitate easier interaction with the browser's content.

Privacy settings, while important, mainly focus on controlling the user's data visibility and tracking but do not directly aid in making the browser more navigable for blind users.

Appearance settings can alter the look of the browser but are limited to visual customization that does not necessarily translate to usability improvements for those without sight.

Bookmarks simplify accessing frequently visited sites but do not address the unique interaction challenges faced by blind users.

Correct Answer: B. Accessibility

## CHAPTER 22

Artificial Intelligence
Objective 3.5: Identify common uses of artificial intelligence (AI)

Artificial intelligence (AI) is rapidly transforming the landscape of knowledge work. Algorithms capable of analyzing data to make predictions and generating text, code, and other content enable knowledge workers to be more efficient and effective.

In this chapter, you'll learn everything you need to know about Tech+ objective 3.5:

▶ **AI chatbots**
▶ **AI assistants**
▶ **Generative AI**
▶ **AI predictions and suggestions**

ARTIFICIAL INTELLIGENCE, MACHINE LEARNING, AND DEEP LEARNING

We often hear the terms *artificial intelligence*, *machine learning*, and *deep learning* being used almost interchangeably to describe any sort of technique where computers are working with data. Now that you're entering the world of data science, it's important to have a more precise understanding of these terms.

Artificial intelligence (AI) includes any type of technique where we are attempting to get a computer system to imitate human behavior. As the name implies, we are trying to ask computer systems to artificially behave as if they were intelligent. Now, of course, it's not possible for a modern computer to function at the level of complex reasoning found in the human mind, but we can try to mimic some small portions of human behavior and judgment.

Machine learning (ML) is a subset of artificial intelligence techniques. Machine learning techniques attempt to apply statistics to data problems in an effort to discover new knowledge. Or, in other terms, machine learning techniques are artificial intelligence techniques designed to learn the hidden patterns in our data.

Deep learning is a further subdivision of machine learning that a set of complex techniques, known as *neural networks,* are used to discover knowledge in a particular way. It is a highly specialized subfield of machine learning that is most commonly used for image, video, and sound analysis.

Figure 22.1 shows the relationship between these three technologies.

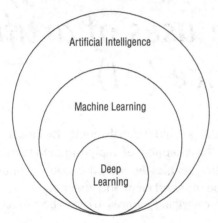

FIGURE 22.1 Relationship between artificial intelligence, machine learning, and deep learning

AI APPLICATIONS

AI has many diverse applications that have impacted numerous industries, including healthcare, finance, transportation, and entertainment. Examples include personalized recommendations in shopping, autonomous vehicles, fraud detection systems, and tailored medical treatment plans. Let's take a look at some of the important applications of AI that you need to know as you prepare for the Tech+ exam.

AI Chatbots

AI *chatbots* are programs that can simulate a conversation with human users. These bots are widely used in customer service to handle inquiries, support tickets, and frequently asked questions, providing immediate responses to customers 24/7. They may hand customers off to a live agent if the customer's needs are beyond the abilities of the chatbot.

AI Assistants

AI *assistants*, such as Apple's Siri and Amazon's Alexa, understand natural language and perform tasks for users. They can manage calendars, control smart homes, provide real-time information like weather updates, and even support decision-making with data-backed suggestions. These assistants are available through smartphone interfaces as well as dedicated hardware devices, such as the smart speaker shown in Figure 22.2.

FIGURE 22.2 Smart speaker powered by an AI assistant

VicTycoon/Adobe Stock

AI Predictions and Suggestions

AI's predictive capabilities are used in many different applications such as stock market analysis, weather forecasting, and predictive maintenance. AI systems analyze historical data to make future predictions, helping organizations to plan ahead and make informed decisions.

Generative AI

Generative AI is a revolutionary branch of artificial intelligence that focuses on creating new content, whether it be text, images, code, or even music. This technology has garnered significant attention because not only can it generate content that feels authentic, but it can also tailor that content to specific styles or requirements.

Content Creation

Text generation is one of the most common uses of generative AI. Using models trained on vast datasets, these AI systems can write essays, reports, articles, and even poetry. They can mimic specific writing styles, adapt to different tones, and understand and generate various languages. This capability is transforming content creation, enabling more personalized and interactive experiences, and even aiding in educational tools by providing tutoring or writing assistance.

Generative AI also excels in creating visual content. It can design realistic images, artworks, or renderings from textual descriptions, known as text-to-image generation. These AI-generated images can range from product prototypes to imaginary landscapes, offering invaluable tools for designers, artists, and marketers. The technology behind this visual creativity often involves complex models, which learn to produce visuals that are increasingly difficult to distinguish from those created by humans.

Figure 22.3 shows an example of the ChatGPT generative AI platform creating text and an image describing the Tech+ exam.

ChatGPT 4

You
Write a paragraph describing the CompTIA Tech+ exam. Include details about the exam itself as well as the type of person who would benefit from this certification.

ChatGPT
The CompTIA Tech+ exam is designed as an entry-level certification aimed at individuals seeking to establish a foothold in the IT industry. This exam assesses foundational technology skills, including understanding basic IT infrastructure, software troubleshooting, and security practices. It is particularly well-suited for individuals new to tech who are aiming to demonstrate their readiness for IT support roles. The certification can also benefit career changers looking to verify their tech knowledge and educators or trainers who need to validate their technical expertise. By covering broad technology concepts, the CompTIA Tech+ exam provides a stepping stone for further specialized certifications and career advancement in the rapidly evolving tech landscape.

You
Create an image of a student preparing for the Tech+ exam.

ChatGPT

Here is the image of a student preparing for the Tech+ exam. You can see the focused and determined approach as the student studies in a well-organized setting.

FIGURE 22.3 ChatGPT describing the Tech+ exam

Code Creation

Another groundbreaking application of generative AI is in the realm of coding and software development. AI systems can now understand programming languages and assist in writing and optimizing code. They can autogenerate boilerplate code, detect and suggest fixes for bugs, and even help in developing complex algorithms. This not only speeds up the development process but also makes it more accessible, allowing people with less experience to contribute to software projects. Figure 22.4 shows an example of ChatGPT being used to create code in Python.

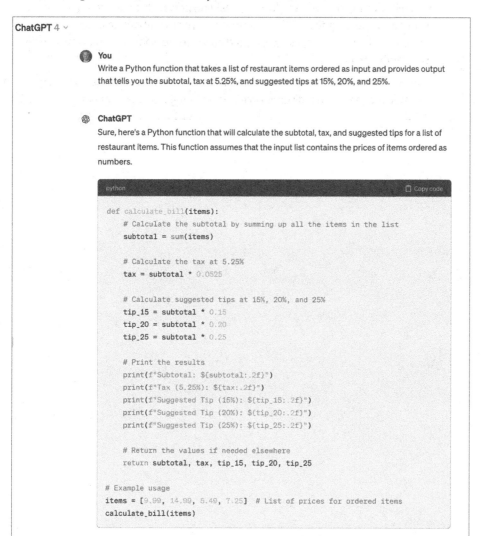

ChatGPT 4 ˅

You
Write a Python function that takes a list of restaurant items ordered as input and provides output that tells you the subtotal, tax at 5.25%, and suggested tips at 15%, 20%, and 25%.

ChatGPT
Sure, here's a Python function that will calculate the subtotal, tax, and suggested tips for a list of restaurant items. This function assumes that the input list contains the prices of items ordered as numbers.

```python
def calculate_bill(items):
    # Calculate the subtotal by summing up all the items in the list
    subtotal = sum(items)

    # Calculate the tax at 5.25%
    tax = subtotal * 0.0525

    # Calculate suggested tips at 15%, 20%, and 25%
    tip_15 = subtotal * 0.15
    tip_20 = subtotal * 0.20
    tip_25 = subtotal * 0.25

    # Print the results
    print(f"Subtotal: ${subtotal:.2f}")
    print(f"Tax (5.25%): ${tax:.2f}")
    print(f"Suggested Tip (15%): ${tip_15:.2f}")
    print(f"Suggested Tip (20%): ${tip_20:.2f}")
    print(f"Suggested Tip (25%): ${tip_25:.2f}")

    # Return the values if needed elsewhere
    return subtotal, tax, tip_15, tip_20, tip_25

# Example usage
items = [9.99, 14.99, 5.49, 7.25]  # List of prices for ordered items
calculate_bill(items)
```

FIGURE 22.4 ChatGPT creating Python code

CERTMIKE EXAM ESSENTIALS

▶ Artificial intelligence uses computer code in an attempt to simulate human intelligence. Machine learning is a subset of artificial intelligence that uses statistical methods to learn from data, and deep learning is a subset of machine learning that uses neural networks for tasks like image and sound analysis.

▶ AI applications span various industries, enabling personalized shopping recommendations, autonomous vehicles, customer service chatbots, smart assistants for tasks and information, as well as predictive analytics for stock markets and weather forecasts.

▶ Generative AI is an AI that can create new, realistic content, including text, images, and code that are often indistinguishable from human-created content.

Practice Question 1

Ryan's organization is experimenting with the use of automated techniques to create text and images for use in marketing campaigns. Which one of the following tools is mostly likely to meet his organization's need?

A. Deep learning
B. Machine learning
C. Adversarial AI
D. Generative AI

Practice Question 2

What differentiates machine learning from other artificial intelligence techniques?

A. Machine learning focuses exclusively on robotics.
B. Machine learning uses statistical methods to learn from data.
C. Machine learning does not require any data.
D. Machine learning cannot make predictions.

Practice Question 1 Explanation

Generative AI is most likely to meet the need for automated creation of text and images for marketing campaigns, as it specializes in generating new content.

Deep learning and machine learning are subsets of AI that could be involved in the functioning of generative AI models, but on their own, they don't specify the generation of new content.

Adversarial AI, meanwhile, refers to a system that learns to make decisions within a competitive framework, but the term by itself doesn't capture the creation aspect that is central to the needs of a marketing campaign.

Correct Answer: D. Generative AI

Practice Question 2 Explanation

Machine learning is characterized by its use of statistical methods to learn from data, enabling the system to make predictions or decisions without being explicitly programmed to perform the task. This is different from other artificial intelligence techniques that may rely on hard-coded rules or logic.

Robotics, although it can incorporate machine learning, is not exclusive to this field; it also encompasses other aspects of AI and engineering that are not solely related to learning from data.

The claim that machine learning does not require any data is incorrect, as data is fundamental to a machine learning algorithm's ability to learn.

The ability to make predictions is a core capability of machine learning.

Correct Answer: B. Machine learning uses statistical methods to learn from data.

Domain 4.0: Software Development Concepts

Software Development Concepts is the fourth domain of CompTIA's Tech+ exam. In it, you'll learn the basics of programming, including the use of different programming languages and the basic structure of code. This domain has four objectives:

4.1 Compare and contrast programming language categories

4.2 Identify fundamental data types and their characteristics

4.3 Explain the purpose and use of programming concepts

4.4 Identify programming organizational techniques and logic concepts

Questions from this domain make up 13% of the questions on the Tech+ exam, so you should expect to see approximately 10 questions on your test covering the material in this part.

## CHAPTER 23

Programming Languages

Objective 4.1: Compare and contrast programming language categories

Software developers write code in programming languages to create software that meets an organization's business objectives. These programming languages each have different commands and formatting and focus on different types of development.

In this chapter, you'll learn everything you need to know about Tech+ objective 4.1:

▶ Interpreted
▶ Compiled programming languages
▶ Query languages
▶ Assembly language

PROGRAMMING LANGUAGE CATEGORIES

Computers execute code in different ways depending on the type of *programming language* used. They may either interpret the code directly or first compile it into a format that can be executed.

In either case, programmers develop applications by writing instructions in a language that looks somewhat similar to English. Figure 23.1 shows an example of code written in the R programming language, which is commonly used for statistical and machine learning applications. Don't worry about the content of the code. At this point, I just want you to have an idea what code looks like.

Exam Tip

You won't find any questions on the exam that require you to know how to write code in any specific language. The questions you encounter will either test you on general concepts or ask you to read pseudocode that is written in a generic way.

```
library(tidyverse)
library(stringr)
library(lubridate)

# Read in the dataset
disability <- read_csv("ssadisability.csv")
head(disability)

# Convert it to a long dataset
disability <- disability %>%
  gather(month, applications, -Fiscal_Year)
head(disability)

# Separate the month from the filing type
disability <- disability %>%
  separate(month, c("month", "format"), "_")
head(disability)

# Look at the month values
unique(disability$month)
```

FIGURE 23.1 Code written in the R programming language

The difference between interpreted and compiled code occurs when it comes time to execute that code.

Interpreted Code

When you use *interpreted code*, the computer reads the actual instructions written by the developer as it executes the code. The computer does this by using software called an *interpreter* that is designed to understand a specific language. We'll talk about two subcategories of interpreted languages: scripting languages and markup languages.

Scripting Languages

Scripting languages are often used by administrators to automate actions on a computer and for a variety of general programming tasks. Here are some examples of scripting languages:

- ▶ PowerShell
- ▶ Perl
- ▶ R

▶ Python
▶ Ruby
▶ JavaScript
▶ VBScript

Markup Languages

The second category of interpreted language is the *markup language*. These are languages that provide tags that you can use to mark up text documents. The two most common examples of these are the *Hypertext Markup Language (HTML)*, which is used to create web pages, and the *Extensible Markup Language (XML)*, which is used to exchange structured data between systems.

Figure 23.2 shows an example of a web page written in HTML. If you notice all of the text highlighted in blue, these are the tags that represent different types of formatting that should be applied to the text. These tags usually appear in pairs. The first tag includes the instruction inside of less-than and greater-than brackets, and the second tag is exactly the same, except there is a forward slash after the less-than symbol. Any text that appears between the two tags is given the formatting indicated by the tag.

```
<HTML>
<BODY>

This is <B>bold text</B>.

For more certification
information, visit <A
HREF="https://www.certmike.com">
the CertMike website</A>

</BODY>
</HTML>
```

FIGURE 23.2 Web page written in HTML

Figure 23.3 shows an example of a document written in XML. This document provides a set of data elements that are going to be exchanged between systems. XML uses tags just like those in HTML to provide names for each of the data elements.

Remember that scripting and markup languages are both examples of interpreted languages.

Compiled Code

In languages that use *compiled code,* the programmer runs a tool called a *compiler* on their program to produce an *executable file*. This executable file contains instructions in *machine language* that carry out the programmer's instructions. When a user wishes to run the program, they launch the executable file, rather than the programmer's original source code.

```
<PERSON>
 <FIRSTNAME>George</FIRSTNAME>
 <LASTNAME>Parker</LASTNAME>
 <AGE>28</AGE>
 <SALARIED>true</SALARIED>
</PERSON>

<PERSON>
 <FIRSTNAME>Theresa</FIRSTNAME>
 <LASTNAME>Monaghan</LASTNAME>
 <AGE>32</AGE>
 <SALARIED>false</SALARIED>
</PERSON>
```

FIGURE 23.3 Document written in XML

Exam Tip

In an interpreted language, the computer directly executes the source code written by the developer using a program called an *interpreter*. In a compiled language, a program called a *compiler* must first be used to convert the source code into an executable file. Compiled code normally runs faster than interpreted code.

Examples of compiled languages are as follows:

▶ C and C++
▶ Java
▶ Go
▶ Julia
▶ FORTRAN

Exam Tip

Be sure that you are able to identify whether a language is compiled or interpreted when you take the exam. Java, C, C++, Go, Julia, and FORTRAN are all compiled languages. PowerShell, Perl, R, Python, Ruby, JavaScript, and VBScript are all interpreted languages.

SPECIALIZED LANGUAGES

There are two other categories of language that we need to talk about, but they're for special use cases.

Assembly Languages

Assembly language allows programmers to write code that works directly with the hardware, bypassing the use of a compiled or interpreted language. Each type of processor you might use has a different assembly language, and it is fairly rare to actually write code in assembly language for this reason (and because it's pretty difficult to use). Assembly language isn't quite the same as machine language, but they're very close. Today, the only time you see people writing assembly language is when they're working with specialized hardware, such as embedded devices or Internet of Things devices.

Query Languages

Query languages are used to ask questions of databases, and the main language in this category is Structured Query Language (SQL). We're going to cover SQL in much more detail in Part V of this book, so I won't discuss it now.

IDENTIFYING LANGUAGES

I know we covered a lot of different categories and languages, and you do need to know which language fits in which category for the exam. The summary chart in Figure 23.4 will help you remember the major languages that you might see on the exam.

FIGURE 23.4 Language summary chart

CERTMIKE EXAM ESSENTIALS

▶ Interpreted languages are executed from source code using an interpreter. Interpreted languages may be either scripting languages (such as PowerShell, Perl, R, Python, Ruby, JavaScript, and VBScript) or markup languages (such as HTML and XML).

▶ Compiled languages use a compiler to convert source code into executable machine language. Compiled languages include C, C++, Java, Go, Julia, and FORTRAN.

▶ Structured Query Language (SQL) is used to interact with relational databases.

▶ Assembly language is written to work on a specific hardware processor.

Practice Question 1

Which one of the following languages requires a compiler to create executable code?

A. SQL

B. Python

C. C++

D. Perl

Practice Question 2

You are upgrading the hardware and operating system on a server that runs some custom code that was created by the software development team in your organization. Which one of the following types of code is most likely to need to be rewritten for the new server?

A. Interpreted language

B. Compiled language

C. Scripting language

D. Assembly language

Practice Question 1 Explanation

This question is asking you to recognize which category each programming language falls into. From the knowledge you gained in this chapter, you should know that C and C++ are compiled languages. In these languages, the developer writes source code in that language and then uses a compiler to create a machine language file that may be executed.

Python and Perl are interpreted scripting languages. In those languages, the code written by a software developer is directly executed by the language's interpreter. SQL is a query language used to send commands to a relational database.

Correct Answer: C. C++

Practice Question 2 Explanation

Code that is written in assembly language is written to work on a specific hardware processor. A server upgrade that changes the processor is likely to require new assembly language code that is designed to work on the new processor.

Software written in compiled languages does not need to be rewritten. Instead, the developer can take the original source code and recompile it to work on the new processor.

Similarly, interpreted languages do not need to be rewritten. The system administrator simply needs to ensure that an appropriate interpreter is installed on the new server.

Query languages, such as Structured Query Language (SQL), are not hardware-specific, and as long as the same database server is installed on the server, existing SQL commands should continue to execute in the same way that they did on the old server.

Correct Answer: D. Assembly language

## CHAPTER 24

Data Types

Objective 4.2: Identify fundamental data types and their characteristics

While computers are designed to directly work with binary code, operating systems and applications are written with human users in mind. In Chapter 2, "Notational Systems," you learned how binary bits can be used to represent different decimal, hexadecimal, and text values. In this chapter, you'll discover the different types of data objects that you can use when creating software to run on a computer.

You'll learn everything you need to know about Tech+ objective 4.2, including the following topics:

▶ **Char**
▶ **Strings**
▶ **Numbers**
▶ **Boolean**

DATA TYPES

Each data object used by an application has an associated *data type* that tells the computer how to handle the data that it encounters. This is how we tell the difference between numeric values, character strings, and other types of data that we might have stored in memory or on disk.

Exam Tip

Expect to see exam questions that ask you to identify the best data type to use in a given situation. When you face a question like this, you should first determine whether the data is numeric, text, or binary. If the data is numeric and a whole number, then choose integer values. If the data is numeric with a decimal, then choose floating-point values. If the data is text, choose char if it will be a single character or string if it will be more than one character. If the data requires only a single binary bit, such as a yes/no, on/off, or true/false value, use a Boolean data type.

Boolean Data

The most basic data type is the *Boolean* object. A Boolean data element consists of only a single bit, so it can only have two possible values—0 and 1. That might sound pretty limiting, but Boolean data types are widely used in computer systems to represent values that are either true or false. The value 0 represents FALSE and the value 1 represents TRUE.

When we're designing software, we often refer to these Boolean values as *flags* and use them for a wide variety of purposes. For example, if I'm storing data about products that I maintain in my store's inventory, I could have a flag called Taxable that represents whether sales tax should be charged when the product is sold or whether it is exempt from tax. Products that are taxable would have a 1 in the taxable field, making the taxable value TRUE, whereas products that are not taxable would have a 0, making the taxable value FALSE.

Numeric Data

We also commonly store numeric values in memory. They come in two basic forms: *integers* and *floating-point numbers*.

Integers

Integers are values that do not have decimal or fractional values. They are whole numbers, such as 1, 2, and 3. They may also take on negative values, such as –123.

Floats

Floating-point numbers, or floats, are numbers that do have decimal places associated with them. The precision of a floating-point number indicates how many decimal places may be used with that number. The more precision we use, the more memory a floating-point number consumes.

Examples of floating-point numbers include 1.2, 3.6, and 150.0. Note that it is possible to store numbers with no decimal content in a floating-point value, such as 150.0. However, it is more efficient to store this type of data in an integer, and software will treat floats and integers differently when performing some types of calculation.

Text Data

Finally, we often store text values in memory and on disk. A single character of text uses the *char* data type and, in the ASCII encoding system, consumes a single byte of memory.

Character strings consist of one or more characters strung together, such as in a word, sentence, or paragraph, and they consume 1 byte per character.

> **WARNING**
>
> Tech+ candidates often become confused about the appropriate data type to use for ZIP codes. ZIP codes are 5- or 9-digit values that consist entirely of numbers. However, they should *always* be stored as character strings and not numeric values. The reason for this is that they are not used in computation, and because some ZIP codes start with the digit 0, numeric data types would truncate this digit, making the ZIP code invalid. For example, 07717 is the ZIP code for Avon-by-the-Sea, New Jersey. If this ZIP code were stored in an integer field, it would be truncated to 7717, which is not a valid ZIP code.

Tying It All Together

You should be prepared to answer questions where you are provided with a scenario and are asked to choose the best data type for that situation. Figure 24.1 shows a flowchart that you can use to make these decisions.

Table 24.1 provides an example of the types of information that a store might maintain about the products that it sells. Review this table and each of the data elements. What data type do you think should be used for each one?

TABLE 24.1 Product information

Product Name	Price	Quantity	Taxable	Discounted
Bicycle	899.49	47	Yes	TRUE
Helmet	49.99	13	Yes	FALSE
Handlebars	62.99	85	No	FALSE
Seat	104.99	19	No	TRUE

As you look through this table, consider each of the columns:

▶ Product Name is text data. The field contains words, which are multiple characters strung together, so it should be stored using a string data type.

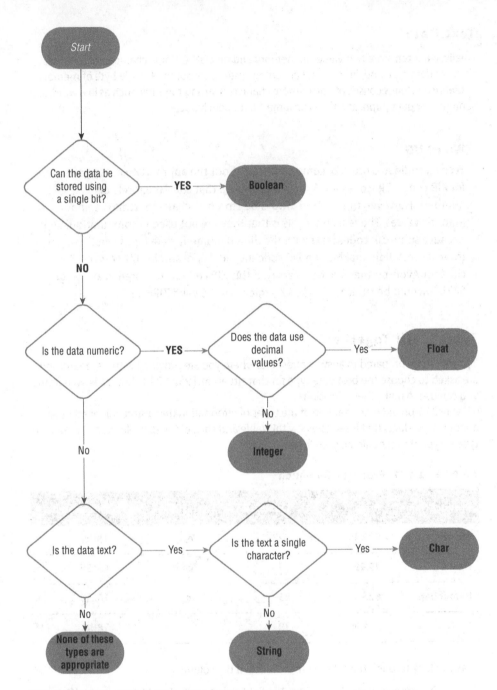

FIGURE 24.1 Data type flowchart

- ▶ Price is monetary data. It contains numeric data that includes decimal values, so it should be stored using a floating-point data type.
- ▶ Quantity is also numeric data, but it contains only whole numbers, so it should be stored as an integer data type.
- ▶ Taxable is a Yes/No field, so it may be stored using a single binary bit, where 1 represents Yes and 0 represents No. Therefore, it should be stored as a Boolean value.
- ▶ Discounted is a TRUE/FALSE field and it may be treated the same way, encoding the value TRUE as 1 and the value FALSE as 0. It should also be stored as a Boolean value.

CERTMIKE EXAM ESSENTIALS

▶ Data that will be used in computations should be in numeric form. Numeric data may be either whole numbers, stored as integers, or decimal numbers, stored as floating-point values.

▶ Text data may be stored in character data types if it will be a single character or in character strings if the text will be multiple characters joined together, such as a word, sentence, or paragraph.

▶ Data elements that can be represented as a single binary digit (bit) should use the Boolean data type to conserve storage and memory.

Practice Question 1

You are creating a new software program for your organization that will track the number of times a customer visits your store. The program will contain a variable called visits that will maintain the tally.

What data type would be *best* suited for the visits variable?

A. Boolean
B. String
C. Integer
D. Float

Practice Question 2

You are working with a software developer who is creating a database that will track information about the guests who stay at a hotel. One of the variables that you wish to track is whether each guest is a member of the hotel loyalty program. You will track this in a variable called loyalty.

What data type would be *best* suited for the loyalty variable?

A. Boolean
B. String
C. Integer
D. Float

Practice Question 1 Explanation

In this question, we're asked to choose the most appropriate data type for a given situation. We can approach this using the flowchart method discussed in this chapter. Let's walk through that flowchart together.

First, we're asked if we can store the data in a single binary bit. This would allow us only two possible values, such as 0/1, true/false, or yes/no. The number of times a customer visits a store may take on many possible values, so we cannot store it in a bit and a Boolean data type is not appropriate.

Next, we're asked if the data is numeric. The number of times that a customer visits a store is numeric data, so we then ask the follow-up question of whether it uses decimal values. It wouldn't make sense for the number of customer visits to be a decimal number (what would 1.5 visits mean?), so a float is not appropriate. We then decide to use an integer value as the most appropriate data type.

The only other possible answer choice here is a string value, which is not appropriate because this data is numeric and we would very likely want to perform calculations on it, such as tallying the average number of visits per customer or the total number of visits per month.

Correct Answer: C. Integer

Practice Question 2 Explanation

This question also calls for the use of the flowchart shown in Figure 24.1. We begin the flowchart by asking the question: "Can this data be stored using a single bit?"

The variable will store data about whether a customer is a member of the loyalty program. There are only two possible answers to this question: yes and no. Therefore, it is possible to store this data in a single bit, so a Boolean data type would be the best choice.

You could also use any of the other data types listed to store this data. You could use character strings to store the words "yes" and "no." You could also use integers or floating-point numbers to store 0 and 1 values. However, these are not the best choices because those data types will use more storage than a single Boolean bit with no added value. That's why the flowchart directs us to use Boolean values whenever we can store data using only a single bit.

Correct Answer: A. Boolean

## CHAPTER 25

Programming Concepts

Objective 4.3: Explain the purpose and use of programming concepts

As you prepare for the Tech+ exam, you won't need to know how to write code, but you will need to be familiar with the basic concepts of programming. You'll encounter questions that ask you to understand and interpret pseudocode, and that requires understanding the use of variables, arrays, vectors, functions, and objects.

In this chapter, you'll learn the material that you need to know about Tech+ objective 4.3. The topics covered in this chapter include:

▶ Identifiers
▶ Arrays
▶ Functions
▶ Objects

IDENTIFIERS AND ARRAYS

Variables and arrays are the basic constructs that we use to store data in memory. They're crucial to the understanding and execution of code written in any programming language.

Identifiers

Identifiers are one of the core concepts in any programming language. They allow developers to store information in memory using a descriptive name and then later reference that information in their script. Identifiers come in two forms: variables and constants. *Variables* contain values that may change during the execution of code whereas *constants* contain values that do not change. Variables can store integers, decimal numbers, Boolean (true/false) values, dates and times, character strings, and virtually any other type of information that you might need.

Let's take a look at how we might use a variable in some pseudocode. Imagine that we have a small store that normally sells cupcakes for $2 but offers a 50 percent discount on Tuesdays. We might need a script that calculates Tuesday's price, like this one:

```
cupcake_price = 2

cupcake_price = cupcake_price / 2

print "The price of a cupcake is ", cupcake_price
```

In this script, cupcake_price is a variable. The first line of the script sets the value of that variable equal to 2.00. The next line changes the price to one-half of its current value. The last line prints the price of the cupcake, which will be $1 on Tuesday.

That's a simple example of a variable in action. Remember, when we execute a script containing a variable, the script interpreter performs a substitution, using the value stored in that variable's memory location in place of the variable name.

We sometimes have values that will never change. In those cases, we don't have to put them in a variable, but we can use a similar data structure called the *constant*. Constants are values that don't ever change in our code. Otherwise, we can use them basically the same way that we use a variable.

Arrays

In some cases, we need to keep track of many related variables at the same time. For example, we might have the ages of all students in a high school programming class. We might create a separate variable to keep track of each student's age, but that would make things very complicated. We'd have to remember the names of all those variables. *Arrays* offer a helpful way to store that information together. For example, we might create an array called ages using this code:

```
ages = [16,15,18,15,16,14,13,17,13,14]
```

This creates an array with 10 elements, each one corresponding to the age of a single student. We can pull out individual values from the array and inspect or manipulate them. For example, if we want to access the first element in the array, we can use this code, which would give us the value 16:

```
ages[0]
```

Now you might be wondering why I used the number 0 to reference the first element of the array. When programmers count elements in an array, they usually begin with 0 instead of 1. This means that a 10-element array has elements numbered 0 through 9.

If our first student has a birthday, we could increment that student's age with this command:

```
ages[0] = 17
```

That changes a single element of the array. Alternatively, if we wanted to add 1 to all of the students' ages, we could use this command to create the array and then perform a simple arithmetic operation:

```
ages = [16,15,18,15,16,14,13,17,13,14]

ages = ages + 1
```

This would result in an array with the values shown here:

```
ages [17,16,19,16,17,15,14,18,14,15]
```

DATA TYPES

In most programming languages, each variable has an associated data type that tells the computer how to handle it. This is how we tell the difference between numeric values, character strings, and other types of data that we might have stored in memory or on disk.

Numeric Data

Numeric data is, as the names implies, data that uses numbers. You might use a numeric data type to store the number of products you have remaining in stock, the weight of a person in pounds or kilograms, the length of a boat, or any other value that we can measure quantitatively.

There are two major subtypes of numeric data:

▶ *Integers* are values that do not have decimal or fractional values. They are whole numbers, such as 1, 2, and 3. They may also take on negative values, such as −145.
▶ *Floating-point numbers*, or floats, are numbers that do have decimal places associated with them. They're decimal numbers. The precision of a floating-point number indicates how many decimal places may be used with that number. The more precision we use, the more memory a floating-point number consumes because the computer has to store the values in all those extra decimal places.

Text Data

We also commonly work with *text data*—that is, data made up of characters. We use text for so many different purposes, ranging from small fields such as people's names or addresses, to large blocks of text that might make up a paragraph, article, or even an entire book.

Computers store text using a data type known as a *character string*. This simply means that it is a sequence, or string, of one or more characters put together to create a block of text. You can create strings of different lengths in databases, spreadsheets, and programming languages.

Character strings may contain either plain text, consisting only of letters and symbols, or they may contain alphanumeric text that mixes together numeric digits with letters and symbols. One important thing to understand is that if you have numeric data stored in a string, you can't perform mathematical operations on that data. The data might look like a number to us, but to the computer it's simply the text characters that make up those numbers.

ZIP Codes

One really interesting and tricky example of data types are the ZIP codes that we use as postal codes in the United States. These are five-digit or nine-digit numbers that uniquely identify a town or an area of a city for the delivery of mail. Since these are numbers, you might be tempted to store them using a numeric data type.

However, the problem is that many ZIP codes start with the digit 0. If you store those in a numeric data type, the computer will ignore the leading 0 and truncate the ZIP code to be only four digits! For that reason, you should always store ZIP codes as text.

Boolean Data

The final data type that you should be familiar with for the exam is the *Boolean* data type. This is just a fancy way of saying that a variable can only contain two values: True and False. We might have a Boolean value stored in a database of employees indicating whether or not an employee is salaried. If the value is set to True, the employee is salaried. If the value is set to False, the employee is not salaried.

Exam Tip

As you prepare for the exam, it's really important that you understand these different data types and that you're able to select the most appropriate data type for a given situation. That's a common topic that might appear on the test.

FUNCTIONS

In software development, we often wind up needing to use the same code over and over again. *Functions* provide us with an opportunity to create reusable pieces of code that can be easily called multiple times.

For example, in Chapter 26, "Programming Organizational Techniques," we look at an algorithm for converting temperatures from Fahrenheit to Celsius. Here's that algorithm written in pseudocode:

```
Input: T (a temperature in Fahrenheit)

T = T - 32

T = T * 5

T = T /9

Output: T (a temperature in Celsius)
```

If I had to do this conversion many times in my code, I could just copy and paste these steps over and over again, but that's not very efficient. It's a lot of typing for me, and if I made a mistake in my algorithm, I'd have to go correct it in many different places.

Instead, I might create a function that performs the conversion. I just name my function and provide the code that should be executed and the names of any variables it will take as input. This function takes a Fahrenheit temperature as input and returns the Celsius equivalent:

```
Function FahrenheitToCelsius(T)

{

T = T - 32

T = T * 5

T = T /9

return T

       }
```

Then whenever I want to use this code, I can just call the function with the Fahrenheit temperature. For example, if I call this function:

```
FahrenheitToCelsius(50)
```

it will go through the math and subtract 32 from 50, multiply it by 5, and divide it by 9 to get this result:

```
10
```

Similarly, if I call

`FahrenheitToCelsius(90)`

I get the result:

`32.2`

Functions can be used any time we want to have reusable code, and they may be used by a single developer, shared within a team or company, or even included in public libraries, where anyone can download them.

OBJECTS

Some programming languages are *object-oriented*. In this model, we don't write all our code in a step-by-step fashion, giving the computer a series of actions to take in order. Instead, we create a series of *objects* that each have some common components.

Objects have two major components:

▶ *Attributes* are the properties or variables associated with an object.
▶ *Methods* are the functions or procedures that can be taken on the object. They're similar to the functions that exist in other programming languages, but they are tied to an object rather than being generally available.

So let's think about this in a concrete example. Suppose we are writing code that deals with the different products sold in a store. We might create an object called `Product` that looks something like the one shown in Figure 25.1. `Product` has some attributes associated with it—things like the name of the product, the weight of the product, the price, a description, and so on.

Product
Name: Weight: Price: GetPrice()   SetPrice()

FIGURE 25.1 The Product object

We can then interact with the object through methods. We'd have methods for anything someone might want to do to a product. For our purposes, let's just focus on price. There are two main things someone might want to do with the price: Check the price of the product, and change the price of the product. So, we'd write two methods that contain that code:

▶ A GetPrice() method that returns the current price of a product
▶ A SetPrice() method that changes the price of the product to a specific value

When we use this code, we would create copies of this object for each product that we sell. Each of these copies is called an *instance* of the object. Then we could reference each of them by name and call the methods of the object. For example, we might create instances of the Product object for a bicycle and a television, as shown in Figure 25.2.

Bicycle
Name: Bicycle
Weight: 50 lbs
Price: $142
GetPrice()
SetPrice()

TV
Name: TV
Weight: 92 lbs
Price: $700
GetPrice()
SetPrice()

FIGURE 25.2 Instances of the Product object for a bicycle and a TV

If we wanted to get the price of a bicycle, we'd reference the Bicycle object and call the getPrice() method to get the result of $142:

```
Bicycle -> getPrice()
$142
```

If we wanted to change the price of the television to $800, we'd call the setPrice() method on TV and pass the value $800:

```
TV -> setPrice($800)
```

which would change the underlying price in that instance, as shown in Figure 25.3.

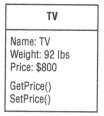

Bicycle
Name: Bicycle
Weight: 50 lbs
Price: $142
GetPrice()
SetPrice()

TV
Name: TV
Weight: 92 lbs
Price: $800
GetPrice()
SetPrice()

FIGURE 25.3 Updated instances of the Product object for a bicycle and a TV

Exam Tip

When you take the exam, you should be familiar with the concept of an object and know that the characteristics of an object are stored in attributes and that we can take actions on objects using methods.

CERTMIKE EXAM ESSENTIALS

▶ Variables are used to hold data in memory during a program's execution. They may contain numeric data, text data, or Boolean values. Arrays are collections of multiple variables of the same type stored together.

▶ Functions contain reusable code that may be called multiple times from within a program and may be shared across programs.

▶ Object-oriented programming uses instances of objects that contain two components. Attributes are variables stored within the object, and methods are functions that may be used to manipulate and retrieve those attributes.

Practice Question 1

You are creating a variable for use within a program. The variable will contain the number of children that a person has. What data type would be most appropriate for this variable?

A. Floating-point number
B. String
C. Boolean
D. Integer

Practice Question 2

You are looking at the source code for a program written in an object-oriented language and find an object class used to represent an employee in that program. The object contains the employee's pay rate in a variable called `salary` and has the ability to give the person a raise and increase their salary using a function called `GrantRaise()`. Which one of the following statements is correct?

A. Both `salary` and `GrantRaise()` are attributes.
B. `Salary` is an attribute and `GrantRaise()` is a method.
C. `Salary` is a method and `GrantRaise()` is an attribute.
D. Both `salary` and `GrantRaise()` are methods.

Practice Question 1 Explanation

The number of children that an individual has is a whole number and should, therefore, be stored as an integer value.

Floating-point numbers contain decimal places. It would not make sense to store a fractional number of children, such as 1.5, so it would not be logical to use a floating-point number for this purpose, since doing so could lead to nonsensical values being stored.

While you could use a text string to store the number of children, in the form "1" or "2", this is not the best way to store the data. It would not be possible to manipulate that number mathematically, such as incrementing it to mark the birth of a new child or adding several values together to find the combined number of children among a group of people.

Boolean values can only be True or False, so it would not be possible to store the number of children that an individual has in a Boolean. A Boolean value could be used for a field named HasChildren that is only used to record the fact that a person does or does not have children.

Correct Answer: D. Integer

Practice Question 2 Explanation

There are two important facts about objects that you need to know to answer this question. First, objects have attributes that are the properties or variables associated with an object. Second, objects have methods that are the functions or procedures that can be taken on the object.

In this case, `salary` is a property of the employee, so it is an attribute. `GrantRaise()` is a function that may be used to manipulate `salary`, so it is a method.

Correct Answer: B. Salary is an attribute and GrantRaise() is a method.

## CHAPTER 26

Programming Organizational Techniques

Objective 4.4: Identify programming organizational techniques and logic concepts

As software developers begin to create code, they use some standard tools to organize their work. These tools include pseudocode, which allows them to write code that is not yet in any specific programming language, and flowcharts, which show the general flow of software-based decision-making.

In this chapter, you'll learn the first half of the material that you need to know about Tech+ objective 4.4. The remaining material for this objective is covered in Chapter 27, "Logic Components." The topics covered in this chapter include:

▶ Pseudocode concepts
▶ Object-oriented methods
▶ Comments and documentation
▶ Flowchart concepts

PSEUDOCODE

Software developers use a fairly consistent process for creating new pieces of software. The majority of their work is dedicated to creating what we call *algorithms*. Algorithms are just a fancy term for the step-by-step instructions that a computer should follow when it is executing the code.

Let's write a basic algorithm together that will convert temperatures from Fahrenheit into Celsius. First, I'll make sure that you understand the process for performing this conversion. Our algorithm will receive a single piece of input: a temperature in Fahrenheit. Then it will perform a series of calculations on that input. It will subtract 32 from the Fahrenheit temperature, then multiply that result by 5 and divide that result by 9. That produces the output as the equivalent temperature in Celsius.

The previous paragraph is an algorithm. It's written in text form, which isn't a standard way to write an algorithm, but it is an algorithm nonetheless because it describes the sequence of steps that we need to follow. If I gave you a temperature in Fahrenheit and asked you to convert it to Celsius, you could simply follow the process outlined here to perform that conversion. And I can also program a computer to do the same thing.

Pseudocode is a more common way to write an algorithm. Pseudocode is simply a plain English description of an algorithm that a software developer can take and use as the basis for a program written in any language. Here's an example of that same algorithm written in pseudocode:

```
Input: T (a temperature in Fahrenheit)


T = T - 32

T = T * 5

T = T /9

Output: T (a temperature in Celsius)
```

This algorithm isn't written in any specific programming language. I could write code in Python, Java, C, or another programming language to execute this code, but I haven't done that yet. All I've done here is write the steps out in plain English using a programming style.

EXAM TIP

There aren't "correct" and "incorrect" ways to write pseudocode. Unlike code written in a programming language, there's no syntax to worry about. When you're writing pseudocode, you're just trying to document your ideas in a way that communicates clearly to yourself and others what you've done.

FLOWCHARTS

Flowcharts are another common design tool used by programmers to help them understand the sequence of steps that a program will follow when it has to make decisions.

For example, Figure 26.1 shows a flowchart that I might use to adjust the temperature in a building so that it stays within the range of 65 to 70 degrees. I enter at the top of the flowchart and then I get to the first decision: Is the temperature greater than 70? If it is, I turn on the air conditioning and then end the program.

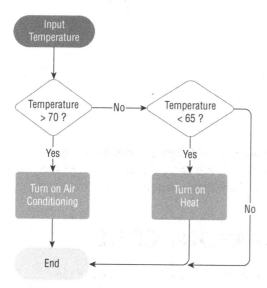

FIGURE 26.1 **Temperature adjustment flowchart**

If the temperature is not greater than 70 degrees, I get to the next decision: Is the temperature less than 65 degrees? If it is, then I turn on the heat and end the program. If it is not, then the temperature is within the range of 65 to 70, so I don't take any action and just end the program.

When you're creating a flowchart, there are three basic symbols you can use (see Figure 26.2):

▶ Ovals, which are used as terminators. They mark either the beginning or the end of an algorithm.

▶ Rectangles, which are used as process steps. Rectangles are used to mark some type of action that is taking place.

▶ Diamonds, which are used as decision steps. Diamonds pose a question and then have outputs that are followed depending on the answer to the question. In most flowcharts, these questions are Yes/No questions that have only two possible answers, so there are two arrows leaving the diamond: one path to follow if the answer is yes, and another to follow if the answer is no.

FIGURE 26.2 **Common flowchart shapes**

COMMUNICATING ABOUT CODE

Clear communication is crucial in software development. Effective communication ensures that code is understandable not just for current team members but also for future developers. The two main communications tools available to developers are thoughtful comments and comprehensive documentation. These tools are essential for maintaining code clarity and enhancing its usability across different stages of development and deployment.

Comments

Comments are annotations within the code itself that are ignored by the compiler or interpreter. Comments help developers explain what the code does, why certain decisions were made, and outline steps that might not be immediately obvious. Different languages use different syntax for comments. For example, in Python, you can begin a comment with the # symbol.

Here's an example of some Python code that implements the algorithm from earlier in this chapter but includes comments to explain what is being done:

```
def convert_fahrenheit_to_celsius(fahrenheit_temp):
    # Subtract 32 from the Fahrenheit temperature
    intermediate_temp = fahrenheit_temp - 32

    # Multiply the result by 5
    intermediate_temp = intermediate_temp * 5

    # Divide the result by 9 to get the Celsius temperature
    celsius_temp = intermediate_temp / 9

    return celsius_temp
```

Documentation

While comments are meant for developers looking directly at the code, *documentation* is often a separate document, intended for both end users and developers. Documentation provides a detailed description of the software's functionality and API interfaces. It describes how to use the software, as well as how to interact with the system from other code. Documentation can be in the form of text files, user manuals, or online help pages.

OBJECT-ORIENTED METHODS

Object-oriented methods are also a programming organizational technique that you should understand as you prepare for the Tech+ exam. We covered those in Chapter 25, "Programming Concepts."

CERTMIKE EXAM ESSENTIALS

▶ Pseudocode allows software developers to write out the steps in an algorithm without using any specific programming language. It's a common way to organize work before beginning to write code.

▶ Flowcharts provide a method for visually describing the logical flow of code. In a flowchart, ovals represent the start or beginning of a flowchart. Rectangles represent process steps, and diamonds represent decision steps.

▶ Comments are annotations within code that explain what the code does, why certain decisions were made, and outline steps that might not be immediately obvious.

▶ Documentation provides a detailed description of software functionality and API interfaces. It describes how to use the software, as well as how to interact with the system from other code.

Practice Question 1

A software developer is beginning to design a new application and would like to develop a flowchart that will map out the process. They reach a step in the middle of the algorithm where the code will evaluate the number of items in inventory and either reduce the price of the item if the inventory is too high or order more of the item if the inventory is too low.

What shape would they use in a flowchart to represent the step where this evaluation is performed?

A. Rectangle
B. Diamond
C. Oval
D. Circle

Practice Question 2

A programmer recently completed the pseudocode for a new piece of software that they are writing and is ready to convert it into real code. What is responsible for converting the pseudocode into actual code?

A. Compiler
B. Interpreter
C. Assembler
D. Programmer

Practice Question 1 Explanation

This is clearly a decision step in the flowchart. The application must evaluate the current inventory level and then make a decision as to whether the inventory is too high or too low. Decision steps are represented in flowcharts using diamond shapes.

Once the software has made this decision, it may then move on to take the appropriate action. Those action steps are process steps and would be represented by rectangles. The portion of the flowchart that carries out this part of the code is shown here:

Ovals are used to represent the start and end of the flowchart, as they are terminator symbols. The scenario describes this as a step in the middle of the algorithm, so it would not be appropriate to use a terminator here.

Correct Answer: B. Diamond

Practice Question 2 Explanation

There is no automated tool that converts pseudocode into actual code. This is the work that programmers themselves must undertake. The purpose of pseudocode is to provide the programmer with a roadmap for creating actual code.

The other tools mentioned here play different roles in the software development process. Compilers are used to convert source code written in a compiled language into machine language. Assemblers convert assembly language into machine language. Interpreters are used to directly execute code written in an interpreted language.

Correct Answer: D. Programmer

## CHAPTER 27

Logic Components

Objective 4.4: Identify programming organizational techniques and logic concepts

When writing code, developers use special instructions to control the logical flow of the code's execution. Branching, or conditional execution, allows the developer to set the code up to perform different actions based on the circumstances. Looping allows the same code to be executed repeatedly until one or more conditions are met.

In this chapter, you'll learn the second half of the material that you need to know about Tech+ objective 4.4. The first half of the material for this objective was covered in Chapter 26, "Programming Organizational Techniques." The topics covered in this chapter include:

▶ Branching
▶ Looping

BRANCHING

Conditional execution allows developers to write code that executes only when certain logical conditions are met. The most common conditional execution structure is the `if..then..else` statement. The general idea of the statement is summarized in this pseudocode:

```
if (logical_test1) then
  command1
else if (logical_test2) then
  command2
```

```
else if (logical_test3) then
  command3
else
  command4
```

Here's how this works. Each of the logical tests contained in this pseudocode is a question that can be answered with "yes" or "no" or, in logical terms, "true" or "false." For example, `logical_test1` might be the question "Is *x* greater than 3?" Each of the commands in the pseudocode is an action that the program should take if the preceding logical test is true.

When the program executes this code, it first checks to see if `logical_test1` is true. If it is, then it executes *command1* and the entire code statement is complete without performing any additional checks.

If `logical_test1` is false, then the program checks `logical_test2`. If that is true, then *command2* executes. If `logical_test2` is false, the program checks `logical_test3`. If that test is true, then *command3* executes.

If all of the logical tests are false, then *command4*, contained within the `else` clause, executes. This logical testing, working with values of true and false, is an example of performing *Boolean* operations.

An `if..then..else` statement may have one, many, or no `else if` clauses. The `else` clause is also optional. It's important to remember that, no matter how many clauses you have in your statement, only one can execute.

TIP

When you execute an `if..then..else` statement, only one of the actions is executed. If multiple logical tests are true, then the code only executes the first true test that it encounters.

Let's look at an example of an `if...then...else` statement in action. Here's some code that prints different statements depending on the current temperature:

```
if (temperature > 90) then
  print "It's very hot!"
else if (temperature > 70) then
  print "It's somewhat hot."
else
  print "It's not hot."
```

If we run this code when the temperature is 95 degrees, the first test is true and the code prints "It's very hot" and then exits.

If we run the code when the temperature is 75 degrees, the first test is false, so we move on to the next `else if` statement. That one is true, so we print "It's somewhat hot" and then exit.

If we run the code when the temperature is 30 degrees, the first test is false, so we move on to the second test, which is also false, and then we hit the `else` statement, which we execute and print "It's not hot" before exiting.

LOOPING

Looping operations allow you to repeat the same block of code more than one time. For example, you might want to run a certain piece of code 25 times, or once for each variable in a list.

for Loops

The *for loop* is one way that you can insert looping into your code. Here's a pseudocode example of how `for` loops are structured:

```
for variable = start to finish
    code statements
```

This `for` loop will create a new variable with the name `variable` and give it the starting value specified in `start`. It will then run the code statements the first time. After they complete, it will add 1 to the value of `variable` and execute the code statements again. This process will repeat until variable takes on the value of `finish`.

The exact behavior of this statement, including whether it executes the code one more time when the value of `variable` is equal to `finish`, depends on the programming language used.

Here's a more concrete example, still written in pseudocode:

```
for i = 0 to 10
    print i
```

This `for` loop would produce these results:

```
0
1
2
3
4
5
6
7
8
9
```

Again, it may print one more line containing the value 10, depending on the programming language.

while Loops

The *while loop* is another type of looping statement. Similar to for loops, while loops repeat a block of code multiple times. Instead of repeating a fixed number of times, they repeat until a condition is no longer true. They use the general format shown here:

```
while (condition)
     code statements
```

The code statements will perform some modification to the variable(s) checked in the condition statement. The while loop will then repeat continuously until condition evaluates as false.

For example, this while loop will execute as long as the value contained in the variable i is greater than 90:

```
i = 100
while (i > 90)
     print i
     i = i - 1
```

If we set i to 100 and then execute this code, the loop will run until i is not greater than 90, resulting in this output:

```
100
99
98
97
96
95
94
93
92
91
```

CERTMIKE EXAM ESSENTIALS

▶ Branching allows you to execute different code statements based on logical conditions. The primary mechanism for branching is the if..then..else statement.

▶ for loops allow you to execute the same code segment repeatedly a certain number of times. while loops work similarly but execute the code segment as long as a logical condition remains true.

Practice Question 1

Examine the pseudocode shown here:

```
if (x > 2) then
  print "We have enough inventory."
else if (x > 3) then
  print "We have too much inventory."
else if (x = 0) then
  print "We have no inventory."

else
  print "We do not have enough inventory."
```

If the value of x is set to 4 before this code executes, what will be the output?

A. We have enough inventory.
B. We have too much inventory.
C. We have no inventory.
D. We do not have enough inventory.

Practice Question 2

You are writing pseudocode for a new program and would like to check the temperature of a room. In your code, you would like to keep the air conditioning on until the room reaches 68 degrees Fahrenheit and then you would like to turn the air conditioning off.

Here is partial pseudocode to solve this problem:

```
COMMAND (temperature > 68)
    keep air conditioning on

    turn off air conditioning
```

What type of statement should you use where it currently says COMMAND to complete this code?

A. if
B. for
C. while
D. else

Practice Question 1 Explanation

When you encounter a question like this, you should walk through the pseudocode step by step, reading each line carefully without jumping to conclusions.

If you were to look at this code without following that process, you might quickly come to the conclusion that x is indeed greater than 3, so the code would print the statement "We have too much inventory." That, however, is not the correct answer.

The reason for this is that the conditions in an if..then..else statement are tested sequentially and the command corresponding to the first true condition is executed. In this case, the first test is asking if x > 2. The value of x is 4, which is greater than 2, so the code prints the line "We have enough inventory."

In this pseudocode, the reality is that the statement "We have too much inventory" will never print because any value of x that satisfies the test x > 3 will also satisfy the test x > 2 and will trigger the command to print "We have enough inventory."

Correct Answer: A. We have enough inventory.

Practice Question 2 Explanation

In this code, you would like to keep the air conditioning on until the temperature is lowered to 68 degrees. The command to complete this code is a while statement, as shown here:

```
while (temperature > 68)
    keep air conditioning on


    turn off air conditioning
```

The code will remain in the while loop until the temperature reaches 68 degrees. Then it will exit the while loop and turn off the air conditioning.

A for loop would execute the command a certain number of times, instead of waiting until a logical condition is met, so it would not be appropriate here. The use of an if statement would test the logical condition, but it would only do so once, so it would turn the air conditioning on and then immediately turn it off. An else statement cannot be used here because it may only be used as a component of an if..then..else statement.

Correct Answer: C. while

Domain 5.0: Data and Database Fundamentals

Data and Database Fundamentals is the fifth domain of CompTIA's Tech+ exam. In this domain, you'll learn about the purpose of databases and the techniques available to users who need to create, read, update, and delete (CRUD) database information. This domain has four objectives:

5.1 Explain the value of data and information

5.2 Explain database concepts and the purpose of a database

5.2 Compare and contrast various database structures

5.4 Explain basic data backup concepts

Questions from this domain make up 13% of the questions on the Tech+ exam, so you should expect to see approximately 10 questions on your test covering the material in this part.

## CHAPTER 28

The Value of Data
Objective 5.1: Explain the value of data and information

In today's economy, information is often one of a business's most valuable assets. From product plans to customer records, every business has sensitive information and protecting that information is a crucial business concern. If that information falls into the wrong hands, it could damage the organization's reputation, injure its customers, or cause financial losses.

In this chapter, you'll learn everything you need to know about Tech+ objective 5.1, including the following topics:

▶ Data and information as an asset
▶ Data-driven business decisions
▶ Data monetization
▶ Data analytics
▶ Big data

DATA AND INFORMATION

As an IT professional, you're responsible for protecting the information that your organization values. The first key step to that is recognizing that data and information are indeed assets that have value to your business, just like your vehicles, buildings, and other equipment.

Data

Let's talk a bit about the difference between data and information. *Data* is the raw facts that our systems and processes generate and collect on a regular basis. You can think of data as just bits of knowledge. For example, we might put a thermometer in our factory to monitor a piece of sensitive equipment. That thermometer might record a temperature reading every 10 minutes to determine the temperature inside the equipment.

The end result would be a spreadsheet or database table containing all of the temperature recordings over time, such as the one shown in Figure 28.1. Each of these temperature readings is one fact and all of this is data. We have a spreadsheet providing data about our temperature readings.

Time	Temperature
1/10/2022 0:00	107
1/10/2022 0:30	108
1/10/2022 1:00	101
1/10/2022 1:30	103
1/10/2022 2:00	107
1/10/2022 2:30	110
1/10/2022 3:00	101
1/10/2022 3:30	110
1/10/2022 4:00	101
1/10/2022 4:30	104
1/10/2022 5:00	102
1/10/2022 5:30	102
1/10/2022 6:00	110
1/10/2022 6:30	104
1/10/2022 7:00	110
1/10/2022 7:30	107
1/10/2022 8:00	109
1/10/2022 8:30	105
1/10/2022 9:00	104
1/10/2022 9:30	100

FIGURE 28.1 A spreadsheet of temperature readings is only data.

Information

Information is data that has been processed and analyzed. A system or person has put some effort into putting that data in the context of the business so that it is useful to us. The spreadsheet of temperature information in Figure 28.1 is all correct, but it isn't very useful to us. It's just a collection of data that isn't in any context.

Figure 28.2 shows what happens if we create a plot showing how the temperature of this equipment changes over time. Now we start to have some information.

Data-Driven Business Decisions

Looking at Figure 28.2 we can quickly see that the temperature in this machinery spikes to dangerously high levels every afternoon around 2 p.m., as shown in Figure 28.3.

Temperature vs. Time

FIGURE 28.2 Plotting data over time is one way we can transform it into information.

Temperature vs. Time

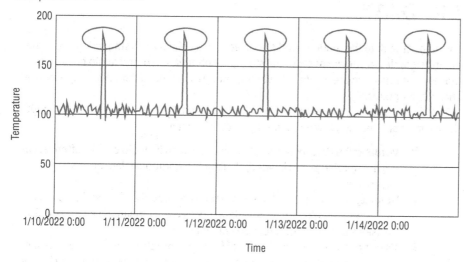

FIGURE 28.3 Information can drive action.

That's information that we can act upon. We can tell the people responsible for this equipment that they need to figure out what is going on every afternoon that's causing this potentially dangerous situation.

That story is an example of a data-driven business decision. When have the right information at our disposal, we can act upon it to improve our business. This process consists of the following stages:

1. We first capture and collect data that might have meaning to our business. Whether that's temperature data like our previous example, data about our customers, products, or the operating environment, there are many different kinds of data that might be valuable to us.
2. Once we have that data, we can correlate it, performing analysis to help find the meaningful information that it contains.
3. With that information in hand, we can provide reports to business leaders, helping them make data-driven business decisions.

Data Monetization

As you've read, data and information are critical assets to any business. One significant way that companies derive value from these assets is through *data monetization*. Data monetization refers to the process of using data to achieve measurable economic benefits. This can be done through direct methods, such as selling data directly to third parties, or indirect methods, such as using data to improve marketing strategies, enhance business operations, or create personalized customer experiences that can increase sales or reduce costs.

BIG DATA

The amount of data the modern world generates on a daily basis is staggering. From the organized tables of spreadsheets to the storage of photos, video, and audio recordings, modern businesses create an almost overwhelming avalanche of data that is ripe for use in analytics programs.

The idea of *big data* isn't just about the amount of data that we have at hand. It's about three core characteristics, known as the "Three Vs" of big data:

▶ **Volume:** Big data involves data collection at an incredible scale, often reaching into terabytes and beyond, challenging traditional data processing capabilities.
▶ **Velocity:** The speed at which new data is generated and moved around is staggering. Thanks to real-time data processing, companies can make quick decisions based on the latest information.
▶ **Variety:** Data comes in all types of formats, from structured, numeric data in traditional databases to unstructured text, emails, videos, audios, stock ticker data, and financial transactions.

ANALYTICS

Analytics is the process of discovering and interpreting patterns in data. It's a discipline that merges statistical analysis, data science, and predictive modeling to extract valuable information for decision-making. Let's take a look at the major categories of analytics techniques.

Descriptive Analytics

Descriptive analytics simply seek to describe your data. For example, if you perform descriptive analytics on your customer records, you might ask questions like, what proportion of your customers are female? And how many of them are repeat customers?

Predictive Analytics

Predictive analytics seek to use your existing data to predict future events. For example, if you have a dataset on how your customers respond to direct mail, you might use that dataset to build a model that predicts how individual customers will respond to a specific future mailing. That might help you tweak that mailing to improve the response rate by changing the day you send it, altering the content of the message, or even making seemingly minor changes like altering the font size or paper color.

Prescriptive Analytics

Prescriptive analytics seek to optimize behavior by simulating many scenarios. For example, if you want to determine the best way to allocate your marketing dollars, you might run different simulations of consumer response and then use algorithms to prescribe your behavior in that context. Similarly, you might use prescriptive analytics to optimize the performance of an automated manufacturing process.

SECURING DATA

Information technology professionals are responsible for securing data of many different kinds. This includes the intellectual property that belongs to the organization as well as other sensitive information, such as the personal information of the company's customers and employees.

You'll learn much more about securing data in Part VI of this book, as security is an entire domain of the Tech+ exam.

CERTMIKE EXAM ESSENTIALS

▶ Data consists of raw facts that may be transformed into information. Together, data and information are among a business's most valuable assets.

▶ Businesses may use data to make data-driven business decisions. To do this, they must first capture/collect data, then correlate that data with other sources, and finally provide reporting to decision-makers.

Practice Question 1

Your organization has collected extensive data on sales performance across different regions and products for the past five years. The data science team has been asked to analyze this data to forecast sales for the upcoming quarter, considering factors such as market trends, economic forecasts, and past sales performance.

What type of analytics is the team performing?

A. Big data analytics
B. Prescriptive analytics
C. Descriptive analytics
D. Predictive analytics

Practice Question 2

Which of the following would best be described as information rather than data? (Select two.)

A. Receipt from a customer transaction
B. Arrival time of a bus
C. Average customer purchase size
D. Population of a country
E. Amount of rainfall in a city yesterday
F. Per capita income of a country

Practice Question 1 Explanation

The data science team is performing predictive analytics, which involves using historical data, statistical models, and algorithms to forecast future outcomes, in this case, the upcoming quarter's sales figures.

Descriptive analytics would merely summarize past data without making predictions.

Prescriptive analytics would go further by suggesting actions to achieve desired outcomes based on predictions.

Big data refers to the large volume and variety of data being analyzed and is not a type of analytics itself.

Correct Answer: D. Predictive analytics

Practice Question 2 Explanation

This question is asking us to select more than one correct answer. You'll likely see a few of these questions on the Tech+ exam. You should handle these questions by noting the number of correct answers and then walking through each option one by one to see if you think it is correct. If you find "extra" answers, remember that you're looking for the *best* answer choices.

Remember that data consists of raw facts while information has been processed and analyzed.

A receipt from a customer transaction is simply data—we haven't gathered any meaningful information from it. The average customer purchase size for a business is, however, analyzed information, so that would be a correct answer.

The arrival time of a bus and the amount of rainfall in a city yesterday are also just facts. They're data that has not been turned into information.

The population of a country is also just a fact and is data by itself, but when we use that data to compute the per capita income of a country, that becomes analyzed information.

Correct Answers: C. Average customer purchase size, F. Per capita income of a country.

## CHAPTER 29

Database Concepts

Objective 5.2: Explain database concepts and the purpose of a database

Organizations use databases to maintain centralized stores of data that are available to all users who need them and are protected against unauthorized access and accidental damage.

In this chapter, you'll learn everything you need to know about Tech+ objective 5.2, including the following topics:

▶ **Database uses**
▶ **Flat file vs. database**
▶ **Database records**
▶ **Storage**
▶ **Data availability**

DATABASES

Databases provide organizations with a way to store their data centrally in organized tables so that many people can access it at the same time. Popular database platforms include Microsoft SQL Server, Oracle, and MySQL.

> **EXAM TIP**
>
> Expect to see exam questions that ask you to decide the best way to store data in a given situation. If the question references any of the core advantages of a database over a flat file (i.e., multiple concurrent users, scalability, speed, and variety of data), you'll want to store the data in a database. If the data does not seem like it would easily be organized into tables, a database is probably not the best choice.

Databases vs. Flat Files

Databases offer an excellent alternative to *flat files*, which are files created in other applications that are stored on a hard disk without the benefit of a database server to help organize them. This approach works well for data used by a single person and in small quantities, but databases work better in many situations. Here are the four key characteristics of databases:

Databases allow multiple concurrent users to store and retrieve data.
If you've ever tried to access a file stored on a hard drive or server and edit it at the same time as other people, you know that this can be really challenging. Databases manage all of that for us, allowing everyone to share concurrent access.

Databases are very scalable.
That means that they can grow with our data. You can have a small database supporting just your department or an enormous database that serves thousands of people at the same time.

Databases have a speed advantage over flat files.
They're designed to help you find and retrieve the data that you need very quickly. There's no need to hunt through many files looking for the right data—databases allow you to search for the information you want using Structured Query Language (SQL).

Databases store a variety of data elements.
You can put text, numeric data, and even photos, videos, and other binary files into a database.

Structuring Data into Tables

It's important to remember that databases structure data into *tables*. Each row within a table is known as a *database record*. If you have a situation where data is not organized into tables, it might fit better into a flat file format. For example, if you have a list of courses offered by a university, you can design a table that contains the key characteristics of each course. It might look something like Table 29.1.

TABLE 29.1 Course table example

Department	CourseNumber	CourseName	Semester	Credits	Professor
CHEM	101	Introduction to Chemistry	Fall 2024	3.0	Smith
ECON	220	Macroeconomics	Spring 2025	4.0	Hutchinson
PHIL	220	Modern Philosophy	Spring 2025	3.0	Kolessar

That course data is easily organized into a table. On the other hand, imagine that you had driving directions between the White House and the U.S. Capitol in Washington, DC. Those directions are step by step and would not easily fit into a table. It would better fit into a word processing document as a list, such as this one:

1. Head east on H Street NW.
2. Turn right onto 14th St. NW.
3. Turn left onto Independence Ave. SW.
4. Turn slight left onto Maryland Ave. SW.
5. At the traffic circle, take the first exit onto First St. SW.
6. Arrive at the U.S. Capitol.

Imagine if you tried to organize that information into a table. It would be quite difficult. You might try to create a table with six columns—one for each step of the directions. But what would happen if you tried to add another set of directions that had seven or eight steps? This type of information is just better suited for a flat file than a database.

DATABASE USES

Configuring and working with the data stored in a database consists of four major stages:

1. First, you need to create the database. This involves getting a computer to act as the database server. That computer will do all the processing for your database. The server will also contain one or more hard drives that will physically store the data that's maintained in the database. The use of hard drives is what makes database storage permanent. In IT terminology, we call that permanent storage *data persistence*.
2. Next, you need to get data into your database. This might be accomplished by *importing* existing datasets, such as loading data stored in comma-separated values (CSV) files or spreadsheets into database tables, or it may involve users *inputting* data directly into the database through a web application or other means.
3. Once your data is in the database, users can run queries and reports against the data. *Queries* are questions that users ask of the database. They're written in SQL, a special programming language.
4. *Reports* are predefined queries that you execute on a regular basis. For example, you might write a query that returns all the sales made by your organization in the last 24 hours. You could then set up a report that runs every night, producing a PDF file or spreadsheet of all those sales, and automatically send that report to sales managers.

DATA AVAILABILITY

Data availability refers to how quickly and reliably users can access data, regardless of their physical location. Achieving high data availability is critical for organizations to ensure continuous operation and to make real-time decisions. This availability can be influenced by the choice between cloud-based versus local storage solutions and online versus offline access methods.

Cloud vs. Local

You have two options for the location where your data is stored: cloud storage or local storage.

Cloud storage places the data on remote servers managed by a service provider or on systems located within an organization's premises. Cloud storage is scalable and accessible from anywhere, making it ideal for businesses with fluctuating needs and remote teams, and it offers cost efficiency by reducing upfront hardware investments.

> **EXAM TIP**
>
> When you use a cloud-based application, data is not stored locally. Using the application requires Internet access, and the data will be stored on the cloud server.

Local storage uses hardware owned by the company and maintained in a data center. Using local storage provides organizations with full control over their data and infrastructure, leading to potentially enhanced security and performance due to reduced latency. This makes it suitable for operations that require rapid data access and have high security needs, despite the higher initial costs and physical space requirements.

Online vs. Offline

Databases may also be stored online or offline. An *online database* is constantly connected to a network, granting users the ability to engage with the database in real time. This immediate access is indispensable for dynamic systems that depend on up-to-the-minute data, such as online retailing platforms or operational dashboards, where the current state of information is pivotal. An *offline database* can be engaged with even in the absence of a network connection. Users can query, update, and manipulate the data offline, with the changes being stored locally. These alterations are then synchronized with the central database once network connectivity is reestablished. Offline access is particularly helpful in cases where networks are unreliable, allowing work to continue until the connection is restored.

CERTMIKE EXAM ESSENTIALS

► Database software allows the centralized storage and retrieval of information that is organized into tables.

► When you use a cloud-based application, data is not stored locally. Using the application requires Internet access, and the data will be stored on the cloud server.

► You should use a database instead of a flat file when you will have multiple concurrent users, when you require scalability or speed, and/or when you have a variety of data to store.

► Data availability refers to how quickly and reliably users can access data, regardless of their physical location. When making availability decisions, IT professionals choose between local versus cloud storage and online versus offline databases.

Practice Question 1

You are the IT manager for a mid-sized company and are helping the sales team develop a new solution for managing customer contacts. They would like a system that allows many different sales people to access records at the same time and for changes made by one salesperson to be immediately visible to other salespeople.

What type of software would *best* meet this need?

A. Spreadsheet software
B. Accounting software
C. Database software
D. Instant messaging software

Practice Question 2

You are helping a chain of restaurants design a data management strategy. You are identifying, as the first stage of that project, the types of information that would best fit into a database and those that would be better suited by other storage mechanisms.

Of the categories of data listed, which would be *least* well suited for storage in a database?

A. Customer contact information
B. Recipes used in the kitchen
C. Restaurant locations
D. Product inventory

Practice Question 1 Explanation

This question is asking us to identify the software that would *best* meet the described need. This is a common format for CompTIA exam questions, and you should be prepared to evaluate all the possible answer choices and find the one that is better than the others.

Let's evaluate these choices one at a time.

First, we have the possibility of using spreadsheet software. This is a possible solution. The sales team could create a spreadsheet of all customer contacts and have each team member update that spreadsheet when they have new information. We can't eliminate this choice up front, so we'll keep it alive for now.

Next, we have accounting software. That doesn't seem like a very good fit. Accounting software is designed to support accounting departments, so it's not going to be designed for supporting a sales team. We can eliminate that possibility.

Database software sounds like a very good fit for this situation. Databases are good at storing information that is organized into tables, and we could organize customer information into a set of tables. A spreadsheet could also handle that information, but databases are also great for applications where multiple users need concurrent access to data. So that makes a database a better solution than a spreadsheet. We'll keep databases alive and eliminate spreadsheets as a possible answer.

Finally, we have instant messaging software. That software is helpful for communicating among the team, but instant messaging software doesn't store data, so it's not a great choice here.

Correct Answer: C. Database software

Practice Question 2 Explanation

This question is asking you to identify which type of information is not well suited for storage in a database. Let's approach this by asking the opposite question for each data element: Is this element well suited for storage in a database? We can answer that question by determining how easy it would be to store that information in a table as opposed to a flat file.

The first item is customer contact information. We could easily imagine storing this information in a table. That table might look something like Table 29.2.

TABLE 29.2 Customer contact information stored in a database table

FirstName	LastName	Email	Phone
Mike	Chapple	mike@certmike.com	574-555-1212
Jane	Adams	jadams@yahoo.com	212-555-1212
Mary	Smith	msmith@gmail.com	516-555-1212

So it seems that customer contact information can be stored in a table, and we can eliminate that as a possible answer.

Next, imagine recipes used in the kitchen. These are a series of ingredients and sequential steps, such as the one shown in Figure 29.1.

Gingerbread

75g butter
3 1/2tbsp golden syrup
60g light soft brown sugar
175g plain flour
1/4 tsp bicarbonate of soda
2tsp ground ginger

• Add butter, golden syrup and light brown sugar to a pan. Stir on a low heat until sugar has dissolved.

• Add flour, bicarbonate of soda and ginger to a mixing bowl then stir together. Make a well in the centre and pour in the sugar and butter mixture.

• Stir together to form a dough (it might be easiest to use your hands).

• Wrap in clingfilm and let chill for 30mins to firm up.

• Lay the dough between two sheets of baking parchment. Press dough lightly with a rolling pin. Give a quarter turn than repeat.

• Give it a final quarter turn, then start to roll backwards and forwards, giving regular quarter turns. Until dough is roughly thickness of a £1 coin.

• Using a biscuit cutter cut out the shapes. Bake at 190°C (170°C fan) mark 5 for 10 to 12min, until lightly golden brown.

• The biscuits won't be firm but will harden when left to cool outside the oven.

FIGURE 29.1 Recipe example

This recipe presents a very different situation. It's not easy to imagine how you might structure this in a database table. For that reason, we're going to suspect that this might be the correct answer, but let's continue ruling out the other options.

The third data item is restaurant locations. As with our customer data, we can imagine storing that data in a table like Table 29.3.

TABLE 29.3 Restaurant location information stored in a database table

RestaurantID	City	State	ZIP
102	Sea Cliff	NY	11579
103	Miami	FL	33131
104	Chicago	IL	60604

Finally, we have product inventory. Table 29.4 shows how a product inventory table might be stored in a database.

TABLE 29.4 Product inventory information stored in a database table

ProductName	Quantity	Last restocked
Chickens	12	1/14/2024
Cucumbers	9	1/16/2024
Eggs	102	1/19/2024

Evaluating all of these options, it seems that the recipes are the least well suited for storage in a database table, so we will choose that as our correct answer.

Correct Answer: B. Recipes used in the kitchen.

## CHAPTER 30

Database Structures
Objective 5.3: Compare and contrast various database structures

The data we work with every day comes in varying degrees of structure and may be in different formats as we store and process it. All data resides on a spectrum, ranging from highly structured tables to very unstructured, poorly organized, data. We store this data in different types of databases, both relational and nonrelational systems.

In this chapter, you'll learn the material that you need to know about Tech+ objective 5.3. The topics covered in this chapter include:

▶ Structured vs. semi-structured vs. nonstructured
▶ Relational databases
▶ Nonrelational databases

STRUCTURING DATA

When you think of data, chances are that spreadsheets come to mind, such as the Microsoft Excel spreadsheet shown in Figure 30.1. Spreadsheets are valuable tools that allow us to organize our data in tabular form. That's an easy way for us to think about our data, and it's the most common way that we store data for use in analytics.

This approach, in which we organize our data into well-defined tables, describes a category of data known as *structured data*. Not only do we find this structured approach to data in spreadsheets, but we also find it in relational databases.

Relational databases allow us to create many different tables of data, each containing information about a single type of person, object, event, or other data subject. Database designers then create relationships between those different tables that describe how the data interacts.

	A	B	C	D	E
1	service_date	day_type	bus	rail_boardings	total_rides
2	1/1/01	U	297192	126455	423647
3	1/2/01	W	780827	501952	1282779
4	1/3/01	W	824923	536432	1361355
5	1/4/01	W	870021	550011	1420032
6	1/5/01	W	890426	557917	1448343
7	1/6/01	A	577401	255356	832757
8	1/7/01	U	375831	169825	545656
9	1/8/01	W	985221	590706	1575927
10	1/9/01	W	978377	599905	1578282
11	1/10/01	W	984884	602052	1586936
12	1/11/01	W	995561	607503	1603064
13	1/12/01	W	1018985	605252	1624237
14	1/13/01	A	591791	270056	861847
15	1/14/01	U	373091	174842	547933
16	1/15/01	W	675845	412149	1087994
17	1/16/01	W	1024367	622163	1646530
18	1/17/01	W	1018690	620343	1639033
19	1/18/01	W	1006996	618832	1625828
20	1/19/01	W	909964	583851	1493815
21	1/20/01	A	582348	263815	846163
22	1/21/01	U	378381	172107	550488
23	1/22/01	W	1005936	598777	1604713
24	1/23/01	W	1019983	610352	1630335

FIGURE 30.1 Microsoft Excel spreadsheet

Figure 30.2 shows an example of a very complex *database schema*. This is the schema for the AdventureWorks database, a database designed by Microsoft to mimic the operations of a bicycle manufacturing company. Each one of the boxes on this diagram represents a different table of data, and each one of the arrows represents a relationship between two tables. You don't need to worry about the complexity of this diagram. I just want you to understand that the data we use in our day-to-day business operations is highly structured.

At the other end of the spectrum, we have *unstructured data*. This is data that doesn't fit neatly into the table model. For example, we might have a collection of photographs, video recordings, word processing documents, and other data sources where users simply enter or collect data without the highly structured framework of a table. While it's true that most of the data that we use in analytics is structured data that lives in spreadsheets and databases, most of the data that exists in the world today is unstructured. It lacks the defined fields of more structured datasets.

Unstructured data often comes from machine data sources. Internet of Things devices, smartphones, tablets, personal computers, and servers all create digital footprints of their activity and often do so in unstructured form. This data can be a treasure trove for analysts seeking to find new data sources for use in their analysis, and organizations that take advantage of their unstructured data may achieve a real competitive edge.

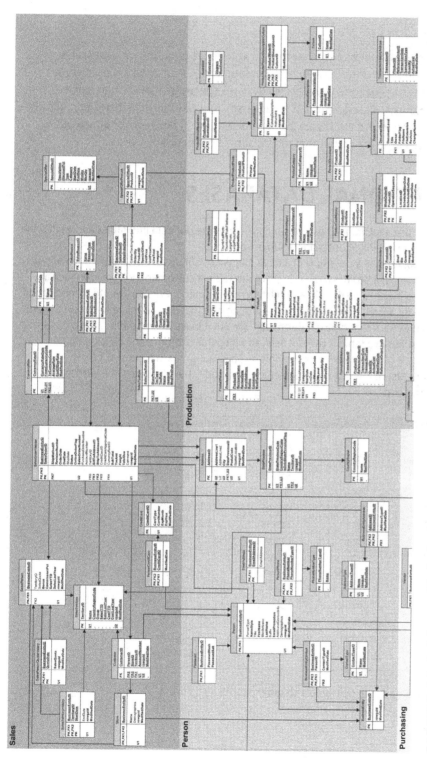

FIGURE 30.2 AdventureWorks database schema

NOTE

We like to put things into clear categories, and it's tempting for data professionals to try to describe any data source as either structured or unstructured. However, the reality is that data resides on a spectrum, where it can range from highly structured, such as a database table, to highly unstructured, such as an audio recording. There's also plenty of room in between for data that has elements of structure but that retains some unstructured elements.

RELATIONAL DATABASES

Databases use a *relational model* in which we organize our data into tables and each table contains information about a single subject or topic.

Figure 30.3 shows an example of a table that we might use to track information about the customers of a business. The subject of this table is customers, and you don't see any information in the table that doesn't relate to a customer. There's no inventory information, weather data, store phone numbers, or anything else that doesn't relate to our customers. If we need to track that type of information, we put it in a different table.

Each column in a table is called a *field*, and it contains information about a single characteristic of the subject. For example, we have columns in Figure 30.3 for the customer's first name, last name, street address, and other attributes that we'd like to track about customers.

	CustomerID	Cust First Name	Cust Last Name	Cust Street Address
1	1001	Suzanne	Viescas	15127 NE 24th, #383
2	1002	William	Thompson	122 Spring River Drive
3	1003	Gary	Hallmark	Route 2, Box 203B
4	1004	Robert	Brown	672 Lamont Ave
5	1005	Dean	McCrae	4110 Old Redmond Rd.
6	1006	John	Viescas	15127 NE 24th, #383
7	1007	Mariya	Sergienko	901 Pine Avenue
8	1008	Neil	Patterson	233 West Valley Hwy
9	1009	Andrew	Cencini	507 - 20th Ave. E. Apt. 2A
10	1010	Angel	Kennedy	667 Red River Road
11	1011	Alaina	Hallmark	Route 2, Box 203B
12	1012	Liz	Keyser	13920 S.E. 40th Street
13	1013	Rachel	Patterson	2114 Longview Lane
14	1014	Sam	Abolrous	611 Alpine Drive
15	1015			

FIGURE 30.3 Customers database table

Each row in the table is called a *record* and it contains information about a single instance of the table subject. In Figure 30.3, our table subject is customers, so each row corresponds to an individual customer. The first row is about Suzanne Viescas, the second row is about William Thompson, and so on.

The rows and columns in a database table are very well defined. That's how databases extend the relational model used by spreadsheets. Data is still organized into single-subject tables, with each column representing a characteristic of the subject and each row representing an instance of the subject.

Database Keys

Every database table contains at least one *key*. Keys are special-purpose database fields that play important roles in the relational model. They help to organize the information in tables and also define the relationships between tables. You need to know about two different types of keys as you prepare for the Tech+ exam: primary keys and foreign keys.

Primary Keys

The *primary key* is the most important field in a database table. Its purpose is to allow the database to uniquely identify the records in a table. When we define a primary key field for a table, we must choose something that will always be unique. Every row in a table must have a unique value for the primary key.

The database enforces a business rule, called a *constraint*, that prevents us from inserting two rows into a table that have the same primary key value. Constraints are technical and business rules that define what values we can enter in a column, and the rule that says primary keys have only unique values is an example of a database constraint. We could create another constraint, for example, that limits us to entering reasonable birthdates for living people. For example, we might say that someone living today must have been born within the last 120 years.

> **EXAM TIP**
>
> Constraints are used to limit the values that may be entered into a database field. They enforce business rules and restrict data entry to valid values.

Foreign Keys

The second type of key we need to discuss is the *foreign key*. Foreign keys define the relationships between tables. For example, Figure 30.4 shows a table, *Orders*, that contains information about orders placed at a company. It has a primary key called `OrderNumber`. It also has fields that contain references to other tables.

For example, `CustomerID` in the *Orders* table is a reference to the customer ID field in the *Customers* table. The second record in the *Orders* table indicates that the order was placed by customer number 1001. That's Suzanne Viescas. We can use this field to combine information from related tables. We already know that CustomerID is the primary key for the *Customers* table. When we use it in this way in the *Orders* table, we call it a foreign key. So CustomerID is the primary key of the *Customers* table and it is a foreign key from the *Orders* table to the *Customers* table, as shown in Figure 30.5.

	OrderNumber	OrderDate	ShipDate	CustomerID	EmployeeID
1	1	2012-09-01 00:00:00.000	2012-09-04 00:00:00.000	1018	707
2	2	2012-09-01 00:00:00.000	2012-09-03 00:00:00.000	1001	703
3	3	2012-09-01 00:00:00.000	2012-09-04 00:00:00.000	1002	707
4	4	2012-09-01 00:00:00.000	2012-09-03 00:00:00.000	1009	703
5	5	2012-09-01 00:00:00.000	2012-09-01 00:00:00.000	1024	708
6	6	2012-09-01 00:00:00.000	2012-09-05 00:00:00.000	1014	702
7	7	2012-09-01 00:00:00.000	2012-09-04 00:00:00.000	1001	708
8	8	2012-09-01 00:00:00.000	2012-09-01 00:00:00.000	1003	703
9	9	2012-09-01 00:00:00.000	2012-09-04 00:00:00.000	1007	708
10	10	2012-09-01 00:00:00.000	2012-09-04 00:00:00.000	1012	701
11	11	2012-09-02 00:00:00.000	2012-09-04 00:00:00.000	1020	706

FIGURE 30.4 *Orders* database table

EXAM TIP

This approach is very common where the foreign key in one table references the primary key in another table.

FIGURE 30.5 CustomerID is a foreign key from the *Orders* table to the *Customers* table.

NONRELATIONAL DATABASES

Most databases are relational databases, but there are other types of databases that don't rely on the relational model. These *nonrelational databases* help us with some specialized data storage needs.

Key-value pairs are an example of a semi-structured approach to data storage. They provide a lightweight way to store data that throws away many of the rules of relational databases. They don't have to be organized into tables. The only requirement is that we have a key that can be used to index the data and one or more values that we wish to store in the database. Each record can have different values and even different numbers of values.

Key-value stores are databases designed specifically to provide efficient storage and very fast retrieval of key-value pairs. They're often used in applications where the data is simple and the most important feature of the database is being able to get at that information quickly.

Figure 30.6 shows a simple example of a table created in DynamoDB, a key-value store from AWS. This table contains some simple information about individuals and their skills. Notice that different people have different numbers of skills. When you first look at this table, you might think that it simply has fields labeled skill1, skill2, and skill3 and that the last field is blank for people who have only two skills. However, if you look at the two records that I've excerpted on the right side of the table, you'll notice that Hercules Mulligan has only two skill items associated with his record. There is no skill3 item. In this simple example of a key-value store, the employee ID is the key, and all the other fields are values.

Document databases (or document stores) are specialized databases designed to store larger documents, such as data in HTML, JSON, or XML format, and index them using a key. They are structured similarly to a key-value store but are optimized for storing extensive documents.

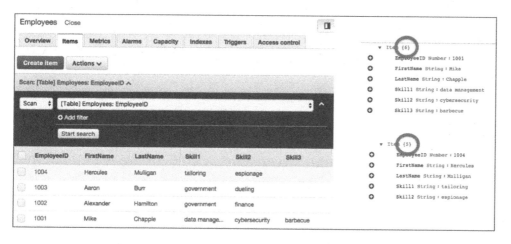

FIGURE 30.6 Table from a key-value store

EXAM TIP

Those are just a few examples of nonrelational databases. As you prepare for the exam, you won't need to know the implementation details of these databases, but you should be aware that they exist and that they primarily give up some of the constraints of a relational database to achieve speed and performance gains.

CERTMIKE EXAM ESSENTIALS

▶ Relational databases structure data into tables of related data. Each column in a table represents an attribute and each row in a table represents an instance.

▶ The primary key of a database table uniquely identifies the rows in that table. A foreign key defines the relationship between two tables. It is common for the foreign key in one table to reference the primary key in another table.

▶ Constraints are used to limit the values that may be entered into a database field. They enforce business rules and restrict data entry to valid values.

▶ Key-value stores are a nonrelational database type that provide efficient storage and very fast retrieval of key-value pairs. Document databases work similarly to key-value stores but are optimized to store large documents.

Practice Question 1

Consider the two tables shown here.

Books

BookID	Title	Publication Year	AuthorID	Price
1	Tech+ Essentials	2024	101	$40.00
2	CISSP Study Guide	2021	101	$70.00
3	Practical Machine Learning in R	2020	103	$40.00

Authors

AuthorID	FirstName	LastName
101	Mike	Chapple
102	David	Seidl
103	Fred	Nwanganga

Which one of the following statements most likely describes the relationship between these tables?

A. BookID is a foreign key from *Books* to *Authors*.
B. BookID is a foreign key from *Authors* to *Books*.
C. AuthorID is a foreign key from *Books* to *Authors*.
D. AuthorID Is a foreign key from *Authors* to *Books*.

Practice Question 2

You are examining the database used by a concert promoter and find that there is a table in that database named *Concerts*. Examining the table, you see that it contains information about all of the different events run by that promoter. Where would you expect to find the information about a single event?

A. In one column of the *Concerts* table
B. In several columns of the *Concerts* table
C. In one row of the *Concerts* table
D. In several rows of the *Concerts* table

Practice Question 1 Explanation

These tables aren't labeled with information about which fields are primary keys and foreign keys, so we must attempt to figure that out on our own. We know that every table should have a primary key and that the primary key must be unique for each row. Looking at these tables, it seems as if `BookID` is the primary key for the *Books* table and `AuthorID` is the primary key for the *Authors* table.

The question is asking us to identify the relationship between the two tables. We see that `AuthorID` appears in both of these tables, and it would be a natural relationship for a book to have an author.

We can describe this relationship in terms of keys by saying that `AuthorID` is a foreign key from the *Books* table (where it is the foreign key) to the *Authors* table (where it is the primary key).

Correct Answer: C. `AuthorID` **is a foreign key from *Books* to *Authors*.**

Practice Question 2 Explanation

In a relational database table, columns represent attributes of the subject of the table. For example, in a *Concerts* table, you would expect to find columns with names such as *Artist*, *Date*, *Time*, *Venue*, and *City*.

Each row in a relational database table contains information about a single instance of the table subject. Therefore, each row in a *Concerts* table should contain all the information about one concert.

Correct Answer: C. In one row of the *Concerts* **table.**

## CHAPTER 31

Backups

Objective 5.4: Explain basic data backup concepts

Performing backups is one of the core responsibilities of the information technology profession. We face many potential disruptions in our business operations, ranging from natural disasters to human-created threats. Backups help make our businesses resilient against these threats.

In this chapter, you'll learn the material that you need to know about Tech+ objective 5.4. The topics covered in this chapter include:

▶ **Data**
▶ **Location**

DATA BACKUPS

Business continuity efforts are a collection of activities designed to keep a business running in the face of adversity. This may come in the form of a small-scale incident, such as a single system failure, or a catastrophic incident, such as an earthquake or a tornado. Business continuity plans may also be activated by human-made disasters, such as a terrorist attack or hacker intrusion.

While many organizations place responsibility for business continuity with operational engineering teams, business continuity is a core security concept because it is the primary control that supports the security objective of availability. Remember, that's one of the CIA triad objectives of information security: confidentiality, integrity, and availability.

Disaster recovery (DR) is a subset of business continuity activities designed to restore a business to normal operations as quickly as possible following a disruption. Disaster recovery plans (DRPs) may include immediate measures that get operations working again temporarily, but the disaster recovery efforts are not finished until the organization is completely back to normal.

Backups are perhaps the most important component of any disaster recovery plan because most businesses today are built around their data. Whether it's proprietary designs, confidential customer lists, or information databases, data drives businesses. For many organizations, the complete loss of data would be a disaster of tremendous proportions.

Backups provide organizations with a fail-safe way to recover their data in the event of a technology failure, human error, natural disaster, or other circumstances that result in its accidental or intentional deletion or modification. Backups are a crucial safety net for data-driven businesses.

One of the critical ways that IT professionals protect the availability of systems and data is ensuring that they are backed up regularly. *Backups* are copies of data that are made and moved to another location. This provides redundancy for that data. Ideally, organizations will conduct regular backups of their critical data files, operating systems, and databases and place those backups in secure locations.

Backup Media

Organizations can back up their data in many ways. The simplest approach is to copy files from one location to another, but that process is manual and error-prone. Most organizations use a more sophisticated backup strategy.

Local Backups

Traditionally, organizations wrote their backups to magnetic tapes, and this is still a very common practice today. Linear Tape-Open (LTO) tapes, such as those shown in Figure 31.1, are commonly used for this purpose. However, tapes are difficult to manage, and modern

FIGURE 31.1 LTO backup tapes

bigmagic/Adobe Systems Incorporated

backup approaches often use alternative storage that has become much less expensive over the past few years.

Some organizations do *disk-to-disk backups*, which write data from the primary disk to external hard drives set aside for backup purposes. These backup disks may be in a separate facility where it would be unlikely that the same physical disaster would affect both the primary and backup sites. Organizations may also choose to back up some data to flash drives or secure digital (SD) cards for easy transportability of crucial files.

Cloud Backups

A newer trend in backups is to write backups directly to storage provided by cloud computing vendors, such as Amazon Web Services (AWS), Microsoft Azure, or their competitors. Cloud-based storage provides great geographic diversity, as the backup data is stored in separately managed facilities and cloud providers usually per- form their own backups of their systems, providing an added layer of protection for customer data.

EXAM TIP

Remember that if you store data in the cloud, you will need Internet access to read and write that data and that the data will be stored on the cloud provider's servers.

Testing and Restoring Backups

Backups play a crucial role in an organization's disaster recovery strategy, but it's surprising how often organizations fail to properly test those backups to verify that they were completed properly and are ensuring the continued availability of critical business information in the event of a disaster.

One of the most important data protection actions that you can take is regularly verifying your backups to ensure that they are functioning properly. This is true whether you are a cloud service provider testing your own backups or a cloud service customer testing your use of your provider's backup mechanism. In either event, there are several types of backup tests that you should perform.

First, all modern backup software has built-in verification mechanisms that you can use to validate that a backup was successful immediately after creating the backup. This is just the bare bones of backup verification because you are relying on the software that performed the backup to tell you that it worked properly. However, it's amazing how many organizations have this verification feature turned off either because they never bothered to turn it on or because they felt that it took too long to complete the backups with verification turned on.

Another mistake that organizations commonly make even when they do have backup verification turned on is that they don't ever look at the logs where backup errors are recorded. You should configure alerts from backup software to trigger notification to system administrators when a backup fails. Better yet, have any error automatically create an incident in your IT service management system. Even better, use code that verifies that the backup report was received each day so that if the backup fails silently you find out.

In addition to using the built-in verification mechanism, you should perform regular tests of your restoration capabilities. There's no better test than actually attempting to perform a restore to see that it works properly.

A simple test is asking for the restoration of a single file from a specific date. An IT manager or someone else not involved in the backup process should randomly select a file and date and then ask the backup administrator to restore that file. It's a good idea to do this on a regular basis to verify that the restore mechanism functions properly.

A more sophisticated test that you should perform periodically is restoring a server or an entire service from a backup. This simulates a real disaster scenario where you are forced to rebuild a system from backups.

Both tests provide backup administrators, IT managers, and business leaders with the confidence that the backup mechanism is functioning properly and that the business will be able to restore operations in the event of a critical disaster.

EXAM TIP

Regulatory requirements and organization policies may influence your backup decisions. They may dictate testing requirements and locations for storing backup data.

CERTMIKE EXAM ESSENTIALS

▶ Disaster recovery controls are designed to restore normal operations after an event disrupts those normal operations. Disaster recovery picks up the pieces when business continuity efforts fail.

▶ Backups are a crucial component of the organization's disaster recovery plan. Organizations should back up critical data using file backups and system backups. They should test their ability to restore data from those backups.

▶ Backups may be stored locally using tapes, external hard drives, flash drives, or SD cards. They may also be stored in the cloud for added redundancy.

Practice Question 1

Which of the following statements is correct about cloud-based data backups?

A. Storing backups in the cloud provides geographic diversity.
B. Storing backups in the cloud offers limited storage capacity.
C. Storing backups in the cloud does not require a high-bandwidth network connection.
D. Storing backups in the cloud reduces data restoration time.

Practice Question 2

You are helping your organization recover from a major disaster. At what point would the organization normally consider the disaster recovery effort complete?

A. Backup data has been fully restored.
B. Operations are resumed at a temporary facility.
C. The organization is functioning at pre-disaster conditions.
D. The operations team has assumed responsibility.

Practice Question 1 Explanation

Storing backups in the cloud provides geographic diversity, ensuring that data is not susceptible to being lost due to local disasters since cloud providers typically store data across multiple locations.

The statement that cloud backups offer limited storage capacity is misleading; cloud services often offer scalable options that allow storage capacity to grow with user needs.

A high-bandwidth network connection is usually necessary for cloud backups, especially for large datasets or businesses with continuous backup requirements, because significant amounts of data need to be transferred efficiently.

Depending on various factors, including the amount of data, the bandwidth available, and the specifics of the cloud provider's architecture, storing backups in the cloud can sometimes increase data restoration time rather than reduce it.

Correct Answer: A. Storing backups in the cloud provides geographic diversity.

Practice Question 2 Explanation

The organization would normally consider the disaster recovery effort complete when it is functioning at pre-disaster conditions, as this indicates a return to normalcy and operational stability.

Having backup data fully restored is a crucial step, but it does not signify the end of recovery if other operational aspects are still compromised.

Resuming operations at a temporary facility is part of the continuity plan to ensure immediate recovery post-disaster, but it's a temporary measure, not a completion of the recovery process.

Lastly, while the operations team assuming responsibility is part of managing the recovery, it is more about governance and process rather than a sign of complete recovery.

Correct Answer: C. The organization is functioning at pre-disaster conditions.

Domain 6.0: Security

Security is the sixth domain of CompTIA's Tech+ exam. In this domain, you'll learn the tools and techniques that IT professionals use to protect the confidentiality, integrity, and availability of information and systems under their care. This domain has five objectives:

6.1 Explain fundamental security concepts and frameworks

6.2 Explain methods to secure devices and security best practices

6.3 Explain password best practices

6.4 Identify common use cases for encryption

6.5 Given a scenario, configure security settings for a small wireless network

Questions from this domain make up 19% of the questions on the Tech+ exam, so you should expect to see approximately 14 questions on your test covering the material in this part.

Domain 6.0: Security

## CHAPTER 32

Confidentiality, Integrity, and Availability

Objective 6.1: Explain fundamental security concepts and frameworks

Information plays a vital role in the operations of the modern business, and we find ourselves entrusted with sensitive information about our customers, employees, internal operations, and other critical matters. As IT professionals, we must work with information security teams, other technology professionals, and business leaders to protect the security of that information.

In this chapter, you'll learn part of the material that you need to know about Tech+ objective 6.1. The topics covered in this chapter include:

▶ **Confidentiality, integrity, and availability**

The remaining material for this objective is covered in Chapter 33, "Privacy," and Chapter 34, "Authentication, Authorization, Accounting, and Nonrepudiation."

THE CIA TRIAD

When we talk about cybersecurity, we're referring to three main concerns: the confidentiality of information, the integrity of information, and the availability of information. You can remember these three main goals by thinking of the CIA triad shown in Figure 32.1. Each side covers one of the three main goals. The remainder of this chapter explores each of these concerns in detail.

FIGURE 32.1 The CIA triad summarizes the three main concerns of cybersecurity: confidentiality, integrity, and availability.

CONFIDENTIALITY

Confidentiality ensures that only authorized individuals have access to information and resources. This is what most people think of when they think about information security—keeping secrets away from prying eyes. And it is, in fact, how security professionals spend the majority of their time. Let's take a look at some of the main threats to confidentiality.

> **EXAM TIP**
>
> As you prepare for the exam, you'll need to understand the main threats against each of the cybersecurity objectives. For confidentiality, we have five main concerns: snooping, dumpster diving, eavesdropping, wiretapping, and social engineering.

Snooping

Snooping is exactly what the name implies. The individual engaging in snooping wanders around your office or other facility and simply looks to see what information they can gather. When people leave sensitive papers on their desks or in a public area, it creates an opportunity for snooping.

Organizations can protect against snooping by enforcing a *clean desk policy*. Employees should maintain a clean workspace and put away any sensitive materials whenever they step away, even if it's just for a moment.

Dumpster Diving

Dumpster diving attacks also look for sensitive materials, but the attacker doesn't walk around the office. Instead they look through the trash, trying to find sensitive documents that an employee threw in the garbage or recycling bin.

You can protect your organization against dumpster diving attacks using a pretty simple piece of technology: a paper shredder! If you destroy documents before discarding them, you'll protect against a dumpster diver pulling them out of the trash.

Eavesdropping

Eavesdropping attacks come in both physical and electronic types. In a physical eavesdropping attack, the attacker simply positions themselves where they can overhear conversations, such as in a cafeteria or hallway, and then listens for sensitive information.

We can protect against eavesdropping attacks by putting rules in place limiting where sensitive conversations may take place. For example, sensitive conversations should generally take place in a closed office or conference room.

Wiretapping

Electronic eavesdropping attacks are also known as *wiretapping*. They occur when an attacker gains access to a network and monitors the data being sent electronically within an office.

The best way to protect against electronic eavesdropping attacks is to use encryption to protect information being sent over the network. If data is encrypted, an attacker who intercepts that data won't be able to make any sense of it. You'll learn more about encryption in Chapter 39, "Encryption."

Social Engineering

The last type of confidentiality attack you need to know about is *social engineering*. In a social engineering attack, the attacker uses psychological tricks to persuade an employee to give them sensitive information or access to internal systems. They might pretend that they're on an urgent assignment from a senior leader, impersonate an IT technician, or send a phishing email.

It's difficult to protect against social engineering attacks. The best defense against these attacks is educating users to recognize the dangers of social engineering and empowering them to intervene when they suspect an attack is taking place. You will learn more about social engineering in Chapter 35, "Security Awareness."

INTEGRITY

Security professionals are also responsible for protecting the *integrity* of an organization's information. This means that there aren't any unauthorized changes to information. These unauthorized changes may come in the form of a hacker seeking to intentionally alter information or a service disruption accidentally affecting data stored in a system. In either case, it's the information security professional's responsibility to prevent these lapses in integrity. Let's take a look at some of the main threats to integrity.

EXAM TIP

As you prepare for the exam, you'll need to know about four types of integrity attacks: the unauthorized modification of information, impersonation attacks, on-path attacks, and replay attacks.

Unauthorized Information Alteration

The unauthorized modification of information occurs when an attacker gains access to a system and makes changes that violate a security policy. This might be an external attacker, such as an intruder breaking into a financial system and issuing themselves checks, or it might be an internal attack, such as an employee increasing their own salary in the payroll system.

Following the principle of *least privilege* is the best way to protect against integrity attacks. Organizations should carefully consider the permissions that each employee needs to perform their job and then limit employees to the smallest set of permissions possible.

Impersonation

In an *impersonation* attack, the attacker pretends to be someone other than who they actually are. They might impersonate a manager, an executive, or an IT technician in order to convince someone to change data in a system. This is an extension of the social engineering attacks discussed earlier, and the best defense against these attacks is strong user education.

On-path Attacks

Sometimes impersonation attacks are electronic. In an on-path attack, the attacker intercepts network traffic as a user is logging into a system and pretends to be that system. They then sit in the middle of the communication, relaying information between the user and the system while they monitor everything that is occurring. In this type of attack, the attacker might be able to steal a user's password and use it later to log into the system themselves. These attacks can also be used to tamper with data before it reaches its intended destination.

Replay Attacks

In a *replay attack*, the attacker doesn't get in the middle of the communication but finds a way to observe a legitimate user logging into a system. They then capture the information used to log into the system and later replay it on the network to gain access themselves.

The best defense against both replay and on-path attacks is the use of encryption to protect communications. For example, web traffic might use the Transport Layer Security (TLS) protocol to prevent an eavesdropper from observing network traffic.

AVAILABILITY

As a security professional, you must also understand how to apply security controls that protect the *availability* of information and systems. As the third leg of the CIA triad, availability controls ensure that information and systems remain available to authorized users when needed. They protect against disruptions to normal system operation or data availability. Let's take a look at some of the main threats to availability.

Denial-of-Service Attacks

Denial-of-service (DoS) attacks occur when a malicious individual bombards a system with an overwhelming amount of traffic. The idea is to send so many requests to a server that it is unable to answer any requests from legitimate users.

We can protect our systems against DoS attacks by using firewalls that block illegitimate requests and by partnering with our Internet service providers to block DoS attacks before they reach our networks.

Power Outages

Power outages can occur on a local or regional level for many different reasons. Increased demand can overwhelm the power grid, natural disasters can disrupt service, and other factors can cause power outages that disrupt access to systems.

We can protect against power outages by having redundant power sources and backup generators that supply power to our systems when commercial power is not available.

Hardware Failures

Hardware failures can and do occur. Servers, hard drives, network gear, and other equipment all fail occasionally and can disrupt access to information. That's an availability problem.

We can protect against hardware failures by building systems that have built-in redundancy so that if one component fails, another is ready to pick up the slack.

Destruction

Sometimes equipment is just outright destroyed. This might be the result of intentional or accidental physical damage, or it may be the result of a larger disaster, such as a fire or a hurricane.

We can protect against small-scale destruction with redundant systems. If we want to protect against larger-scale disasters, we may need to have backup data centers in remote locations or in the cloud that can keep running when our primary data center is disrupted.

Service Outages

Finally, sometimes *service outages* occur. This might be due to programming errors, the failure of underlying equipment, or many other reasons. These outages disrupt user access to systems and information and are, therefore, an availability concern.

We can protect against service outages by building systems that are resilient in the face of errors and hardware failures.

CERTMIKE EXAM ESSENTIALS

▶ Confidentiality ensures that only authorized individuals have access to information and resources. Major confidentiality threats include snooping, eavesdropping, wiretapping, social engineering, and dumpster diving.

▶ Integrity protects information from unauthorized changes. Major threats to integrity include on-path attacks, replay attacks, impersonation, and unauthorized information alteration.

▶ Availability ensures that information and systems are available for authorized use. Major threats to availability include denial-of-service attacks, power outages, hardware failure, destruction, and service outages.

Practice Question 1

Which one of the following security risks would most likely be considered an availability issue?

A. Replay attack
B. Power outage
C. Social engineering
D. Snooping

Practice Question 2

What are the three major objectives of cybersecurity programs?

A. Confidentiality, integrity, and availability
B. Confidentiality, integrity, and authorization
C. Confidentiality, infrastructure, and authorization
D. Communications, infrastructure, and authorization

Practice Question 1 Explanation

Availability issues affect the ability of authorized users to gain access to information, systems, or other resources that they need. All of the issues listed here are cybersecurity risks that you need to be aware of when you take the Tech+ exam, but only power outages are classified as an availability risk. This is because a power outage can easily disrupt access to systems and information by causing those systems to be offline.

Replay attacks allow an unauthorized individual to impersonate a legitimate user and are primarily considered integrity risks.

Social engineering and snooping attacks may allow an attacker to gain access to sensitive information, and they are primarily considered confidentiality risks.

Correct Answer: B. Power outage

Practice Question 2 Explanation

The three major objectives of any cybersecurity program are protecting the confidentiality, integrity, and availability of systems and information.

Confidentiality ensures that only authorized individuals have access to information and resources. Integrity protects information from unauthorized changes. Availability ensures that information and systems are available for authorized use.

Correct Answer: A. Confidentiality, integrity, and availability

## CHAPTER 33

Privacy

Objective 6.1 Explain fundamental security concepts and frameworks

Objective 6.2 Explain methods to secure devices and security best practices

In the digital era, the organizations we deal with collect a lot of information about individuals and their actions. From credit card transactions to educational records, each of us generates a significant trail of data, and we are rightfully concerned about the *privacy* of that information.

In this chapter, you'll learn about privacy. This topic is spread across two different objectives on the Tech+ exam: objective 6.1 from which this chapter covers the topic:

▶ Privacy

And objective 6.2 from which this chapter covers the topic:

▶ Privacy considerations

PRIVACY

As an IT professional, you have a few interests in how organizations collect and use personal information:

> ▶ You are obviously concerned about the privacy of your own personal information.
> ▶ You have a responsibility to educate the users in your organization about how they can protect their own personal information.
> ▶ You have a responsibility to assist the privacy officials within your organization with the work they need to do to protect the personal information entrusted to your organization.

Types of Private Information

Private information may come in many forms. Two of the most common elements of private information are personally identifiable information and protected health information:

> ▶ *Personally identifiable information (PII)* includes all information that can be tied back to a specific individual. Examples of PII include Social Security numbers (SSN), driver's license numbers, and passport numbers.
> ▶ *Protected health information (PHI)* includes healthcare records that are regulated under the Health Insurance Portability and Accountability Act (HIPAA).

Expectation of Privacy

Privacy programs are based on a legal principle known as the *reasonable expectation of privacy*. Many laws that govern whether information must be protected are based on whether the person disclosing the information had a reasonable expectation of privacy when they did so and whether the disclosure would violate that reasonable expectation of privacy.

When you put content on social media, whether it be a post on a social networking site or a comment on a shared video, you generally have no reasonable expectation of privacy. You're posting that content publicly or to a large group of people, and a reasonable person would assume that is not a private conversation.

However, when you send a message to someone over email or instant messaging, or share a file through a file sharing site with a specific person or small group, you do have an expectation of privacy. If you don't encrypt the message, you do run the risk that others will eavesdrop on the message, but you have a more reasonable expectation of privacy.

At the other end of the spectrum, when you provide private information to a government agency through their website, such as completing your taxes or registering for a medical insurance program, you have a much greater expectation of privacy. In those cases, you expect that the agency collecting information will treat that information with care and not share it without your permission. And, in fact, most countries have laws that require this information be kept private.

When you're using a computer or network that belongs to your employer, you generally do not have a reasonable expectation of privacy. The employer owns that equipment and is normally legally entitled to monitor the use of their systems. If you're using software on your employer's desktop computer, accessing business information over a corporate network, or even using the Internet at work for personal use, you generally should not expect to have privacy for your communication.

As an IT professional, you should communicate to users clearly and accurately about their privacy expectations. It's important to reinforce that when employees of your organization are using systems or networks that belong to the organization, they should not have an expectation of privacy.

You also need to ensure that you and your organization are appropriately handling confidential information. In addition to protecting personal information about employees and customers, you should take steps to safeguard other sensitive information, including passwords and the company's confidential information.

COOKIE CONSENT

Cookies are essential tools that help website operators enhance the user experience by storing small data files on visitors' devices. These files help the website store information about users' browsing habits, enabling features like remembering login details, preserving user preferences, and delivering personalized content. While beneficial, the use of cookies requires careful handling of personal information due to privacy implications.

To comply with privacy laws like the *General Data Protection Regulation (GDPR)* in the European Union (EU), it is crucial to inform visitors about your use of cookies through a cookie consent banner or notification. This banner should clearly explain that cookies are being used and for what purposes, giving visitors the opportunity to consent to or decline the storage of cookies on their devices.

When visitors click Accept on a cookie consent banner, they agree to let the website store and manage their data according to its privacy policy. If they choose to decline, websites must limit the use of cookies, which may affect the personalization and efficiency of the browsing experience. Website owners should provide transparency and control, offering clear information about data collection practices and allowing users to customize their cookie preferences. This not only ensures compliance with privacy regulations but also builds trust with your users by respecting their privacy choices.

Privacy and Artificial Intelligence

Artificial intelligence (AI) has become a significant factor in the discussion of privacy. AI systems can process vast amounts of data, including personal information, at unprecedented speeds and scales. This capability has raised new concerns about the reasonable expectation of privacy.

When interacting with AI systems, users might not always be aware of the extent to which their data is being collected, processed, and analyzed. For example, AI-driven platforms and applications often gather data to improve user experiences or for targeted advertising. This data collection can include location data, browsing habits, and even voice recordings.

As AI systems become more integrated into everyday life, organizations should be transparent about their data collection practices and ensure they comply with privacy laws and regulations. Users should be informed about what data is being collected, how it is being used, and how long it will be retained. Organizations should also implement robust security measures to protect the data collected by AI systems from unauthorized access and breaches. This includes using encryption, anonymization, and regular security audits.

Privacy Regulations

Whenever we work with sensitive information, we encounter laws and regulations that govern the ways that we store, process, and transmit that information. One of the first things that we need to figure out when working with sensitive data is what specific laws and regulations apply to us. While that might sound straightforward at first glance, the question of which jurisdictions have authority to regulate data is actually quite complicated and compliance risks can impact an organization's risk posture.

The EU says that the GDPR applies to the personal information of all EU residents, wherever they might be located. This may become complicated because the GDPR includes complex data subject rights, including the right to be forgotten, which allows data subjects to request that companies holding their data purge their personal information from their records, which can be technically complicated.

Of course, GDPR isn't the only law that you'll need to follow. IT professionals should be aware of the different global standards as well as national, local, and regional laws that apply to their operations.

> **EXAM TIP**
> While GDPR isn't the only law that you'll need to follow, it *is* the only law that you need to know for the Tech+ exam. GDPR is the only law specifically mentioned in the FC0-U71 exam objectives.

This is very important work because the consequences of noncompliance can be significant. They may include fines and other sanctions, contractual obligations, and reputational damage.

CERTMIKE EXAM ESSENTIALS

▶ IT professionals have an obligation to protect the privacy of personal information, particularly when the individuals involved have a reasonable expectation of privacy.

▶ The types of personal information that must be safeguarded include personally identifiable information (PII), which is any personal information that may be tied to an individual, and protected health information (PHI), which includes medical records.

▶ The EU General Data Protection Regulation (GDPR) protects the privacy of personal information of EU residents. It includes the right to be forgotten, which allows data subjects to request that companies delete their personal information.

Practice Question 1

Which of these people would have the least expectation of privacy?

A. A patient discussing medical records with a nurse
B. An employee sending an email to a friend over the office network
C. A student discussing grades with a teacher
D. Two people having a private conversation

Practice Question 2

What law governs the privacy of personal information belonging to European Union residents?

A. GLBA
B. HIPAA
C. GDPR
D. FERPA

Practice Question 1 Explanation

A patient discussing medical records with a nurse is in a situation where there is a strong expectation of privacy. These records are protected health information (PHI) and should be treated very carefully. Of the situations listed, this is likely the one with the greatest expectation of privacy.

A student discussing grades with a teacher and two people having a private conversation are also in situations where they should have some expectation of privacy.

An employee of an organization sending an email at work has no expectation of privacy. The employer is entitled to inspect any information sent or received using the office network, even if that information is of a personal nature.

Correct Answer: B. An employee sending an email to a friend over the office network.

Practice Question 2 Explanation

The General Data Protection Regulation (GDPR) governs the privacy and protection of personal information for individuals within the EU. It establishes strict guidelines on data processing and grants individuals significant rights over their data.

The Gramm–Leach–Bliley Act (GLBA) and the Health Insurance Portability and Accountability Act (HIPAA) are both U.S. regulations, focusing on financial institutions and healthcare information privacy respectively, thus not directly applicable to general personal data in the EU.

The Family Educational Rights and Privacy Act (FERPA) also pertains to educational records in the United States and does not extend to general data privacy concerns for EU residents.

Note that the incorrect answer choices given here are distractors only. GDPR is the only law specifically mentioned in the Tech+ exam objectives.

Correct Answer: C. GDPR

## CHAPTER 34

Authentication, Authorization, Accounting, and Nonrepudiation
Objective 6.1: Explain fundamental security concepts and frameworks

Protecting access to systems and other resources requires that we allow authorized individuals to access that data while blocking any unauthorized access attempts. In order to do this, we must have confidence that a user is who they claim to be and know what they are allowed to do. The authentication and authorization processes provide us with this confidence.

In this chapter, you'll learn part of the material that you need to know about Tech+ objective 6.1. The topics covered in this chapter include:

▶ **Authentication, authorization, accounting, and nonrepudiation concepts**

The remaining material for this objective was covered in Chapter 32, "Confidentiality, Integrity, and Availability," and Chapter 33, "Privacy."

ACCESS CONTROL

As IT professionals, one of the most important things that we do is ensure that only authorized individuals gain access to information, systems, and networks under our protection. The *access control* process consists of three steps that you must understand: identification, authentication, and authorization.

Identification

During the first step of the process, *identification*, an individual makes a claim about their identity. The person trying to gain access doesn't present any proof at this point; they simply make an assertion. It's important to remember that the identification step is only a claim and the user could certainly be making a false claim! Imagine a physical world scenario in which you want to enter a secure office building where you have an appointment. During the identification step of the process, I would walk up to the security desk and say, "Hi, I'm Mike Chapple."

Authentication

Proof comes into play during the second step of the process: *authentication*. During the authentication step, the individual proves their identity to the satisfaction of the access control system. In our office building example, the guard would likely wish to see my driver's license to confirm my identity.

Authorization

Just proving your identity isn't enough to gain access to a system, however. The access control system also needs to be satisfied that you are *allowed* to access the system. That's the third step of the access control process: *authorization*. In our office building example, the security guard might check a list of that day's appointments to see if it includes my name.

Digital Authentication and Authorization

So far, we've talked about identification, authentication, and authorization in the context of gaining access to a building. Let's talk about how they work in the electronic world. When we go to log into a system, we most often identify ourselves using a username, most likely composed of some combination of the letters from our names. When we reach the authentication phase, we're commonly asked to enter a password.

Finally, in the electronic world, authorization often takes the form of *access control lists (ACLs)* that itemize the specific filesystem permissions granted to an individual user or group of users. Users proceed through the identification, authentication, and authorization processes when they request access to a resource.

Accounting

In addition to this process, access control systems provide accounting functionality that allows administrators to track user activity and reconstruct it from logs. This may include tracking user activity on systems and even logging user web browsing history or geographic location. Any tracking that takes place as part of an organization's monitoring program should fit within the boundaries set by the law and the organization's privacy policy.

> **NOTE**
> Together, the activities of authentication, authorization, and accounting are commonly described as AAA, or "triple A."

As you design access control systems, you need to think about the mechanisms that you use to perform each of these tasks. You also want to consider the environments supported by identity and access management mechanisms. In a modern computing environment, where organizations combine resources from both cloud and on-premises systems, you'll want an *identity and access management (IAM)* system that can work across both environments.

AUTHENTICATION FACTORS

Computer systems offer many different authentication techniques that allow users to prove their identity. Let's take a look at three different authentication factors:

- ▶ Something you know
- ▶ Something you are
- ▶ Something you have

Something You Know

By far, the most common authentication factor is *something you know*. We've already talked about how passwords are the most commonly used authentication technique. This is a something-you-know factor because the password is something that the user remembers and enters into a system during the authentication process. Personal identification numbers (PINs) and the answers to security questions are also examples of something you know.

Something You Are

The second authentication factor is *something you are*. *Biometric* authentication techniques measure one of your physical characteristics, such as a fingerprint, eye pattern, face, or voice. Figure 34.1 shows an example of a smartphone fingerprint reader performing biometric authentication.

Figure 34.2 shows a more complex eye scan being performed as a biometric access control for entering a facility.

Something You Have

The third authentication factor, *something you have*, requires the user to have physical possession of a device, such as a smartphone running a software token application or a hardware authentication token keyfob. These devices generate one-time passwords that are displayed to the user and allow them to prove that they have access to a physical device.

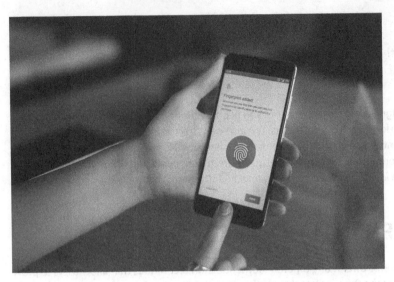

FIGURE 34.1 Fingerprint authentication on a smartphone

artiemedvedev/Adobe Systems Incorporated

FIGURE 34.2 Eye scan authentication entering a facility

demphoto/Adobe Systems Incorporated

Multifactor Authentication

When used alone, any one of these techniques provides some security for systems. However, they each have their own drawbacks. For example, an attacker might steal a user's password through a phishing attack. Once they have the password, they can then use that password to assume the user's identity. Other authentication factors aren't foolproof either.

If you use smartcard authentication to implement something you have, the user may lose the smartcard. Someone coming across it may then impersonate the user.

The solution to this problem is to combine authentication techniques from multiple factors, such as combining something you know with something you have. This approach is known as *multifactor authentication (MFA)*.

Take the two techniques we just discussed: passwords and smartcards. When used alone, either one is subject to hackers gaining knowledge of the password or stealing a smartcard. However, if an authentication system requires both a password (something you know) and a smartcard (something you have), it brings added security. If the hacker steals the password, they don't have the required smartcard, and vice versa. It suddenly becomes much more difficult for the attacker to gain access to the account. Because something you know and something you have are different factors, this is multifactor authentication.

We can combine other factors as well. For example, a fingerprint reader (something you are) might also require the entry of a PIN (something you know). That's another example of multifactor authentication.

When evaluating MFA, it's important to remember that the techniques must be *different* factors. An approach that combines a password with the answer to a security question is *not* multifactor authentication because both factors are something you know.

EXAM TIP

When you take the exam, you'll likely find a question about multifactor authentication. Be careful to ensure that the authentication techniques come from two different factors. Mistaking two something-you-know techniques for multifactor authentication is a common exam mistake!

Single Sign-On

The last authentication concept we need to discuss is *single sign-on (SSO)*. This technology shares authenticated sessions across systems. Many organizations create SSO solutions within their organizations to help users avoid the burden of repeatedly authenticating. In an SSO approach, users log onto the first SSO-enabled system they encounter and then that login session persists across other systems until it reaches its expiration. If the organization sets the expiration period to be the length of a business day, it means that users only need to log in once per day and then their single sign-on will last the entire day.

AUTHORIZATION

Authorization is the final step in the access control process. Once an individual successfully authenticates to a system, authorization determines the privileges that individual has to access resources and information.

Least Privilege

Before we discuss the different ways that you can implement authorization, let's cover an important underlying principle: the principle of *least privilege*. This principle states that an individual should only have the minimum set of permissions necessary to accomplish their job duties.

Least privilege is important for two reasons:

▶ Least privilege minimizes the potential damage from an insider attack. If an employee turns malicious, the damage they can cause will be limited by the privileges assigned to them by job role. It's unlikely, for example, that an accountant would be able to deface the company website because an accountant's job responsibilities have nothing to do with updating web content.

▶ Least privilege limits the ability of an external attacker to quickly gain privileged access when compromising an employee's account. Unless they happen to compromise a system administrator's account, they will find themselves limited by the privileges of the account that they steal.

ACCOUNT TYPES

Access control systems contain several types of accounts, and each category requires different types of controls.

User Accounts

Most of the accounts that we manage are standard user accounts. They're assigned to an individual user and grant routine access to resources. Everyone from the receptionist to the CEO in an organization typically has a standard user account, even though those accounts may have dramatically different privileges. User accounts should be subject to routine monitoring for compromise and should follow a life cycle management process for creation and removal.

Administrator Accounts

Some accounts belong to system administrators and have extensive privileges to modify system configurations. These accounts are highly sensitive and should be carefully guarded using a process known as *privileged account management*. Generally speaking, you should log every action performed by a privileged account and treat any suspicious activity occurring on a privileged account as a high priority for investigation.

It's easy for users with privileged access to make mistakes and cause unintended but drastic consequences. Also, the more that you use an account, the higher the likelihood of compromise. Therefore, administrative users who require privileged access typically have standard user accounts that they use for most of their routine activity and then manually elevate their account to privileged status when they need to issue an administrative command. The exact mechanism for this elevation will vary depending on the access control system, but it may consist of logging in with a different account or assuming an administrative role.

Guest Accounts

Guest accounts provide users with temporary access to resources. For example, you might use guest accounts to grant a visitor access to your wireless network. Guest accounts should be tied to unique individuals and should expire after a reasonable period of time.

Shared/Generic Accounts

Shared or generic accounts are accounts where more than one individual has access to use the account. Generally speaking, these accounts are a bad idea. It is difficult to trace who performed an action with a shared account, and every user has plausible deniability when several people have access to an account.

Service Accounts

Service accounts are a special type of account used internally by a system to run a process or perform other actions. These accounts typically have privileged access and should be carefully controlled. You should configure service accounts so that they may not be used to log onto the system interactively, and their passwords should not be known by anyone.

NONREPUDIATION

Another important focus of some security controls is providing *nonrepudiation*. Repudiation is a term that means denying that something is true. Nonrepudiation is a security goal that prevents someone from falsely denying that something is true.

For example, you might agree to pay someone $10,000 in exchange for a car. If you just had a handshake agreement, it might be possible for you to later repudiate your actions. You might claim that you never agreed to purchase the car or that you agreed to pay a lower price.

We solve this issue by using signed contracts when we sell a car. Your signature on the document is the proof that you agreed to the terms, and if you later go to court, the person selling you the car can prove that you agreed by showing the judge the signed document. Physical signatures provide nonrepudiation on contracts, receipts, and other paper documents.

There's also an electronic form of the physical signature. *Digital signatures* use encryption technology to provide nonrepudiation for electronic documents. You won't need to know the details of how digital signatures work on the Tech+ exam, but you should know that digital signatures provide nonrepudiation for electronic documents.

> **EXAM TIP**
> The goal of nonrepudiation is to make it so that people can't deny that an event took place. In other words, it provides proof that someone or something performed a specific action.

There are other ways that you can provide nonrepudiation as well. You might use biometric security controls, such as a fingerprint or facial recognition, to prove that someone was in a facility or performed an action. You might also use video surveillance for that same purpose. All of these controls allow you to prove that someone was in a particular location or performed an action, offering some degree of nonrepudiation.

CERTMIKE EXAM ESSENTIALS

▶ The access control process consists of three major steps. Identification is when a user makes a claim of identity. Authentication is when the user proves that identity claim. Authorization is when the system determines that the user is allowed to perform a requested action.

▶ Accounting processes create a record of who performed which actions on a system and are useful when investigating security incidents.

▶ Multifactor authentication combines authentication techniques with at least two of the three factors: something you know, something you have, and something you are.

▶ Nonrepudiation uses technical measures to ensure that a user is not able to later deny that they took some action.

Practice Question 1

You are considering deploying a multifactor authentication system to protect access to your organization's virtual private network (VPN). Which one of the following combinations of controls would meet this requirement?

A. Password and PIN
B. Fingerprint and eye scan
C. Smartcard and fingerprint
D. Keyfob and smartcard

Practice Question 2

You are working with a home loan provider who needs a system that will ensure they can prove in court that a user signed a contract. What type of requirement are they most directly trying to achieve?

A. Authentication
B. Authorization
C. Accounting
D. Nonrepudiation

Practice Question 1 Explanation

Before we can answer this question, we must identify the authentication factors in use here.

Passwords and PINs are both examples of something you know.

Fingerprint and eye scans are both examples of something you are.

Keyfobs and smartcards are both examples of something you have.

The only answer option that combines techniques from two different factors is the use of a smartcard (something you have) with a fingerprint (something you are).

Correct Answer: C. Smartcard and fingerprint

Practice Question 2 Explanation

This is a tricky question because the user is technically performing all of these actions. Before allowing a user to sign a contract, the system must be confident in their identity, and it gains this confidence through the authentication process. It must also be sure that the user is allowed to enter into the contract, which it does through the authorization process. And the lender will definitely want to keep a record of the action, which is done through the accounting process.

However, this question is about proving to a third party that the user signed the contract. This is preventing the user from denying the action and is a nonrepudiation requirement.

Correct Answer: D. Nonrepudiation

## CHAPTER 35

Security Awareness

Objective 6.2 Explain methods to secure devices and security best practices

Security awareness training is a crucial part of any cybersecurity strategy. It's an ongoing process that equips people to recognize and respond to threats, including social engineering, which manipulates individuals into divulging sensitive information. The training also emphasizes the importance of robust password protection. Understanding and adopting these measures can significantly improve an organization's defense against cyberthreats, turning every individual into a proactive participant in maintaining security.

In this chapter, you'll learn part of the material that you need to know about Tech+ objective 6.2. The topics covered in this chapter include:

▶ Security awareness

The remaining material for this objective is covered in Chapter 33, "Privacy," Chapter 36, "Securing Devices," and Chapter 37, "Software Licensing."

SOCIAL ENGINEERING

Digital threats aren't the only issue facing information security professionals seeking to protect their organizations. Some of the most dangerous risks come from the human threat of *social engineering*. These are also some of the hardest threats to protect against.

Social engineering attacks use psychological tricks to manipulate people into performing an action or divulging sensitive information that undermines the organization's security. For example, an attacker posing as a help desk technician might use social engineering to trick a user into revealing their password over the telephone. Social engineering attacks are the online version of running a con.

Social engineering attacks are successful for the following reasons:

▶ Authority and trust
▶ Intimidation
▶ Consensus and social proof
▶ Scarcity
▶ Urgency
▶ Familiarity and liking

Authority and Trust

Countless psychological experiments have shown that people will listen and defer to someone who is conveying an air of *authority*. Displaying outward signs of authority, such as dressing in a suit or simply having a look of distinguished age, creates a trust among those without such symbols.

Well-known hacker Kevin Mitnick describes an example of authority and trust in his book *The Art of Intrusion* (Wiley, 2005). He tells of a social engineer who simply walked right into a casino security center and started issuing orders. Because he did so with an air of authority, the staff complied with his commands.

Intimidation

The second reason that social engineering works is *intimidation*. It's simply browbeating people into doing what you want by scaring them and threatening that something bad will happen to them and/or the organization.

A social engineer might call a help desk posing as an administrative assistant demanding that they reset the password on an executive's account. When the help desk asks to speak to the executive, the assistant might just start yelling, "Do you know how busy he is? He is going to be very angry if you don't just do this for me!" That's intimidation.

Consensus and Social Proof

The third social engineering tactic is *consensus and social proof*. When people don't know how to react in a situation, they often look to the behavior of others and follow their example. It's the herd mentality. This is what happens when someone is attacked in the street and nobody calls 911.

It's also how riots occur. Most normal people would never think of burning a car or looting a store. But once the crowd gets going and they see this behavior around them, many people join in.

Scarcity

The fourth tactic is *scarcity*: making people believe that if they don't act quickly, they will miss out. You see this each time a major consumer electronics company releases a new product. Why will people wait in line overnight just to get a new phone? Because they want to get one before they run out.

A social engineer might use scarcity to trick someone into allowing them to install equipment in an office. Perhaps they show up with a Wi-Fi router and say that they are upgrading the Wi-Fi in adjacent offices with a brand-new technology and had a leftover router. If the office staff would like, they can install it here. If they agree, they think they're getting early access to new technology, while the hacker is establishing a foothold on the network.

Urgency

Urgency is the fifth tactic of social engineers. With this tactic, the hacker creates a situation where people feel pressured to act quickly because time is running out.

For example, a hacker might show up at an office and say they are a network technician who is there to perform a critical repair and need access to a sensitive networking closet. When staff refuses to grant access, the hacker can say they have another appointment and can't waste time. If the staff member will open the door now, the hacker will perform the repair; otherwise, the network will probably go down, and they'll be out of luck.

Familiarity and Liking

The final tactic is simple: *familiarity and liking*. People want to say yes to someone they like. Social engineers will use flattery, false compliments, and fake relationships to get on a target's good side and influence their activities.

The best way to protect your organization against social engineering attacks is user education. Everyone in the organization must understand that social engineers use these tactics to gain sensitive information, and they must be watchful for outsiders trying to use these tactics.

SECURITY EDUCATION

Security depends on the behavior of individuals. An intentional or accidental misstep by a single user can completely undermine many security controls, exposing an organization to unacceptable levels of risk. Security training programs help protect organizations against these risks.

Security education programs include the following two important components:

> ▶ *Security training* provides users with the detailed information they need to protect the organization's security. Training may use a variety of delivery techniques, but the bottom-line goal is to impart knowledge. Security training takes time and attention from students.

▶ *Security awareness* is meant to remind employees about the security lessons they've already learned. Unlike security training, it doesn't require time to sit down and learn new material. Instead, it uses posters, videos, email messages, and similar techniques to keep security top-of-mind for those who've already learned the core lessons.

Figure 35.1 shows an example of a security awareness poster.

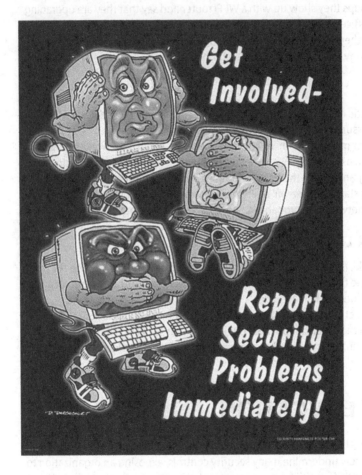

FIGURE 35.1 A security awareness poster

NOAA / https://www.wrc.noaa.gov/wrso/posters/Security_Awareness_
Posters-i0020.htm / last accessed under June 07, 2024

Organizations can use a variety of methods to deliver security training. This may include traditional classroom instruction, providing dedicated information security course material, or it might insert security content into existing programs, such as a new employee orientation program delivered by Human Resources. Students might also use online computer-based training providers to learn about information security, or attend classes offered by vendors. Whatever methods an organization uses, the goal is to impart security knowledge that employees can put into practice on the job.

> **EXAM TIP**
>
> Two very important topics to include in security education programs are defending against social engineering attacks and protecting users from malicious or compromised content. In fact, both of these topics are specifically mentioned in the Tech+ exam objectives, so be sure to remember them!

While all users should receive some degree of security education, organizations should also customize training to meet specific role-based requirements. For example, employees handling credit card information should receive training on credit card security requirements. Human Resources team members should be trained on handling personally identifiable information (PII). IT staffers need specialized skills to implement security controls. Training should be custom-tailored to an individual's role in the organization.

You'll also want to think about the frequency of your training efforts. You'll need to balance the time required to conduct training with the benefit from reminding users of their responsibilities. One approach used by many organizations is to conduct initial training whenever an employee joins the organization or assumes new job responsibilities, and then use annual refresher training to cover the same material and update users on new threats and controls. Awareness efforts throughout the year then keep this material fresh and top-of-mind.

> **EXAM TIP**
>
> The team responsible for providing security training should review materials on a regular basis to ensure that the content remains relevant. Changes in the security landscape and the organization's business may require updating the material to remain fresh and relevant.

CERTMIKE EXAM ESSENTIALS

▶ The main strategies that social engineers leverage—authority and trust, intimidation, consensus, scarcity, urgency, and familiarity—exploit human psychology to circumvent technical security controls. Training programs should emphasize the nature of these tactics, teaching employees to recognize and respond appropriately to potential social engineering attempts.

▶ Security training programs serve as the frontline defense in cybersecurity, empowering employees to recognize and prevent security incidents. Training efforts must continuously adapt to the evolving landscape of cyberthreats, ensuring that employees remain informed about current risks and effective mitigation strategies.

▶ An effective training program covers a diverse array of topics, including general cybersecurity principles and role-specific responsibilities. Broad topics like social engineering and password protection form a foundation of awareness for all employees, whereas role-based training equips individuals with the specific knowledge and skills necessary to safeguard information within their unique job functions.

Practice Question 1

As a part of your company's security education program, you are asked to update the security training material. What is the main reason for keeping the training material updated?

A. To maintain the interest of the trainees

B. To ensure the training material remains relevant in an evolving threat landscape

C. To provide a refresher course for the employees

D. To cover more security topics in the training

Practice Question 2

A person contacts your help desk pretending to be a top executive's assistant, and demands immediate assistance in resetting the executive's password. The person warns that the executive will be very upset if their request isn't fulfilled promptly. Which social engineering tactic is being used?

A. Intimidation

B. Consensus and social proof

C. Familiarity and liking

D. Scarcity

Practice Question 1 Explanation

While maintaining interest, providing refresher courses, and covering more topics can be beneficial, the main reason for keeping training material updated is to ensure it remains relevant in an evolving threat landscape. The nature of cyberthreats is constantly changing, and outdated training material might leave employees unprepared to deal with new types of attacks.

Correct Answer: B. To ensure the training material remains relevant in an evolving threat landscape.

Practice Question 2 Explanation

The scenario presents a situation where a person posing as an executive's assistant leverages the potential of the executive's anger to compel the help desk to act quickly on their demand. This tactic, where a threat or fear is used to manipulate the victim into compliance, is known as intimidation. While elements of authority and trust could be present due to the impersonation of the executive's assistant, the primary manipulation here is the threat of the executive's displeasure.

Correct Answer: A. Intimidation

## CHAPTER 36

Securing Devices
Objective 6.2: Explain methods to secure devices and security best practices

We make use of many different types of computing devices in our businesses. From laptops and desktops to smartphones and tablets, organizations have hundreds or thousands of different devices connected to their networks and handling sensitive information. IT professionals must work to keep these devices secure because a single insecure device can open a network up to attack.

In this chapter, you'll learn some of the material that you need to know about Tech+ objective 6.2. The topics covered in this chapter include:

▶ Securing devices (mobile/workstation)
▶ Device use best practices (software sources, removal of software, safe browsing practices)

The remaining material for this objective is covered in Chapter 33, "Privacy," Chapter 35, "Security Awareness," and Chapter 37, "Software Licensing."

DEVICE SECURITY

Security professionals have a variety of tools at their disposal to protect devices from common security threats. These include antivirus software, host firewalls, passwords, safe web browsing practices, and regular patching and updates.

Antimalware Software

Every device should have *antimalware software* installed that protects it from malicious software, or malware. Viruses, worms, ransomware, Trojan horses, and many other threats roam the Internet and threaten to compromise devices. Antimalware software scans files stored on computers or downloaded from the Internet for common threats and blocks malicious files from running on computers. It's one of the cornerstones of cybersecurity.

Host Firewalls

Devices should also have *host firewalls* that block unwanted inbound connections from elsewhere on the network. The "host" in host firewall simply means that the firewall runs on a specific device and protects only that device, as opposed to a network firewall that protects an entire network. Organizations should use a combination of both host and network firewalls to provide strong protections.

Host firewalls work by restricting the systems and ports that may communicate with a device. The typical end-user computer doesn't need to accept any inbound connections at all—there's simply no need for connections that aren't started by the end user. The most common exception to this is when remote management tools designed to allow remote IT support are installed on systems. In those cases, you may need to configure the host firewall to allow this type of network traffic, but you should limit the access to computers that are part of the help desk and to the specific port used for that remote access. Your networking team can help you figure this out.

Authentication

Passwords are the most basic form of authentication used to restrict access to a computer. You learned about more secure authentication mechanisms in Chapter 34, "Authentication, Authorization, Accounting, and Nonrepudiation," but at the very least, computers and other devices should have passwords enabled. Administrators should also remove any default passwords that came configured on the device to prevent anyone who knows that default password from gaining access.

Updates and Patching

Devices frequently need security updates to continue to protect themselves against new threats. Software and operating system vendors release *patches* that fix security vulnerabilities and protect systems from many types of malware and hacking techniques that exploit old vulnerabilities that remain on systems.

Physical Device Security

Securing the physical devices that connect to our networks is just as important as protecting the network itself. A device that falls into the wrong hands can become an open door to otherwise secure systems and data. To prevent this, we employ physical security measures that are simple yet effective.

For portable devices such as laptops, which are particularly vulnerable to theft, *cable locks*, such as the one shown in Figure 36.1, are a first line of defense. These locks tether a device to a fixed object, like a desk or a table, making it much more difficult for thieves to walk away with the device. They come with either key or combination locks and are especially useful in public or semi-public areas where people may leave devices unattended, such as in offices, at conferences, or in educational institutions.

FIGURE 36.1 Cable lock attached to a laptop

kelly marken/Adobe Systems Incorporated

USB ports can be entry points for unauthorized devices that could be used to copy data or introduce malware. *USB locks* are devices that can be inserted into the USB ports of computers, printers, or any device with a USB connection, to block physical access. These locks prevent the use of USB flash drives or other unauthorized USB-based devices, mitigating the risk of data theft or the introduction of malicious software via USB ports. They can either completely block the port or be part of a managed solution that allows only authorized devices to connect.

SOFTWARE SECURITY

We also face some security risks from the software that we install and run on our systems. Software may contain errors, or even intentional flaws that jeopardize the security of the systems that run them. And if a system runs insecure software and becomes compromised, that could jeopardize the security of the entire network.

For this reason, IT professionals should carefully monitor what types of software run on their systems. When a user wants to use a new software package, it's important to analyze that software for potential security risks and make sure that it's safe before moving forward with the installation.

Software Sources

One of the most important things that you can do when evaluating new software is validate that it came from a legitimate source, such as directly from a trusted vendor or from a trusted *application store*. This may require some research on your part, investigating what company or developer created the software and what it's intended to do. You can be much more trusting of software that comes from a major developer, such as Microsoft, Apple, or SAP, than you might be of software from a company that you've never heard of before.

Also, make sure that you're obtaining software from a trustworthy source. If you're downloading software from the Internet, be certain that you're downloading a copy from the vendor's website and not from a third-party site. If you download software from any source other than the original equipment manufacturer (OEM), then it's possible that a third party modified the software and created a security vulnerability.

Removal of Software

Finally, you should continue to monitor the software installed on your systems and remove software that is suspected to be malicious, that is unwanted, or that is no longer necessary to meet business requirements. The more software packages you have installed on a system, the greater the possibility that the system will have some serious security flaws. This concept of reducing the amount of software on a system to the smallest possible amount is known as reducing the attack surface.

SAFE BROWSING PRACTICES

Finally, systems should be configured to enforce safe web browsing practices. Users should be prompted to confirm that they wish to download software any time a remote website tries to install software on their systems, and any software they accept should be run through a malware scan. Administrators should also use content filtering technology to block users from accidentally visiting malicious websites.

Digital Certificates

In Chapter 21, "Web Browsers," we discussed how web browsers use the HTTPS protocol to securely transfer web pages. Using HTTPS protects against eavesdroppers who might try to view web traffic by protecting it with encryption. This encryption depends on websites having a valid *digital certificate*.

Figure 36.2 shows the digital certificate for my website, www.certmike.com. This certificate is marked as valid by my web browser, and I can be confident that this website is secure.

FIGURE 36.2 Valid certificate for `CertMike.com`

On the other hand, if I visit the website `https://wrong.host.badssl.com`, I see the error message shown in Figure 36.3. This site has an invalid digital certificate. I see a warning message telling me that the certificate is invalid for this site, and that I shouldn't continue accessing it because my communications with the web server will be insecure.

NOTE

If you see a message warning you that a certificate is expired and it has not yet reached its expiration date, check the date and time on your system. If your date is set incorrectly, you may see a lot of these errors!

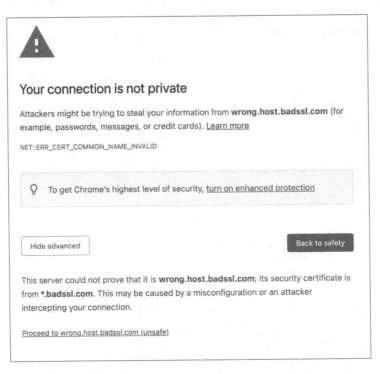

FIGURE 36.3 Invalid certificate warning for `wrong.host.badssl.com`

CERTMIKE EXAM ESSENTIALS

▶ Security professionals are responsible for adopting security controls that protect devices in their organizations. Common device security controls include antimalware software, host firewalls, passwords, safe browsing practices, and patching/updates.

▶ Verify the sources of software used in your organization to validate that it comes from a legitimate source. These sources may include the original equipment manufacturer (OEM), third-party software vendors, or trusted application stores.

▶ Monitor the software installed on systems in your organization and promptly remove any software that is unwanted, unnecessary, or potentially malicious.

▶ Digital certificates enable encryption for websites, allowing them to transfer data using the secure HTTPS protocol instead of the unencrypted HTTP protocol.

Practice Question 1

Which one of the following security controls is *least* likely to prevent the installation of malware on a computer?

A. Antimalware software

B. Safe browsing practices

C. Strong passwords

D. Patching

Practice Question 2

You are working with a user at a branch office and are trying to connect to their system by Remote Desktop. You are unable to make the connection even though the user verified that the software is running on their computer. You are able to connect to the systems belonging to other users in the same office. What component should you check first as the likely source of the problem?

A. Network firewall

B. Antimalware software

C. Content filters

D. Host firewall

Practice Question 1 Explanation

Antimalware software is designed specifically to detect and block malware, so it would definitely be of assistance here. Applying security patches protects systems against common vulnerabilities used to install malware, so it would also be an effective control. Malware often infects systems when users visit malicious websites and unintentionally install it, so safe web browsing practices would also be effective.

While strong passwords are an important security control, they are less likely to protect against malware infections than other types of attack.

Correct Answer: C. Strong passwords

Practice Question 2 Explanation

The immediate conclusion you should come to is that some component is blocking the network connection, and this is the work normally performed by firewalls. Neither antimalware software nor content filters typically interfere with network connection attempts, so we can rule out both of those answer choices from the start.

This leaves us with the possibility that the connection is being blocked by either a network firewall or a host firewall, both of which are reasonable possibilities. However, we also know that you are able to connect to the systems belonging to other users in the same office. All users in an office would be protected by the same network firewall, so it is unlikely that the network firewall is the problem. It is far more likely that this individual computer's host firewall is incorrectly configured and needs to be adjusted to allow remote access.

Correct Answer: D. Host firewall

## CHAPTER 37

Software Licensing

Objective 6.2: Explain methods to secure devices and security best practices

IT professionals often find themselves responsible for installing and managing applications on systems throughout their organization. Let's take some time to talk about the key software licensing concepts that you'll need to understand for the exam.

In this chapter, you'll learn some of the material that you need to know about Tech+ objective 6.2. The topics covered in this chapter include:

▶ **Device use best practices (Licensing)**
▶ **Software piracy**

The remaining material for this objective is covered in Chapter 33, "Privacy," Chapter 35, "Security Awareness," and Chapter 36, "Securing Devices."

LICENSING OPTIONS

Different types of licenses are available that describe the conditions of using the software:

  ▶ Software that we purchase from vendors is considered *proprietary software*. The vendor owns the software and charges for its use.
  ▶ Other software is developed by a community of developers and released as *open source software* that is free for use under the conditions of an open source license agreement. One of the major advantages of open source software is that any developer is free to take an open source package, modify it to meet their own needs, and then even release that modified software as an open source application.

> **EXAM TIP**
> Open source means that the programming code used to design the software is freely available and that anyone may use or modify it.

When you have proprietary software, there are also different types of licensing arrangements that describe how many people may use the software:

- ▶ A *single-user license* allows you to install the software on a computer for a single user to work with.
- ▶ A group-use or *site license* covers many people. It may be the entire organization, a specific team, or a set of named people who may all have access to the software.
- ▶ *Concurrent licenses* also allow multiple people to use the software. The difference is in how those people are counted. For a site license, the license counts the number of people who may have the software installed. A concurrent license counts the number of people who may be using the software at the same time.

Software may be licensed as a one-time purchase where you pay a single up-front fee for perpetual use of the software and then a small maintenance fee to receive support and updates. Or it may be licensed under a subscription model, where instead of paying a large up-front fee, you pay a monthly or annual fee for each user. Cloud services generally tend to use this subscription model.

When you purchase software licenses, you're often given access to a serial number or *product key*. This is basically the password for installing the software under the license, and it is tied to your organization. You want to keep track of that key and protect it. If someone gains access to your license key, they may be able to activate software under your license and use up some of your purchased capacity!

SOFTWARE PIRACY

Software piracy is the illegal copying, distribution, or use of software. It occurs when individuals or organizations violate the terms of a software license agreement by reproducing the software without authorization. There are several common forms of software piracy:

- ▶ **Unauthorized Copying:** Installing software on more than one computer contrary to the terms of a single-user license.
- ▶ **Counterfeit Software:** Selling or distributing fake software that is often misrepresented as genuine.
- ▶ **Client-Server Overuse:** Installing more copies of the software than are licensed for use, typically within a corporate environment.
- ▶ **Internet Piracy:** Distributing software illegally through the Internet, either through file-sharing platforms or unauthorized downloads.

Software piracy not only causes significant financial losses to software developers but also poses security risks to users. Pirated software often lacks proper support and updates, and may contain malware or other security vulnerabilities that can lead to data theft or loss.

Engaging in software piracy exposes individuals and organizations to legal actions, including fines and penalties. It also raises ethical concerns, as piracy undermines the intellectual property rights of developers and the overall integrity of the software industry.

CERTMIKE EXAM ESSENTIALS

▶ Proprietary software is sold by vendors and may only be used under a purchased license. Open source software is developed by a community and is free for use or modification by anyone.

▶ Single-user licenses allow a single named individual to use a software package. Site licenses allow anyone in an organization to use the software. Concurrent licenses also allow anyone in the organization to use the software but limit the number of people who may use it simultaneously.

▶ Software piracy is the illegal copying, distribution, or use of software. It occurs when individuals or organizations violate the terms of a software license agreement by reproducing the software without authorization.

Practice Question 1

You recently purchased a new data visualization software package that will be used by business analysts in your organization. The license allows anyone in the organization to use the software as long as they are using a corporate-owned computer. What term best describes this type of license?

A. Site license
B. Open source license
C. Concurrent license
D. Single-user license

Practice Question 2

Your organization is considering using a new database platform that is developed by a community of developers and released for anyone to use and modify. What term best describes this license arrangement?

A. Open source license
B. Perpetual license
C. Subscription license
D. One-time license

Practice Question 1 Explanation

This is an example of a site license—a license that allows unrestricted use of a software package throughout an organization. The rule that the software may only be installed on corporate-owned devices is a common site license rule to prevent personal use of the software.

The software is not open source because open source software is not purchased. Rather, it is free for use or modification by anyone.

Concurrent licenses restrict the number of users that may use the software at any one time, whereas single-user licenses are for a named individual's use only. Neither of these restrictions appears on this license.

Correct Answer: A. Site license

Practice Question 2 Explanation

An open source license best describes a platform developed by a community of developers and released for anyone to use and modify, as it allows for the free distribution and alteration of the software's source code.

A perpetual license generally grants the user the right to use a software indefinitely after a one-time payment but does not inherently allow for modification or redistribution of the source code.

Subscription licenses require ongoing payments for continued use of the software and typically do not include rights to modify or redistribute the software.

A one-time license involves a single payment for ongoing use of the software, similar to a perpetual license, but like the other incorrect options, it doesn't necessarily include modification or distribution rights, key features of an open source license.

Correct Answer: A. Open source license

## CHAPTER 38

Password Best Practices

Objective 6.3: Explain password best practices

Passwords remain the most common authentication technique used by modern organizations. IT professionals often work with passwords as they assist users in navigating the authentication process.

In this chapter, you'll learn the material that you need to know about Tech+ objective 6.3. The topics covered in this chapter include:

▶ **Password length**
▶ **Password complexity**
▶ **Password history**
▶ **Password expiration**
▶ **Password reuse across sites**
▶ **Password managers**
▶ **Password privacy**
▶ **Password reset process**
▶ **Changing default usernames and passwords**
▶ **Enabling passwords**

PASSWORD POLICIES

When you set a password policy for your organization, you have a number of technical controls available that allow you to set requirements for how users choose and maintain their passwords. Figure 38.1 shows some of the common password policies that may be set in Microsoft Windows.

Let's discuss a few of those mechanisms.

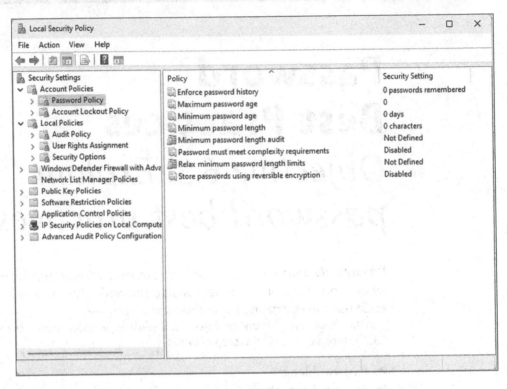

FIGURE 38.1 Windows password policies

Enabling Passwords

First and foremost, passwords or other authentication mechanisms should be enabled on all systems, applications, and services that restrict access to authorized users. You can't enforce strong password policies if you don't require passwords in the first place!

Password Length

The simplest and most common control on passwords is setting the *password length*. This is simply the minimum number of characters that must be included in a password. It's good practice to require that passwords be at least eight characters, but some organizations require even longer passwords. The longer a password, the harder it is to guess.

Password Complexity

Organizations may also set *password complexity* requirements. These requirements force users to include different types of characters in their passwords, such as uppercase and lowercase letters, digits, and special characters. Just as with password length, the more character types in a password, the harder it is to guess.

Password Expiration

Password expiration requirements force users to change their passwords periodically. For example, an organization might set a password expiration period of 180 days, forcing users to change their passwords every six months. These days, many organizations no longer have password expiration requirements, allowing users to keep the same password for as long as they'd like and only requiring that they change it if the password is compromised.

Password History

Password history requirements are designed to prevent users from reusing old passwords. Organizations with password history requirements configure their systems to remember the previous passwords used by each user and prevent them from reusing that password in the future. Password history controls allow the administrator to identify how many old passwords are remembered for each user.

Password Reuse

IT teams should also strongly encourage users not to reuse the same password across multiple sites. This is difficult to enforce, but it does provide a strong measure of security. If a user reuses the same password on many different sites and one of those sites is compromised, an attacker might test that password on other sites, hoping that the password owner reuses the same password.

Password Managers

It's difficult for users to manage unique passwords for every site they visit. That's where *password managers* play a crucial role. These valuable tools are secure password vaults, often protected by biometric security mechanisms that create and store unique passwords. They then automatically fill those passwords into websites when the user visits them. That way users can have unique, strong passwords for every site they visit without having to remember them all.

Figure 38.2 shows an example of LastPass, a popular password manager, being used to create a new, strong password.

Password Privacy

Password privacy is vital for maintaining security within any organization, and a key aspect of this is ensuring that users do not share their passwords. Sharing passwords can lead to unauthorized access and potential data breaches, compromising both individual and organizational security. To prevent this, organizations should enforce strict policies against password sharing, educate employees on the risks associated with it, and implement technical solutions like single sign-on (SSO) and multifactor authentication (MFA), which reduce the need and temptation for users to share their passwords.

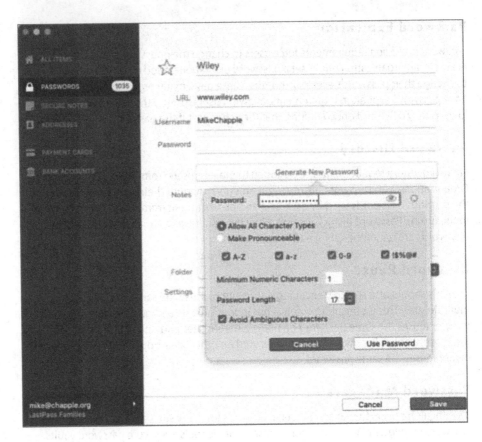

FIGURE 38.2 Creating a password in LastPass

Password Resets

Every organization should allow users to change their passwords quickly and easily. You want users to be able to privately select their own passwords and do so whenever they are concerned that their password may be compromised.

One point of caution is that organizations should carefully evaluate their password reset process for users who forget their passwords. If they're not designed well, these processes can provide an opportunity for attackers to gain access to a system by performing an unauthorized password reset.

Changing Defaults

Changing default usernames and passwords is a crucial security measure for any organization. Default settings are often well-known and publicly documented, making devices vulnerable to attacks. By immediately updating these defaults upon setup and using strong, unique credentials, organizations can significantly enhance their security posture.

This process should involve identifying all devices and software with default settings, using complex passwords and non-obvious usernames, and maintaining a secure record of changes to ensure continuous protection against unauthorized access.

CERTMIKE EXAM ESSENTIALS

▶ Password length requirements set a minimum number of characters that must be in a user's password, and password complexity requirements mandate the use of different character types.

▶ Password history requirements prevent the reuse of old passwords, and password expiration requirements force the periodic reset of existing passwords. Users should be permitted to reset their passwords whenever they wish.

▶ Users should be encouraged not to reuse passwords across multiple sites because this increases the risk of compromise. Password managers provide a convenient tool for managing many unique, strong passwords.

Practice Question 1

Andy is attempting to change his password and has created the following long password:

p7djkqnr2LAD

He receives an error message that he must use a symbol in his password. What password policy is he failing to meet?

A. Password length
B. Password history
C. Password complexity
D. Password reuse

Practice Question 2

You recently learned that a website belonging to one of your competitors was breached, and you are concerned that users with accounts on both sites will have their passwords compromised on your site as well. Which one of the following password policies would best protect against this risk?

A. Password reuse
B. Password complexity
C. Password length
D. Password history

Practice Question 1 Explanation

This is an example of a password complexity requirement. The message is requiring that Andy use a symbol in his password, and password complexity requirements require the use of different character types.

There is no indication that Andy is attempting to reuse an old password that would violate a password history requirement. Nor is he trying to use a password from another site that would violate a password reuse requirement. There is also no indication that his password is too short and does not meet the password length requirements.

Correct Answer: C. Password complexity

Practice Question 2 Explanation

The primary risk here is that some of your customers are using the same password on your competitor's site and your site. If the breach compromised passwords, the attacker would be able to use credentials from the other site to access accounts on your site. A password reuse policy would protect against this risk.

Password length and complexity requirements ensure that users create strong passwords, but the strength of the password is not in question here. If the attacker is able to obtain the passwords from another site, it does not matter how strong they are.

Password history requirements may be of some use in this situation because they would prevent a user from reusing the compromised password at a later date, but that is not the primary threat here. The major risk is that an account will be compromised now because it shares a password with an account on the compromised site.

Correct Answer: A. Password reuse

## CHAPTER 39

Encryption

Objective 6.4: Identify common use cases for encryption

Encryption protects information from prying eyes by making it unreadable to anyone who does not have the required decryption key. We use encryption to protect data that is at rest on a storage device or in motion over a network.

In this chapter, you'll learn the material that you need to know about Tech+ objective 6.4. The topics covered in this chapter include:

▶ Plain text vs. cipher text
▶ Data at rest
▶ Data in transit

CRYPTOGRAPHY

Encryption is one of the most important security controls that we can use to protect the confidentiality of our data. Encryption uses mathematical operations to transform information into a format where it is unreadable by anyone other than the authorized user.

> **EXAM TIP**
>
> The math behind encryption is pretty complex, but the good news is that you won't be responsible for any of that math on the Tech+ exam. You just need to know the basics of what encryption does and how you can use it to protect your organization.

Encrypting Data

When we are encrypting data, we start with some *plain text* information. Plain text is just a fancy way of saying that we have information in normal form. Anyone who looks at that data can read it. Figure 39.1 shows an example of a file containing plain text—the first paragraph from this chapter.

Chapter 38 — vi plaintext.txt — 68×11

```
Encryption protects information from prying eyes by making
 it unreadable to anyone who does not have the required de
cryption key.  We use encryption to protect data that is a
t rest on a storage device or in motion over a network.

~
~
~
~
~
```

FIGURE 39.1 Plain text message

We then take that information and use an encryption algorithm in combination with an encryption key to encrypt the data. The algorithm is the mathematical formula for the encryption, and the key is basically the password to the data. Once we've taken plain text data and encrypted it, we then call the data *cipher text*. Figure 39.2 shows the cipher text obtained by encrypting the plain text message shown in Figure 39.1.

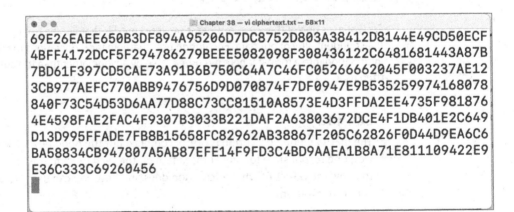

Chapter 38 — vi ciphertext.txt — 58×11

```
69E26EAEE650B3DF894A95206D7DC8752D803A38412D8144E49CD50ECF
4BFF4172DCF5F294786279BEEE5082098F308436122C6481681443A87B
7BD61F397CD5CAE73A91B6B750C64A7C46FC05266662045F003237AE12
3CB977AEFC770ABB9476756D9D070874F7DF0947E9B535259974168078
840F73C54D53D6AA77D88C73CC81510A8573E4D3FFDA2EE4735F981876
4E4598FAE2FAC4F9307B3033B221DAF2A63803672DCE4F1DB401E2C649
D13D995FFADE7FB8B15658FC82962AB38867F205C62826F0D44D9EA6C6
BA58834CB947807A5AB87EFE14F9FD3C4BD9AAEA1B8A71E811109422E9
E36C333C69260456
```

FIGURE 39.2 Cipher text message obtained by encrypting the plain text in Figure 39.1

That cipher text data is completely unreadable to anyone who examines it. It just looks like nonsense, and we can't make heads or tails of it. That stays true until we decrypt the data.

Decrypting Data

When someone wants to *decrypt* the cipher text and turn it back into plain text, they use the decryption algorithm and the decryption key to perform that transformation. If they don't know the correct decryption key, the decryption simply won't work. So protecting the key is vital. As long as unauthorized users don't have access to the decryption key, they won't have access to the data.

> **EXAM TIP**
>
> Encryption is a process that encodes a message, file, or data so that it is only read by those who have access to the appropriate decryption key.

USES OF ENCRYPTION

We use encryption in two different environments. We use it to protect data at rest and we use it to protect data that is in transit.

Data at Rest

Data at rest is simply stored data. We can encrypt individual files, entire disks, or the contents of a mobile device. If someone gains access to one of those encrypted files, disks, or mobile devices, we don't need to worry about the encrypted data because they won't have access to the decryption key.

Full-disk encryption (FDE) is a technology built into some operating systems that automatically encrypts all the data stored on a device. FDE technology is particularly useful for laptops, tablets, smartphones, and other devices that may be lost or stolen. Someone who steals the device will not be able to access the data it contains if that data is protected by full-disk encryption.

Data in Transit

Data in transit is data that's moving over a network. We can protect this data as well by using encryption.

When we access a website using the standard *HTTP* protocol, that data is unencrypted and anyone who observes our network activity can eavesdrop on our web use. However, if we use the secure *HTTPS* protocol, that connection is encrypted and the data being sent over the network is safe from prying eyes.

We can use the same encryption technology to protect the data being sent in email messages or from mobile applications to their servers, or even to protect entire network connections with encryption using a *virtual private network (VPN)*.

EXAM TIP

When you take the exam, you should understand that encryption is used to transform plain text into cipher text and that it protects both data at rest—stored in files or on devices—and data in transit as it is being sent over a network.

CERTMIKE EXAM ESSENTIALS

▶ Encryption is the process of transforming plain text information into cipher text that can't be read by unauthorized individuals. Decryption uses a decryption key to convert cipher text back into plain text.

▶ Encryption may be used to protect data at rest by encrypting individual files or folders. Full-disk encryption (FDE) uses encryption to protect the entire contents of a device.

▶ Encryption may be used to protect data in motion by encrypting it as it travels over a network. The HTTPS protocol encrypts web traffic and is a secure alternative to the unencrypted HTTP protocol. Virtual private networks (VPNs) encrypt entire network connections.

Practice Question 1

You are concerned that users traveling with laptops will have those devices stolen while in transit. What encryption technology would best protect the data stored on those laptops?

A. HTTPS

B. HTTP

C. VPN

D. FDE

Practice Question 2

You have a group of remote users who need to access the corporate network from their homes. You would like to protect the information that they send back and forth to the corporate network, regardless of the application that they use. What encryption technology would best meet this need?

A. HTTPS

B. HTTP

C. VPN

D. FDE

Practice Question 1 Explanation

This question is asking us to identify an encryption technology that will protect data at rest and, in particular, the entire contents of a laptop. Full-disk encryption (FDE) is designed for this use case. FDE encrypts an entire hard drive, rendering the contents inaccessible to an unauthorized individual who steals or finds the device.

HTTP is not an encrypted protocol. HTTPS is a secure, encrypted alternative to HTTP but it is used to protect web traffic, which is an example of data in transit, and would not be effective in protecting a lost or stolen laptop.

Similarly, virtual private networks (VPNs) protect network communications and would not be effective in protecting a lost or stolen laptop.

Correct Answer: D. FDE

Practice Question 2 Explanation

We can begin here by eliminating full-disk encryption (FDE) as an answer choice because FDE is designed to protect the contents of a disk—data at rest. It does not protect data in transit over a network.

The HTTP protocol is unencrypted, so it does not provide any protection. HTTPS is a secure, encrypted alternative to HTTP, but it is used only to protect web traffic. It would protect any web communications from the remote users but would not protect other applications.

Virtual private networks (VPNs) create secure network connections between two locations and would be an effective means of protecting the communications of these remote users.

Correct Answer: C. VPN

## CHAPTER 40

Securing Wireless Networks

Objective 6.5: Given a scenario, configure security settings for a small wireless network

As the use of wireless networks continues to increase, the security of those networks becomes of critical importance. Encryption and other security practices ensure that the sensitive information transmitted using wireless networks remains secure.

In this chapter, you'll learn everything you need to know about Tech+ objective 6.5, including the following topics:

▶ Changing the service set identifier (SSID)
▶ Changing the default password
▶ Encrypted vs. unencrypted

One of the major responsibilities of IT professionals is to secure wireless networks to protect the traffic they carry from eavesdropping attacks and to protect the network from unauthorized access. There are a few best practices you can follow to protect your wireless network.

SSID

Each wireless network has a name that identifies it to users. This name is what you see on your phone or laptop when you're choosing the network you'd like to use. The technical term for this name is the *service set identifier (SSID)*. By default, wireless networks advertise themselves to potential users by broadcasting their SSID, telling everyone in the local area that the network is available and accepting connections.

If you don't want to advertise your network, you can disable SSID broadcasting, hiding the network from users who don't already know that it is there.

Access Point Passwords

Your wireless access point also has an administrative password that allows you to connect to the device and configure the wireless network and its security settings. The access point may have come from the manufacturer with a default password already set that is printed in the user manual or on a label on the device itself. You should, as a matter of habit, immediately change these default passwords to strong passwords known only to you and other network administrators within your organization.

Wireless Access Control

You'll also need to decide what type of wireless network you'd like to run. *Open networks* are available to anyone who comes across them and would like to use them. Other networks use some type of authentication to limit access.

Preshared keys are the simplest kind of wireless authentication and are commonly used on small office/home office (SOHO) Wi-Fi networks. In the preshared key approach, the network uses an encryption key to control access. Whenever a user wishes to connect a device to the network, they must enter the preshared key on the device. If you've ever been at an office or public place where there's a Wi-Fi password posted on the wall, that's an example of a preshared key. Preshared keys have major limitations that prevent them from being used on large networks:

▶ Changing the network encryption key is a tremendous burden. Each time the key changes, users must reconfigure all wireless devices to use the new key. This might not be bad on a home network supporting a handful of users, but it is impractical in most business environments.

▶ The use of a shared key prevents the identification of individual users and the restriction of access by user identity. For example, if a user leaves the organization, network administrators have no way to revoke that user's wireless network access short of changing the preshared key on all wireless devices in the organization.

A common way to approach wireless authentication is through the use of *enterprise authentication*. In this approach, the organization runs an authentication server that verifies user credentials and ensures that only authorized users access the network. In this approach, instead of entering a preshared key, users enter their individual username and password or provide other credentials to access the network.

The third approach to wireless authentication is the use of *captive portals*. You might not be familiar with the term *captive portal*, but you've certainly seen them in use in hotels, airports, coffee shops, and other public locations. Captive portals provide authentication on unencrypted wireless networks. When a user connects to a network using a captive portal, they are redirected to a web page that requires them to authenticate and often acknowledge an acceptable use policy (AUP) before gaining access to the network.

This authentication may be as simple as accepting the terms of service, or it may require an account password or even a credit card payment to escape the captive portal and use the Internet.

WIRELESS ENCRYPTION

Network administrators may choose to add *encryption* to wireless networks to protect communications against eavesdropping. Wireless encryption is a best practice for network security. Encryption hides the true content of network traffic from those without the decryption key. It takes an insecure communications technology—radio waves—and makes it secure. You have several options for wireless encryption.

Wired Equivalent Privacy (WEP)

The original approach to solving this problem was a technology known as *Wired Equivalent Privacy (WEP)*. WEP was used for a long time, but it's now known to suffer from some serious security vulnerabilities. These issues are so significant that security professionals no longer consider WEP secure, and it should never be used on a modern network.

Wi-Fi Protected Access (WPA)

A newer technology called *Wi-Fi Protected Access (WPA)* replaced WEP back in 2003. This first version, just called WPA, used the *Temporal Key Integrity Protocol (TKIP)* to add security that WEP didn't have. TKIP changes the encryption key for each packet, preventing an attacker from discovering the key after monitoring the network for a long period of time. However, as happens with many security technologies, vulnerabilities in WPA have now come to light that also make it a poor choice for use on wireless networks.

Wi-Fi Protected Access v2 (WPA2)

In 2004, *WPA2* was released as an upgrade to WPA. Instead of simply trying to add security on to the old WEP standard, WPA2 uses an encryption protocol that is based on the *Advanced Encryption Standard (AES)*. This mode has a really long name—*Counter Mode Cipher Block Chaining Message Authentication Code Protocol*—but you just need to know it by the acronym CCMP. Security researchers have discovered some potential issues with WPA2, but it is still considered secure and is widely used.

Wi-Fi Protected Access v3 (WPA3)

As of 2020, new wireless devices are required to support the WPA3 standard. WPA3 also supports the CCMP protocol but it adds a new technology called *Simultaneous Authentication of Equals (SAE)*. SAE is a secure key exchange protocol based on the Diffie–Hellman technique to provide a secure initial setup of encrypted wireless communications.

EXAM TIP
You definitely need to know the different wireless encryption mechanisms when you take the exam. Table 40.1 provides a quick reference to help you remember the key facts.

TABLE 40.1 Wireless encryption options

Standard	Security status	Encryption algorithm	Encryption mode
Open	Insecure	None	None
WEP	Insecure	RC4	None
WPA	Insecure	RC4	TKIP
WPA2	Secure	AES	CCMP
WPA3	Secure	AES	CCMP and SAE

If you ever find yourself in a situation where the network available to you is running an insecure encryption algorithm or is run by an untrusted source (such as a hotel or coffee shop), you can enhance the security of an insecure wireless network by using a *virtual private network (VPN)*. VPNs use encryption to create a secure connection back to a trusted network, such as the one in your office.

CERTMIKE EXAM ESSENTIALS

▶ Enterprise authentication allows organizations to authenticate wireless users with their normal usernames and passwords. Preshared keys require the distribution of a common password.

▶ Wireless encryption protects information from eavesdropping while it is traveling over the wireless network. The strongest wireless encryption techniques are WPA2 and WPA3. WEP and WPA should no longer be used.

Practice Question 1

Your organization recently experienced an attack where an outside individual was able to eavesdrop on the wireless connections of network users. Which one of the following security enhancements would best protect against this type of attack?

A. Enabling WPA2
B. Enabling WEP
C. Changing SSIDs
D. Changing channels

Practice Question 2

You are visiting a small branch office of your organization and the users all access a single Wi-Fi access point. There is a sign posted on the wall with the password for the wireless network that all users share. What type of access control is in use on this network?

A. Open network
B. Enterprise authentication
C. Captive portal
D. Preshared key

Practice Question 1 Explanation

This question is asking us to evaluate different changes that we could make to our wireless network. The key here is realizing that eavesdropping on a network connection is best defeated through the use of encryption technology. Two of the answer choices—WEP and WPA2—are options for adding encryption to a wireless network. WEP encryption is outdated and insecure, whereas WPA2 is a secure, robust encryption protocol.

You might look at this question and think that WPA3 is an even better choice. It definitely is! But it's simply not one of the options here, so we should go with adding WPA2 to the network.

Changing the SSID simply changes the name that the network broadcasts to the world, which would have minimal security impact. Changing the channel is a good option if you're experiencing interference on your wireless network, but it won't help with eavesdropping attacks because it's simple for the attacker to find the new channel.

Correct Answer: A. Enabling WPA2

Practice Question 2 Explanation

The access control in use on this network is a preshared key (PSK) system. In a PSK setup, all users access the Wi-Fi network using a shared password that is known to and used by everyone with access to that network, as indicated by the posted sign with the password.

An open network would not require any password at all, allowing anyone within range to connect freely.

Enterprise authentication refers to systems that use individual user credentials for access, typically involving a username and password or other forms of identity verification.

A captive portal typically presents a web page requiring users to take additional steps beyond entering a Wi-Fi password, such as accepting terms of service or entering additional login credentials, which isn't mentioned in this scenario.

Correct Answer: D. Preshared key

INDEX

ONLINE TEST BANK

To help you study for your CompTIA Tech+ certification exam, register to gain one year of FREE access after activation to the online interactive test bank—included with your purchase of this book! All of the practice questions in this book are included in the online test bank so you can study in a timed and graded setting.

REGISTER AND ACCESS THE ONLINE TEST BANK

To register your book and get access to the online test bank, follow these steps:

1. Go to www.wiley.com/go/sybextestprep. You'll see the **"How to Register Your Book for Online Access"** instructions.
2. Click "here to register" and then select your book from the list.
3. Complete the required registration information, including answering the security verification to prove book ownership. You will be emailed a pin code.
4. Follow the directions in the email or go to www.wiley.com/go/sybextestprep.
5. Find your book on that page and click the "Register or Login" link with it. Then enter the pin code you received and click the "Activate PIN" button.
6. On the Create an Account or Login page, enter your username and password, and click Login or, if you don't have an account already, create a new account.
7. At this point, you should be in the test bank site with your new test bank listed at the top of the page. If you do not see it there, please refresh the page or log out and log back in.